A REAPPRAISAL OF
WELFARE ECONOMICS

A REAPPRAISAL
OF WELFARE ECONOMICS

S. K. NATH

Lecturer in Economics
University of Warwick

ROUTLEDGE & KEGAN PAUL
LONDON AND HENLEY

AUGUSTUS M. KELLEY PUBLISHERS
NEW JERSEY

First published in Great Britain 1969
by Routledge & Kegan Paul Ltd
39 Store Street, London WC1E 7DD
and Broadway House, Newtown Road
Henley-on-Thames, Oxon RG9 1EN
Reprinted 1976 and 1980
First published in the United States of America 1969
by Augustus M. Kelley
300 Fairfield Road
Fairfield, N.J. 07006
Printed in Great Britain by
Redwood Burn Limited
Trowbridge & Esher
UK ISBN 0 7100 6251 6

USA *Library of Congress Cataloging in Publication Data*

Nath, S. K.
A reappraisal of welfare economics.

A revised version of the author's thesis, University
of London, 1964.
Includes bibliographies.
1. Welfare economics. I. Title.
[*HB99.3.N39   1976*]   330.15′5   76–18300
ISBN 0–678–06507–1

CONTENTS

v

CONTENTS

PREFACE

This book is a reappraisal of welfare economics because it questions the logic of some of the commonly accepted propositions of *a priori* welfare economics—propositions which have survived earlier appraisals of the subject. At the same time we emphasise the importance of some of its relatively neglected concepts, which are useful even when an *ad hoc* approach to welfare analysis is adopted. We argue for such an approach. Further guidance about the contents of the book will be found in the Introduction and Conclusions.

It remains for me here to thank those from whom I got help and stimulus. The study originated while I was a student at the London School of Economics, and the initial stumulus came from my tutors and supervisors there: Professor Lord Robbins, Dr. E. J. Mishan, Professor K. Lancaster, Mr. K. Klappholz, Dr. B. A. Corry, and Professor G. C. Archibald. The book is a revised version of my thesis approved for a Ph.D. by the University of London in 1964.

I am grateful for their comments on part or whole of a draft of the book to Dr. E. J. Mishan, Mr. Maurice Dobb, Dr. A. G. Ford, Professor F. G. Pyatt, Mr. M. R. Fisher, Professor R. A. Bergstrom, Dr. L. Fishman, and Dr. J. S. Wabe. I have read parts of the book to seminars at Warwick University, Leicester University, and the School of Oriental and African Studies in London University; I am grateful to those who participated for their comments. Parts of the book have also been used for lectures at Leicester University, Bombay University and Warwick University; I am grateful to the students who gave their comments. Needless to say, none of the persons mentioned necessarily agrees with all or any of my arguments, or shares any responsibility for the book's deficiencies.

I would also like to thank the editors of the *Economic Journal*, *Oxford Economic Papers*, and *Journal of Development Studies* for their permission to use here material from articles published by them, the publishers of this book for their kind and efficient co-operation, and Mrs. June Smithies of Warwick University who did most of the typing and performed a very good job. To my wife go the most special thanks for help and encouragement.

S. K. NATH

University of Warwick

vii

To my parents

I

INTRODUCTION

1.1 WELFARE ECONOMICS AND VALUE JUDGMENTS

Let us introduce some concepts which are basic to any kind of welfare economics. We have first the concept of a value judgment. There is by no means general agreement over what it is. We shall adopt a broad definition: any statement which implies a recommendation of any kind is a value judgment. This definition covers all ethical judgments as well as statements which might appear to be merely descriptive, but are in certain contexts recommendatory, persuasive or influential. Some examples of value judgments are: 'a country grows faster if profits are taxed lightly'; 'honesty is the best policy'; 'monopolies need to be controlled'; 'advertising promotes economic growth'; 'fast economic growth is desirable'; 'each individual should be able to order all his economic affairs just as he pleases'; and 'an essential aim of public policy anywhere is a reduction in the inequalities of incomes'.[1]

Value judgments are basic to welfare economics for a number of reasons. First, in welfare economics some propositions are formulated about the *welfare* of individuals comprising a group; since welfare is an ethical term, any theorems incorporating the word welfare are also ethical and must rest on some obvious or hidden value judgments. Some people might deny that welfare is an ethical term and might want to maintain that propositions about it are of the same nature as those about humidity—the only difference being that so far no objective way has been found of measuring welfare the way we can measure humidity. We doubt that an objective way will ever be found of measuring welfare. Since most people consider it an ethical term, even if somebody invented an instrument to measure what he described as welfare, a number of people might object that though the instrument had measured something, that something was not welfare; so long as some people raised such objections, the measure could not be accepted as objective. Hence the basic issue here is whether welfare is an ethical term or not. Our position is that all the following and other similar terms are ethical terms: welfare, 'economic welfare', utility, and satisfaction.

[1] Little [4] argued convincingly that any persuasive statement needs to be regarded as a value judgment.

1

INTRODUCTION

Value judgments are basic to welfare economics also because it has always been considered to be that part of economics where *pre-scriptions* for policy are studied. No prescriptions can ever be made without starting explicitly or implicitly with some notion of what is desirable, good or, simply, the social objective. Again, no objectives can be formulated, or questions of desirability or goodness settled, without implicitly or explicitly assuming some value judgments.

Though value judgments are unavoidable in welfare economics, it is possible to try to pretend that any particular value judgments adopted are so 'widely acceptable', 'general', or 'minimal' that the welfare propositions based on them would be quite general, non-controversial, or 'more-or-less objective'. This indeed has been the usual procedure in the literature of welfare economics. We describe the welfare economics of this kind as *a priori* welfare economics. We shall be arguing (in Chapter VI) that none of the propositions of *a priori* welfare economics is in fact non-controversial (excepting perhaps those concerning technological efficiency), and that the whole procedure of *a priori* welfare economics is invalid on logical grounds. We shall argue that welfare economics has to be *ad hoc*, controversial, and based on the value judgments which particularly appeal to a comment-maker or a decision-maker (see Chapter VI about this distinction); and that properly conceived welfare economics is in-distinguishable from applied economics. We define *ad hoc* welfare economics as a study of problems of applied economics in the light of positive economic theories and some *explicit* value judgments which an economist introduces on his own or which—*if he is doing an assigned job*—are given to him by the 'parliament'; in *either* case the value judgments *are* value judgments and therefore open to argument, criticism, and disagreement. Of course the positive part may also be open to criticism; however, here the argument is about a theory which could conceivably be refuted in practice. As it happens, economic theories are difficult to test, but that does not destroy the distinction between the positive and the normative parts of the discipline; the former does not require any value judgments while the latter does. This question is further discussed in Chapter VI, Section 6.2c.

A social welfare function is another basic concept in welfare economics. Broadly speaking, a social welfare function just shows what the welfare of a society is supposed to depend on; in this sense any statement of what the objectives of a society are is a social welfare function. Though we shall be examining various possible formulations of the idea of a social welfare function, we shall be concluding that for most practical purposes only a workaday concept

2

of a social welfare function is required, where it implies a list of social objectives with some idea of their relative welfare weights. If a social welfare function is written out as an equation, then the dependent variable is social welfare; the independent variables are the targets or objectives which economic policies seek to affect; and the coefficients of the independent variables show their relative importance. In the most commonly used form of the social welfare function the independent variables are individual utility indicators, and the dependent variable is something called 'economic welfare'. We need not say any more about social welfare functions here; a discussion of them is to be found in various parts of the book, but especially in Chapters II and VI.

We regard as trivial a certain question which used to be considered very important in welfare economics; this concerns the measurability and the inter-personal comparability of utility. The neoclassical theory of demand was based on the assumption of measurable individual utility, and Pigou based some welfare propositions about distributions of incomes on the further assumption that interpersonal comparisons of utility are possible in practice. Pigou's assumption provoked strong protests from Robbins and others, who argued that no such inter-personal comparisons could be made in an objective, scientific sense. However, even if those two Pigovian assumptions had been true, no *recommendations* of any kind could be made (and that *also* implies no statements concerning *welfare* could be made) without explicitly or implicitly introducing some *ethical* rule which required that the 'total utility of all individuals' *should* be maximised. Hence Pigou's *recommendations* could no more get away from ethics than can any other *recommendations*. It also has to be admitted that to this day no general undisputed way of measuring individual utility has been found.[1] We may also mention the incidental argument, which we shall be developing in Chapter VI, that no recommendations can be based on a consideration of utility alone; meaningful recommendations have to be in terms of general welfare, which is a broader concept than utility. And welfare is, and will always remain, an ethical concept. Hence the question of whether utility is measurable or not is irrelevant to welfare economics.

So long as our purpose is merely the formulation of the general conditions for the Paretian optima, we need assume only ordinal utility. It was the distinctive mark of Pareto's theorising about

---

[1] For a survey of the various suggested ways of measuring utility, see Rothenberg [7]; no foolproof or practical method emerges. In any case, as we argue in the text, even if utility could be measured, no propositions in welfare economics could ever be formulated without starting from some ethical judgments.

'optimality' that he assumed only ordinal utility. Indeed, as Graaff [3] argues, it need not even be assumed that any kind of individual utility functions exist at all: the theoretical model requires only the assumption that individuals make choices. For deriving the general conditions for Paretian optima, it is not necessary to assume that we know either the individuals' ordinal utility functions or their choice decisions. (Nor is it necessary to make these assumptions to derive the rule for the similar concept of the Pigovian ideal output.) If the social aim is to reach just any Paretian optimum, no further assumptions are required. But if the policy-makers are interested in choosing one particular Paretian optimum from among the many, then it *has to be* assumed that the individual utility functions or choice decisions are *known*.

We owe the explicit formulation of the concepts of a social welfare function and the social optimum (i.e. the point of maximum social welfare) to Bergson [2]. Several different interpretations of the concept of a social welfare function are possible (see Chapter VI), but Bergson argued that we could study something called the 'economic welfare' of a society, instead of its general welfare, and that it could be assumed to depend on individual utility indicators which need only be ordinal; social preferences between different economic situations could then be expressed in terms of them. Bergson agreed that *only ethical* considerations could determine the *particular* functional relationship between 'economic welfare' of a society and the individual ordinal utility indicators. (In other words, only ethical considerations can *determine* any social welfare contours, such as those in fig. 2.3.) Bergson argued that the inter-personal comparisons of utility (which are required for his interpretation of a social welfare function) can be made without having to assume measurability of utility. But this is true *only if* the *fully-defined* individual ordinal utility functions are *known* to whoever is making the inter-personal comparisons of utility.

Therefore, in any application of the theoretical apparatus, it will have to be assumed that the decision-maker or the comment-maker *knows* the fully defined ordinal utility function for each individual. Similarly, if we talk in terms of individual choices instead of utility, again it will have to be assumed that the policy-maker *knows* what each person's choice decisions will be in any situation. (It is for this reason that Graaff [3] has to assume an omniscient observer.) It is impossible to imagine that these assumptions of *known individual* utility functions or choice decisions could ever be true in large communities; we can be quite sure that the economist or the 'parliament' could make only informed guesses about individual utility

4

levels. *These informed guesses would be indistinguishable from ethical assessment in practice.* Hence, once again, we cannot get away from the need for ethical assessments in reaching any welfare conclusions: the new assumptions of *known* ordinal utility functions, or choice decisions, are as ineffectual and irrelevant in this respect as the old assumption of measurable utility. In short, in any *policy* analysis, *ethical* assumptions are inevitable; this is true of both *a priori* and *ad hoc* welfare economics.

1.2 OUTLINE OF THE BOOK

There are, of course, two trends in welfare economics—the Pigovian and the Paretian; the two have somewhat different ethical presuppositions, but their analytical structure is the same. Most of the contemporary work in welfare economics is in the Paretian tradition, so that our discussions will relate mainly to the Paretian form of *a priori* welfare economics, though we shall have several occasions to refer to Pigou's work.[1]

Though in recent years economists have learnt to be a little more aware of their implicit value judgments than seems to have been the practice in the past, it is still not easy to find in the literature on welfare economics a full statement of all the necessary value judgments for Paretian welfare economics; therefore, our Chapter II starts with such a full statement. Chapter II is a detailed and critical review of the standard *a priori* welfare economics on its own terms. We show there that even if all competition were perfect, no uncertainty or externalities existed, and all the Paretian value judgments were acceptable—even then the concept of a Paretian optimum has some important limitations.

In Chapter III some of the assumptions of the second chapter are relaxed: we explore there the consequences of recognising transfers which are not lump-sum, imperfections in the market, and uncertainty on the part of economic agents. A discussion of the second-best theorem belongs to that chapter.

Chapter IV is devoted to externalities. Externalities also qualify the results of the second chapter, just as the considerations of the third chapter do. The concept of an externality is given a rigorous definition; various kinds of externalities are distinguished; and revised conditions for Pareto optimality are formulated. It is maintained that there is no such thing as a pecuniary externality; that the

[1] See Pigou's standard work [5], which was first published in 1920. For an early restatement of Pareto's work in this field which has been translated into English, see [1].

phenomenon which that term was meant to cover is better described as a consequence of uncertainty (on this see Chapter III, Section 3); but that this phenomenon does constitute a very important qualification on the results of the second chapter.

Chapter V critically examines the various *a priori* welfare criteria which have been put forward in the post-Pigou period; but the criticisms there are apart from our fundamental critique of *a priori* norms, which is developed in the next chapter. We also include in the same chapter an explanation of the connection between compensation criteria and some quantity index numbers of national income. That section belongs as much to this chapter as to the ninth chapter, which is about economic development.

In Chapter VI we develop a fundamental critique of the whole attempt to develop an apparently non-political and non-controversial body of welfare propositions about the economic life of any society. We argue that this attempt is ill-founded, and that any welfare propositions are always bound to be relative, political, and controversial. (Incidentally, we also argue that the Paretian value judgments are not all that attractive in any case; but this is very much an incidental point.) In the same chapter the supposed distinction between welfare and economic welfare is examined. We also argue there that both logic and practicability demand that distributive judgments should be in terms of the *economic means* to welfare, rather than welfare *itself*. All this also links up with a detailed discussion of the concept of the social welfare function, of the ambiguous concept of economic efficiency, and of the useful concept of technological efficiency. Through this chapter should emerge an outline of the *ad hoc* welfare economics which we think should come to replace the *a priori* welfare economics.

Chapter VII examines both what *a priori* welfare economics has tended to suggest and what *ad hoc* welfare economics would suggest about the running of public enterprises. In Chapter VIII we have to ignore the fundamental arguments of the sixth chapter while we look at the *a priori* welfare propositions of the gains from trade in order to sort out the valid from the invalid statements in that field. Chapter IX examines the concept of economic development from the welfare standpoint; Section 5 of Chapter V (about index numbers) needs to be read along with this chapter. The chapter concludes by examining some of the famous controversies in the field of development economics and showing how they were caused by value judgments which had failed to be explicit. The book ends with a brief chapter of conclusions. References cited in a chapter have been collected at the end of it.

REFERENCES FOR CHAPTER I

[1] E. Barone, 'The Ministry of Production in the Collectivist State', translation of an original article of 1908, printed in F. A. Hayek, ed., *Collectivist Economic Planning*, London, 1935

[2] A. Bergson, 'A Reformulation of Certain Aspects of Welfare Economics', *Quarterly Journal of Economics*, 1938; also reprinted in his *Essays in Normative Economics*, Cambridge, Mass., 1966

[3] J. de V. Graaff, *Theoretical Welfare Economics*, Cambridge, 1957

[4] I. M. D. Little, *A Critique of Welfare Economics*, 2nd edn., Oxford, 1957

[5] A. C. Pigou, *The Economics of Welfare*, 4th edn., London, 1932

[6] L. C. Robbins, *An Essay on the Nature and Significance of Economic Science*, 2nd edn., London, 1935.

[7] J. Rothenberg, *The Measurement of Social Welfare*

II

THE *A PRIORI* WELFARE THEORY

In this chapter we shall be critically surveying the basic *a priori* welfare theory—taking special care to emphasise the scope and limitations of its theorems, which are so often supposed to be more general than they are. These limitations are quite apart from the fundamental objections to *a priori* normative analysis which we shall develop in Chapter VI. We shall also be coming across in this chapter the important concepts of technological efficiency and the production frontier of an economy. The traditional theory of allocation is static; therefore the bulk of this chapter is based on static assumptions. The existence of time is recognised in a very limited way in Section 10. Some fundamental qualifications to the theorems of this chapter have to be admitted when uncertainty is recognised as well; but a discussion of that aspect is held over until the next chapter.

2.1 THE PARETIAN VALUE JUDGMENTS

Since the Paretian economic-welfare theory of allocation contains propositions about allocations of resources which are meant to be suitable, good, or optimum, it is necessarily based on certain value judgments.[1] They are the following:

(i) The concern is to be with the welfare of all the individuals in the society rather than with that of some mythical entity called 'Society' or 'State', or with that of some special group or class.

(ii) Any non-economic causes affecting an individual's welfare can be ignored. In this chapter, where the traditional Paretian theory is presented in its 'purest' form—i.e. where no externalities are recognised—an individual's utility (which is also referred to as 'economic welfare' in the literature) is assumed to depend only on *his own* income, wealth, and leisure, or, in other words, goods and services which are exchangeable in the market. The part of the traditional theory which deals with *a priori* welfare criteria (which we analyse in Chapter V) is also based on this value judgment. When we come to deal with the possibility of externalities in

[1] The early writers not only failed to point out the underlying value judgments of Paretian welfare economics but also denied that they were necessary. Dobb [5] was the first economist to show that the concept of a Paretian optimum presumed certain value judgments.

consumption (in Chapter IV) this value judgment has to be modified; because we recognise there that an individual's welfare may depend on not just what he buys and sells but also on certain things which are *not* bought and sold (due to legal, technological, or any other reasons—such as ignorance). One of these things may be the income and wealth levels of those richer or poorer than himself; in other words, the pattern of the distribution of income and wealth. See Chapter IV, Section 2; Chapter V, Section 4; and Chapter VI, Section 6.2a.

(iii) An individual should be considered the best judge of his economic welfare; and therefore also of his welfare, in view of the last value judgment. This value judgment is often referred to as that of 'complete consumer sovereignty'—though 'complete consumer and producer sovereignty' would be more appropriate, because an individual is assumed to be the best judge of his welfare in his capacity not only as a consumer but also as a producer.

It is sometimes suggested that the first-value judgment and this third value judgment necessarily go together; that if *individual* welfare alone matters, then the individual must necessarily be considered the best judge of his welfare. Though it is a plausible connection, there is no logical necessity about it. If it is granted that sometimes an individual may not be fully informed or rational, then it is possible that somebody else's decision may increase the individual's welfare more, even *according to himself* (and perhaps necessarily *ex post*), than it would have done if the individual had made his own decision.

There is another point to be noted about this value judgment. Nobody has ever assumed that the theory of allocation is about a world inhabited by adults living singly. But if the theory is about a world inhabited by households, then this third value judgment implies the further (and perhaps somewhat different in flavour) value judgment that the head of a household—the person doing the earning and spending—is the best judge of the economic welfare (and, therefore, also of welfare) of each member of the household; or that, even if he is not the best judge, he should have the right to decide—regarding all things (including education and health) which can be bought and sold on the market—what is most suitable for the welfare of each member of the family.

(iv) If any change in the allocation of resources increases the income and leisure of everyone or at least of one person (or more strictly one household) without reducing those of any other, then the change should be considered to have increased social welfare. This is the best known, and in a sense the most characteristic, value judgment of the Paretian welfare economics. It is sometimes referred to as *the* Paretian value judgment or welfare criterion. In this chapter our task is to state the Paretian set of value judgments and explain the theorems of theoretical welfare economics which have been derived from them. The critical evaluation of these value judgments, the derived theorems and the welfare criteria, is taken up from the next chapter onwards.

Let us assume that there are $(X_1, X_2, \ldots X_n)$ commodities and $(V_1, V_2, \ldots V_m)$ productive services in our economy. There are s individuals; the amount of any commodity or productive service that in any situation is the share of any individual is identified by the superscript; e.g. $x_1{}^3$ is the amount of commodity X_1 which is the share of individual '3'. We also have the following:

$$X_i = x_i{}^1 + x_i{}^2 + \ldots + x_i{}^s \quad (i = 1, \ldots n) \qquad (2.1)$$

and

$$V_j = v_j{}^1 + v_j{}^2 + \ldots + v_j{}^s \quad (j = 1, \ldots m) \qquad (2.2)$$

The first of the four value judgments mentioned above makes it possible to write the following form for the ordinal social welfare function:

$$W = W(U^1, U^2, \ldots U^s) \qquad (2.3)$$

where W is social economic welfare and $U^1, U^2, \ldots U^s$ are the levels of utility of each of the s individuals.[1] The fourth value judgment implies that W is a monotonically increasing function of any U, that is, $\partial W / \partial U^g > 0$. When using this mathematical expression about the relationship between W and U^g, some economists give the impression of considering it a scientific law, but it is in fact one of the many value judgments which could be made about this relationship, and, as we shall be showing later, has very special results in policy evaluation.

The second and third value judgments enable us to write the following ordinal utility functions for each one of the s individuals:[2]

$$U^g = U^g(x_i{}^g, v_j{}^g) \quad (g = 1, \ldots s) \qquad (2.4)$$

[1] W is assumed to be an ordinal function; for any such function, a monotonic transformation would also serve the same purpose. For the purposes of the theory discussed in this chapter, it is not necessary that individual utility should be cardinally measurable, or interpersonally comparable. However, there is further discussion of this question and of the general concept of a social welfare function in Chapter VI.

[2] The values which each of these utility functions may take are assumed to have no cardinal significance, the difference between the utility levels for an individual of different combinations of goods cannot be measured. Only a ranking of

In the light of the third value judgment, each of the individual utility functions incorporates *only the individual's own judgment and discretion; and* because of the second value judgment only the goods consumed by each individual himself (and the productive services or wealth retained by him) are included in his utility function. Any connection (such as through noise or air pollution, etc.) between one person's utility and another's consumption of some good is ignored. Similarly, any connection (such as through envy or compassion, etc.) between one person's utility and his knowledge of the utility levels attained by some other individuals is also ignored. Each of these utility functions, therefore, can also be interpreted as the welfare function of the individual concerned.

2.2 THE BASIC ASSUMPTIONS

Though recently there have been some attempts to work out the implications of its various concepts applied over time (attempts which we shall be discussing later in this chapter), the underlying analytical structure of the welfare theory of allocation is static.

The analysis is about a stationary economy in which everything exactly repeats itself from one period to another. In such a society all decisions are made only once; once made, they are relevant for all time because the things (variables) decided upon (which can be expressed as rates of flow) remain constant for all time. Everything is assumed to take place at a point of time—no time elapses between one event and another; hence there is no future to be uncertain about. In such a timeless world, though there is no uncertainty about the future, there might yet be imperfect knowledge about one another's actions at the present moment of time; but this, too, is assumed away by supposing that there is perfect knowledge. In order to distinguish it from the last assumption (of no uncertainty about the future), it may be called the assumption of 'perfect knowledge about the present'.

It is assumed that there are constant quantities of homogeneous factors of production; no indivisibility is allowed in any factor or product. The size of the working population also remains constant, and there is no involuntary unemployment. Since the quantities of factors stay constant, the model does not include any net investment.

---

different utility levels (with their associated combinations of goods and productive services) of each individual is required. Since these utility functions are assumed to be only ordinal, they are not unique; for each of the utility functions, any monotonic transformation of it would also serve the same purpose.

Further, all production functions are of smooth curvature, and show non-increasing returns to scale with diminishing marginal rate of substitution between any two factors along an iso-product curve. No increase in technical knowledge takes place.

With regard to the consumers both in their capacity as earners and as spenders, the static method implies that individual utility functions, preference maps, or 'tastes' do not change. Since everybody has both perfect certainty and knowledge, there is never any difference between *expected* utility and *realised* utility; hence *ex ante* welfare and *ex post* welfare are also always the same. This last assumption is not usually expressed in the form indicated, it being assumed instead that consumer behaviour (or preference orderings) are consistent. But the assumption of universal consistency in consumer behaviour implies the assumption of perfect foresight. Some other implicit assumptions of the traditional analysis are that no consumer is ever fully satiated, or judges quality (or utility) according to price, or suffers any disutility in making a choice. Along an indifference curve for any two goods the marginal rate of substitution between the goods diminishes for each individual. No two goods are perfect substitutes or perfect complementary goods.

Any *non-market* interdependence (i.e. through instruments other than those which can be and are bought and sold in the market) between production units is assumed away. We have already noted the value judgment that any *non-market* interdependence between individual welfares is not to be regarded as relevant. That value judgment and this assumption together amount to the assumption (or, rather, the value judgment) that there is no divergence between the private and social valuation of economic activities. (See Chapter IV for the exact definition of an externality.)

Lastly, it is assumed that all individuals aim to maximise their individual utility: and also that they are rational and therefore know how to do so. On the production side it is assumed that the business aims are 'cost minimisation' and 'profit maximisation'. All markets are perfectly competitive and at equilibrium. It is also assumed that lump-sum transfers of purchasing power between individuals are possible; the significance of this assumption will be discussed in the first section of the next chapter.

2.3 TECHNOLOGICAL EFFICIENCY

None of the value judgments which underlie welfare economics is needed for a technological concept of efficiency. Given the amounts of factory productive in an economy and the state of technical know-

2.3 TECHNOLOGICAL EFFICIENCY

ledge, there is a technologically efficient allocation of these resources when the output of any commodity cannot be increased without at the same time reducing the output of some other. In such a case we can say there is a technological production optimum. However, there is nothing unique about a technological production optimum; given the resources, there will be an infinite number of technological production optima, each with a different composition of output, all lying on what may be called the technological production frontier.

The definition of technological efficiency, according to some economists, requires the value judgment that more of any output, or less of any input, is, other things being equal, a good thing. This is not entirely convincing. According to this argument, an engineer's concept of efficiency of a unit of equipment (in terms of energy transformation) would depend on the same value judgment. But it is possible to argue that the engineer's definition of efficiency and the economist's definition of technological efficiency depend on the assumption that human action and the management of human affairs are rational. According to this argument, then, the above-mentioned value judgment is not needed, though value judgments are involved in the definition of what are to be the items of output and of inputs. However, it can also be argued that to assume human action to be rational, and then to base the definition of technological efficiency on that assumption is equivalent to saying that human action should be rational.

In any case, there are other reasons which make it difficult to uphold a value-free concept of technological efficiency. First, it rests on the unlikely assumption that (apart from the influence on physical productivity) workers are indifferent to movement between occupations, and that society is indifferent to the movement of the other factors between their alternative uses. Second, it also has to be assumed that individuals' personal efficiency does not depend on the distribution of incomes. This assumption can hardly be true in situations with marked inequalities, so that a number of people have a very low standard of living (as is the case in a number of countries at present). Whenever this second assumption does not hold, the size of the maximum production of any composition depends on the associated distribution of incomes. However, the standard theory is based on these assumptions, and they have been adopted here also.

It is assumed that all the relevant engineering or 'physical' data (including the latest changes) about the relationships between inputs and outputs (or about the production function of each output) are available to the producers, and that there is similar perfect knowledge about factor prices. Production is assumed to take place in farms,

13

factories, firms, and industries which of themselves have no direct welfare significance. Suppose we have the following production function regarding each good:

$$X_i = X_i(v_{ji}) \quad (j = 1, \ldots m) \tag{2.5}$$

where the second subscript indicates the commodity for which a productive service is used. We now have to find the necessary conditions for maximising any commodity (or minimising any input), subject to all other commodities and all inputs being at some arbitrary levels:

$$X_h(v_{jh}) = X_h^0 \quad (h = 1, \ldots n; h \neq i) \tag{2.6}$$

$$v_{j1} + v_{j2} + \ldots + v_{jn} = V_j^0 \tag{2.7}$$

We form the following Lagrangean expression for this purpose:

$$G = X_i(v_{ji}) + \lambda_h[X_h(v_{jh}) - X_h^0] + \mu_j[(v_{j1} + \ldots + v_{jn}) - V_j^0]$$
$$(i \text{ and } h = 1, \ldots n; i \neq h)(j = 1, \ldots m) \tag{2.8}$$

By finding the relevant partial derivatives of this function, and setting them equal to zero, we can derive the following ratios as the necessary conditions for our maximisation problem:

$$\frac{\partial X_i/\partial v_{ji}}{\partial X_i/\partial v_{ki}} = \frac{\partial X_h/\partial v_{jh}}{\partial X_h/\partial v_{kh}} \quad \begin{array}{l} (i \text{ and } h = 1, \ldots n; i \neq h) \\ (j \text{ and } k = 1, \ldots m; j \neq k) \end{array} \tag{2.9}$$

In words, the necessary condition for a technological production optimum is that the ratio between the marginal physical products of any two factors must be the same in the production of all commodities; this also requires that no matter where a commodity is produced, the marginal physical product of a factor is the same. An alternative way of expressing this necessary condition is to say that the marginal rate of substitution between any two factors in the production of any good must be equalised with the marginal rate of substitution between the same two factors in the production of every other good. Since the constraints (2.6) and (2.7) can be at infinitely many levels, there is an infinite number of efficient product combinations.

For diagrammatic illustration of this and other optima, let us assume an imaginary community of two individuals (*g* and *r*), two goods (X_1 and X_2), and two factors of production V_1 and V_2 (say, land and labour). Both the factors are given with perfectly inelastic supply curves.

In fig. 2.1 a box diagram is constructed with width equal to the amount of V_2, and height equal to the amount of V_1. The iso-product curves for commodity X_1 are plotted with 0 as the origin, and those for X_2 with 0* as the origin. At each point of tangency between any

14

two iso-product curves of X_1 and X_2 the marginal rates of substitution between V_1 and V_2 in the production of the two commodities are equalised; each such point is a production optimum. The locus of these points of tangency is the production contract curve.

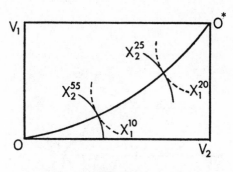

Fig. 2.1

We can exhibit the information provided by this locus differently in fig. 2.2, where each point on the curve shows the maximum possible output for commodity X_2, given varying amounts of the commodity X_1 and the fixed amounts of the factors. That curve is called the (technological) *production possibility frontier* or the *transformation frontier*. The slope of the tangent at any point on it shows the marginal rate of technical transformation between the two commodities.

Reverting to the many goods and many productive services case, the technologically efficient transformation frontier (which gives the maximum amount of output of a good when all inputs and the outputs of all other goods are fixed, or minimum amount of an input when all outputs and all other inputs are fixed, because each point on it satisfies the last equation) can be written in the form of the following implicit function:

$$T(X_1, X_2, \ldots X_n; V_1, V_2, \ldots V_m) = 0 \qquad (2.10)$$

It is worth pointing out that a point on the production frontier is *not* technologically superior to *any* point within the frontier. In fig. 2.2, for example, only the points M and N and any others on the curve between those two are technologically superior to point C within the curve. A point like 0^* on the curve has more of one commodity, as compared with C, *at the expense* of the other commodity. To judge

15

between 0^* and C, other than just technological considerations are required—even if all the assumptions establishing a value-free concept of technological efficiency are given. It should also be noted that it is possible to have transformation functions with a general equation like the last one (2.10) and production frontiers of the shape of

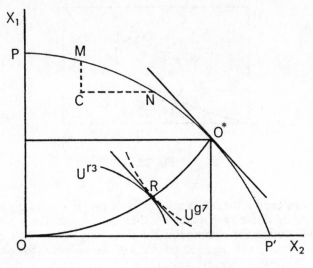

Fig. 2.2

the curve PP' of fig. 2.2, which are *not* the genuine technological production frontier. These other frontiers would lie *within* the true frontier and would be caused by *imperfections in factor markets, imperfect knowledge about technical conditions, and non-cost-minimising behaviour.* (See Chapter III, Section 3, and Chapter VI, Section 3.)

2.4 PARETIAN EXCHANGE OPTIMA

Now we come to a concept which depends on all the value judgments of Section 1. There are given amounts of goods and productive services whose ownership is divided among the individuals of the economy. They are free to exchange them with one another as they like. By free mutual exchange they might reach a point where any further exchange will increase the utility of one person only at the

2.4 PARETIAN EXCHANGE OPTIMA

cost of reducing the utility of some other. Such a division of goods and services is a Paretian exchange optimum. It is important to add the adjective *Paretian* because this particular definition of an exchange optimum does depend on a particular set, namely, the Paretian set of value judgments: that individuals should be free to exchange what they like in any quantities they like, that welfare depends only on exchangeable goods and services and that social welfare is a monotonically increasing function of individual welfares. Any compulsory item of consumption (e.g. milk), or rationing of any goods, would conflict with these value judgments, though they may not with some others. It is to be noted that there is nothing unique about a Paretian exchange optimum; given the amounts of all goods and services, there will be an infinite number of such optima. We have to find the necessary conditions for maximising the utility of any one individual as given by:

$$U^g = U^g(x_i{}^g; v_j{}^g) \quad (i = 1, \ldots n)\,(j = 1, \ldots m) \tag{2.11}$$

subject both to the utility of all other individuals being fixed at some arbitrary levels and to the amounts of all commodities and factors being fixed:

$$U^r(x_i{}^r; v_j{}^r) = U^{r0} \quad (r \text{ and } g = 1, \ldots s; g \neq r) \tag{2.12}$$

$$x_i{}^1 + x_i{}^2 + \ldots + x_i{}^s = X_i{}^0 \tag{2.13}$$

$$v_j{}^1 + v_j{}^2 + \ldots + v_j{}^s = V_j{}^0 \tag{2.14}$$

where U^{r0} stands for the arbitrarily fixed levels of utility of all individuals other than the first; and $X_i{}^0$ and $V_j{}^0$ stand for the fixed amounts of all goods and factors.

We form the following Lagrangean function:

$$H = U^g(x_i{}^g; v_j{}^g) + \lambda_r[U^r(x_i{}^r; v_j{}^r) - U^{r0}] + \\ \mu_i[(x_i{}^1 + \ldots + x_i{}^s) - X_i{}^0] + \pi_j[(v_j{}^1 + \ldots + v_j{}^s) - V_j{}^0] \tag{2.15}$$

$$(g \text{ and } r = 1, 2, \ldots s; g \neq r)$$

By finding the relevant partial derivatives and setting them equal to zero, we can derive the following ratios as the necessary conditions for our maximisation problem:

$$\frac{\partial U^g/\partial x_i{}^g}{\partial U^g/\partial x_h{}^g} = \frac{\partial U^r/\partial x_i{}^r}{\partial U^r/\partial x_h{}^r} \quad \begin{array}{l} (g \text{ and } r = 1, \ldots s; g \neq r) \\ (i \text{ and } h = 1, \ldots n; i \neq h) \end{array} \tag{2.16}$$

and

$$\frac{\partial U^g/\partial v_j{}^g}{\partial U^g/\partial v_k{}^g} = \frac{\partial U^r/\partial v_j{}^r}{\partial U^r/\partial v_k{}^r} \quad (j \text{ and } k = 1, \ldots m; j \neq k) \tag{2.17}$$

17

Equation (2.16) implies that the ratio between the marginal utilities of any two goods (X_i and X_h) to one individual must be the same as the ratio between the marginal utilities of the same two goods to every other individual; it can also be interpreted to imply that the rate of marginal subjective substitution between any two goods must be the same for all individuals. Similarly, equation (2.17) implies that the marginal rate of subjective substitution between any two productive services which they provide must be the same for all individuals. Since the constraint (2.12) can be at infinitely many levels, there is an infinite number of individual utility combinations which are Pareto exchange optimal.

In fig. 2.2 there are given amounts of the two goods X_1 and X_2 as shown by the height and width respectively of the box diagram. The indifference curves of individual g are plotted with 0 as the origin, and those of r with 0* as the origin. The locus of the points of tangency between the two systems of indifference curves (sometimes called the contract curve) is the locus of the Paretian exchange optima. Each point on it shows a different combination of the utility (or preference) levels of the two individuals.

2.5 OVERALL PARETIAN OPTIMA

If both the amounts of labour services and the actual composition of goods produced are allowed to vary as permitted by the efficient transformation function relating to a given state of technology and resources, then from the value judgments of Section 2 a definition follows of a special kind of optimum allocation of resources. So long as any change in the allocation of resources to different uses enables all (*or at least one person*) to move up his scale of preferences, the basic set of value judgments implies that the change is desirable. On the other hand, if an allocation is such that any change in its pattern can move one person or a number of persons up their scales of preference only at the cost of some persons (*or at least one person*) being moved down theirs, then that allocation is as good as any allocation can be in the light of the Paretian value judgments; in other words, such an allocation is an optimum allocation in the light of those value judgments; it has been given the name of (overall) Paretian optimum.

The necessary conditions for a technological production optimum and for a Paretian exchange optimum are combined to get the necessary conditions for an overall Paretian optimum. We have to find the necessary conditions for maximising the utility level of one individual, equation (2.11), subject to the given technologically efficient transformation function, equation (2.10), to any arbitrarily fixed levels of utility of all individuals excepting one, equation (2.12), and to the obvious further conditions that the sum of the amounts of a commodity consumed by each individual, and the sum of the amounts of a factor used in each commodity, must be equal to their available totals from all individuals—as given by equations (2.1) and (2.2). Hence we form the following Lagrangean function:

$$L = U^g(x_i{}^g; v_j{}^g) + \lambda_r[U^r(x_i{}^r; v_j{}^r) - U^{r0}] + \mu_i[(x_i{}^1 + \ldots + x_i{}^s) - X_i] + v_j[(v_j{}^1 + \ldots + v_j{}^s) - V_j] + \pi[T(X_1, \ldots X_n; V_1, \ldots V_m)] \quad (2.18)$$

$$(g \text{ and } r = 1, \ldots s; g \neq r)$$

By finding the relevant partial derivatives and setting them equal to zero, we can derive the following ratios as the necessary conditions for our maximisation problem:

$$\frac{\partial U^g/\partial x_i{}^g}{\partial U^g/\partial x_h{}^g} = \frac{\partial U^r/\partial x_i{}^r}{\partial U^r/\partial x_h{}^r} = \frac{\partial T/\partial X_i}{\partial T/\partial X_h} \quad (i \text{ and } h = 1, \ldots n; i \neq h) \quad (2.19)$$

and

$$\frac{\partial U^g/\partial x_i{}^g}{\partial U^g/\partial v_j{}^g} = \frac{\partial U^r/\partial x_i{}^r}{\partial U^r/\partial v_j{}^r} = \frac{\partial T/\partial X_i}{\partial T/\partial V_j} \quad (j = 1, \ldots m) \quad (2.20)$$

In words, the necessary conditions for an overall Paretian optimum are:

(1) Between any two goods the marginal rate of subjective substitution must be the same for all individuals, and this common rate should also be equal to the marginal rate of technically transforming one of those goods into the other through transferring any factor of production from one of these goods to the other.

(2) For each individual the subjective marginal rate of substitution between any factor of production and a good must be the same; and this common rate should be equal to the marginal technical rate of transformation of that factor into the product in question.

Though this concept is often loosely referred to as an 'optimum allocation' or an 'economic optimum', the only name it can be given if the risk of misleading people is to be minimised is that of a 'Paretian optimum', because the kind of allocation that the concept refers to is optimal only in the light of the Paretian set of value judgments. An allocation which is Paretian optimal might be non-optimal in the light of some other value judgments (see Chapter VI). Given the productive resources of an economy, there will be an infinite number of Paretian optima, each with a different distribution of utility levels. There is nothing unique about a Paretian optimum; this is because the other persons' utilities in equation (2.12) can be fixed at any of the infinitely many levels; the necessary conditions are the same in each case.

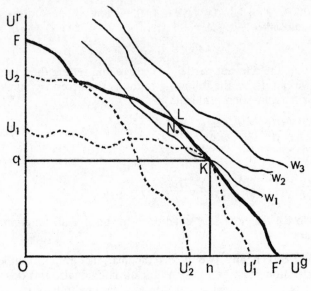

Fig. 2.3

Paretian Situation Utility Possibility Frontier

In fig. 2.3 along the horizontal axis are measured ordinal utility indicators of individual g, and along the vertical, those of r. The information provided by the contract curve of fig. 2.2 is plotted in fig. 2.3. With the amounts of goods X_1 and X_2 fixed (in quantities shown by point 0^* in fig. 2.2), that contract curve shows the maximum level of utility that r can reach with varying specified levels of utility for g. This information is exhibited in fig. 2.3 by the U_1U_1' curve. Such a curve is called a *point utility possibility curve*, because it is drawn with reference to one point on the production possibility frontier (i.e. it is drawn with reference to one given bundle of goods). By sliding point 0^* up and down the production possibility frontier (in fig. 2.2) we can generate a series of contract curves and plot their corresponding point utility possibility curves in fig. 2.3. A number of these curves will overlap. The envelope is the *situation utility possibility frontier*, FF' in fig. 2.3. It is also known as the economic welfare frontier, or the welfare frontier. For different given levels of utility (economic welfare or welfare—if all the value judgments and assumptions we have mentioned are given these terms become equivalent and are treated as such in contemporary welfare economics) of one individual, the frontier shows the maximum possible level of the other. In other words, it is the locus of overall Paretian optima.

Going back to fig. 2.2, each point on the production possibility curve is a production optimum, and each point on the contract curve is a Paretian exchange optimum. But a technologically efficiently produced bundle of goods, which also happens to be distributed so that there is a Paretian exchange optimum, does not qualify to be an overall Paretian optimum unless the marginal rate of technical transformation between the two goods equals the individuals' common marginal rate of subjective substitution.

Generally, there will be only one point on the contract curve where the individuals' common marginal rate of substitution between the two goods of given total amounts is the same as the marginal rate of transformation between them. Such a point is R in fig. 2.2. If the total outputs of goods X_1 and X_2 as given by point 0^* are distributed between g and r in such a manner that each individual is at point R of their preference maps, then 0^* is a point of overall Paretian optimum.

Point utility possibility curve U_1U_1' of fig. 2.3 corresponds to the contract curve 00^* of fig. 2.2. We have just noticed that point R on that contract curve corresponds to an overall Paretian optimum. It follows, then, that on the point utility possibility curve U_1U_1' of fig. 2.3 an overall Paretian optimum exists at the point corresponding to point R of fig. 2.2. Such a point is K in fig. 2.3. With the given bundle of goods with reference to which U_1U_1' is drawn, K is a point of an overall Paretian optimum. Therefore it lies on the utility possibility frontier. Similarly, all those points on the production possibility curve which can (in the light of the individuals' preferences) be overall Paretian optima, generate point utility possibility curves which have at least a point each that lies on the situation utility possibility frontier.

Though each point on the economic welfare frontier is a Paretian optimum, each has a different distribution of economic welfare. Some *specific* function for ranking the different distributions is needed if one particular Paretian optimum is to be chosen as better than others. Indeed, some *specific* social welfare function is needed in general *even* for comparing a Paretian optimum with a position which is *not* such an optimum. For example, in fig. 2.3 point *K*—which is a Pareto-optimum—cannot be declared superior to point *N* *even on the Paretian set of value judgments*. Those value judgments are sufficient to declare *K* superior to any point only within the area *OqKh*. *Hence, a Paretian optimum is not necessarily superior to any non-optimum*.

The concept of a social welfare function which we have already come across briefly in Chapter I, was first introduced by Bergson [3]. It is capable of more than one interpretation, and is a major source of controversy and confusion in the literature; we shall be analysing it in detail in Chapter VI. But for the moment we shall assume, as is the usual practice in the literature, that *somehow* a well-defined schedule or function of the relative deservingness (in terms of economic welfare) of different individuals has been found. Since this function is in terms of individual economic welfare or utility functions, it implies the assumption that *individual utility functions are known* to whoever made the *specific* welfare function. This is so whether ordinal or cardinal utility is assumed. (We shall be examining the significance of this assumption in Chapter VI.) This *specific* welfare function can be depicted by a series of contours in economic welfare space. Since one of the *Paretian* optima is to be chosen, the social welfare function has to be one which is *consistent* with the *Paretian* set of value judgments.

The point where one of these contours (w_1, w_2, etc., in fig. 2.3) just touches the economic welfare frontier is the best of the Paretian optima. That point determines—*in the light of the Paretian set of value judgments and* a social welfare function which is consistent with those value judgments—the best distribution of economic welfare between the two individuals, and therefore the best distribution of the two commodities between them as well as the best composition of output of the two commodities, and therefore the best allocation of the two factors between the production of the two commodities. The best of all positions according to a certain social welfare function is called *the social optimum* according to that welfare function.

The foregoing way of showing the derivation of the conditions amounts to saying that the Pareto-type social welfare function, as given by equation (2.3), is to be maximised subject to the constraint of the Paretian situation utility possibility frontier. The equation of that frontier is the following:

$$P(U^1, U^2, \ldots U^s) = 0 \qquad (2.21)$$

2.5 OVERALL PARETIAN OPTIMA

By forming a suitable Lagrangean function consisting of equations (2.3) and (2.21), we can derive the following necessary conditions for the social optimum:

$$\frac{\partial W/\partial U^g}{\partial W/\partial U^r} = \frac{\partial P/\partial U^g}{\partial P/\partial U^r} \quad (g \text{ and } r = 1, \ldots s; \, g \neq r) \tag{2.22}$$

In words, this necessary condition implies that at the social optimum the ratio between the marginal social significance of the utility levels of any two individuals must be equal to the marginal rate of substitution between their utility levels as given by the utility possibility frontier. The marginal social significance of the utility level reached by any individual is indicated by the exact coefficients of the *fully defined* social welfare function which has been *assumed* to be 'given'. *It is worth emphasising that unless a fully defined social welfare function is given we cannot know the exact shape (or the exact slope at any point) of the welfare contours in fig. 2.3.*

The conditions for the social optimum can also be derived directly without first discovering the Paretian utility possibilities frontier. If we want to refer to our many-goods and many-factors model the derivation of the necessary conditions for the socially optimal allocation can be illustrated as follows. We have to maximise some social welfare function which may or may not be Pareto-type but which has been assumed to be expressed as a function of individual utilities in the form of equation (2.3). The constraints are the social transformation function, equation (2.10), and the two obvious equations (2.1) and (2.2). By forming a suitable Lagrangean expression similar to the ones formed above, or by other methods, the necessary conditions for the social optimum can be shown to be:

$$\frac{\partial W/\partial U^g . \partial U^g/\partial x_i{}^g}{\partial W/\partial U^r . \partial U^r/\partial x_h{}^r} = \frac{\partial T/\partial X_i}{\partial T/\partial X_h} \quad (g, r = 1, \ldots s) \, (i, h = 1, \ldots s) \tag{2.23}$$

$$\frac{\partial W/\partial U^g . \partial U^g/\partial v_j{}^g}{\partial W/\partial U^r . \partial U^r/\partial v_k{}^r} = \frac{\partial T/\partial V_j}{\partial T/\partial V_k} \quad (j, k = 1, \ldots, m) \tag{2.24}$$

In words, the necessary conditions for the social optimum are that for any pair of commodities or factors the ratio between the marginal social significance of their parts going to each of the different individuals must be the same, *and* that this ratio must be equal to the marginal technical rate of substitution between the two commodities or the factors. Further, the marginal social welfare significance of the share of a commodity or a factor going to any person must be the same. (This condition follows if i and h, and j and k are interpreted to be the same good and the same factor respectively in the last two equations.)

It is important here to emphasise again a point that is usually forgotten in the ready application of the arguments and theorems borrowed from the Paretian welfare economics to any discussion of allocation problems in real life. It is that points on the Paretian welfare frontier are relevant for the discovery of the best allocation according to a given welfare function only if that welfare function is consistent with the Paretian value judgments. If the welfare function does not embody, for example, the value judgment that individuals should always be regarded as the best judges of their own welfares or that untraded interdependence of individual welfares should be ignored, then the Paretian welfare frontier ceases to be relevant for allocation; in either of these two examples it would no longer be relevant to ensure a Paretian exchange optimum by making the prices of all goods the same for all individuals. The marginal utility of a good to an individual which appears in equation (2.23) *need not be as judged* by the individual himself in the case of each good; for a number of goods it might be the ethical assessment of the comment-maker or the decision-maker.

The necessary marginal conditions for a Paretian optimum have often been called the *necessary* conditions for the social optimum. But this is persuasive terminology. We have just pointed out that the social optimum according to a non-Paretian welfare function may have very little in common with a Paretian optimum—the only thing in common may be technological efficiency in the allocation of the non-human factors of production. (There is further discussion of this in Chapter VI, Section 4.) The conditions for a Paretian optimum are just conditions for a Paretian optimum; to establish any necessary link between them and the idea of the social optimum is to mislead and to make an already difficult subject more confusing.

Scitovsky Community Indifference Curves

We should digress here to familiarise ourselves with a useful concept —the Scitovsky community indifference curve [25]. In a world of two goods and two individuals the different points on such a curve show the minimum requirements of the two goods for some specified level of utility for each individual; along any one curve the utility level of each individual remains the same. (It is worth recalling that an individual indifference curve is the locus of minimum require-ments of any two goods for an individual who remains at the same utility level.) Since there is an infinite number of ways of combining the different utility levels of even two individuals, there will be an infinity of community indifference curves passing through a point in the two-commodity plane.

24

2.5 OVERALL PARETIAN OPTIMA

For a world of two goods X_1 and X_2, and two individuals g and r, a Scitovsky community indifference curve is derived in the following fashion. Assume that both individuals enjoy some specified levels of utility U^7 and U^9. Assume also that the output of one of the two goods is fixed at a certain level X_1. We then have to find the smallest quantity of the other good, X_2, which is consistent with the specified individual utility levels.

In other words, we have the following problem:

Minimise
$$x_2{}^g + x_2{}^r$$

subject to
$$U^g(x_1{}^g, x_2{}^g) - U^{g7} = 0$$
$$U^r(x_1{}^r, x_2{}^r) - U^{r9} = 0$$

and
$$x_1{}^g + x_1{}^r - X_1{}^0 = 0 \qquad (2.25)$$

Let us form the following Lagrangean function:

$$F = x_2{}^g + x_2{}^r + [U^g(x_1{}^g, x_2{}^g) - U^7] + \mu[U^r(x_1{}^r, x_2{}^r) - U^{r9}] + \nu[x_1{}^g + x_1{}^r - X_1{}^0] \qquad (2.26a)$$

When the first-order partial derivatives of this function with respect to $x_2{}^g$, $x_2{}^r$, $x_1{}^g$, $x_1{}^r$, λ, μ, and ν are set equal to zero the first thing that emerges is that in order for the quantity $X_2 (= x_2{}^g + x_2{}^r)$ to be at a minimum, we must have the following equality:

$$\frac{\partial U^g / \partial x_1{}^g}{\partial U^g / \partial x_2{}^g} = \frac{\partial U^r / \partial x_1{}^r}{\partial U^r / \partial x_2{}^r} \qquad (2.26b)$$

That is, the individuals' subjective marginal rate of substitution between the two goods must be equalised. This can be interpreted as being the same as the necessary condition for a Paretian exchange optimum if it is assumed, *as is usual*, that the marginal utilities (or the partial derivatives of equation (2.26b)) relate to utility functions which incorporate the second and third value judgements of Section 1. By varying the fixed amount of good X_1 in the third constraint, but keeping g and r at the same fixed levels of utility as in the first two constraints, we can find varying minimum amounts of good X_2. If the underlying value judgments are Paretian—and we shall assume they always are for such a curve—the locus of these combinations of X_1 and X_2 is a Scitovsky community indifference curve (C.I.C.—e.g. curve I_1 in fig. 2.4). Since on each point on this curve the marginal subjective rate of substitution between the goods is the same for each individual, and since it is also assumed that this rate diminishes for each individual, the community indifference curve is downward sloping and convex to the origin like an individual indifference curve.

However, unlike an individual indifference map, Scitovsky community indifference curves can cross each other. The combination of X_1 and X_2 shown, for example, by point P in fig. 2.4 can also be associated with a different distribution of utility levels between g and r. Indeed, there is an infinite number of combinations of raised utility levels for g and lowered utility levels for r, and vice versa, while the availability of goods remains as shown by point P. With a different distribution of utility levels, the slope of the C.I.C. at P is

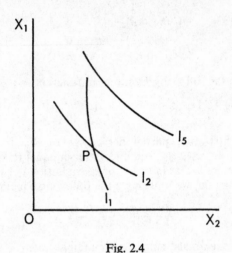

Fig. 2.4

likely to be different if individual tastes are different; hence the common (for the two) marginal rate of subjective substitution—or the common rate of relative subjective evaluation—between the two goods at any point in the diagram is likely to depend on how that commodity bundle is distributed between the two individuals. We shall learn in Section 6 of this chapter that at equilibrium under perfect competition the common rate of subjective substitution between any two goods can be identified with the price ratio between them. Hence we can also say that prices of goods are likely to be a function of the distribution of incomes. These results have to be qualified under two special circumstances. First, when all individual utility functions are homogeneous and identical. Secondly, when different individuals' personal Engel curves are parallel straight lines at the same set of prices; in this case an extra unit of purchasing power is spent in the same way no matter to whom it is given because the marginal propensity to consume any commodity is the same for all individuals. Under either of these assumptions we shall have a map of non-intersecting Scitovsky community indifference curves. See Gorman [7].

If these special assumptions are ignored, as we shall do, then as the distribution of any commodity bundle (or as the composition of national product) alters, then the common (for all individuals) rate of subjective evaluation along a Scitovsky C.I.C. will also alter. Hence

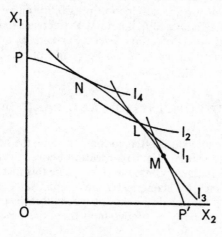

Fig. 2.5

an infinite number of community indifference curves can pass through a point such as P in fig. 2.4. When the amount of one good, say X_1, increases from point P, while the amount of X_2 also increases or at least remains the same, a combination of the utility levels of the two individuals is possible which would enable at least one of them to have a higher level of utility than he had along I_1, without lowering the level of utility of the other. In this case the new community indifference curve (say I_5 in fig. 2.4) does not intersect curve I_1. Such non-intersecting community indifference curves are called Pareto-comparable, because they are comparable on the Paretian value judgments, whereas intersecting community indifference curves are not. On the other hand, the non-intersecting Scitovsky community indifference curves obtained on either of the foregoing two special assumptions will not necessarily be Pareto-comparable; because any two such curves are non-intersecting irrespective of whether on one of them one individual is better off without the other being worse off.

With the help of the concept of Scitovsky community indifference curves we can illustrate the necessary conditions for a Paretian optimum in another way. In fig. 2.5 PP' is the economy's production possibility curve. A technologically efficiently produced bundle of goods (i.e. any point on PP') is a Paretian optimum when a Scitovsky C.I.C. is tangential to it; but it is a Paretian optimum *only with reference to* the distribution of utility levels as shown by *the* community indifference curve which is tangential to it. For example, in fig. 2.5, point L on the production possibility curve is a Paretian optimum with reference to I_1, but not with reference to I_2, which has a different distribution of utility levels. Further, M and N are also Paretian optima; but each of the Paretian optima has a different distribution of utility levels.

2.6 PERFECT COMPETITION AND PARETIAN OPTIMA

We come now to what is often considered to be the heart of welfare economics: a theorem about the relation between perfect competition and the Paretian optima. For a long time this theorem was given great importance by economists; and significant corollaries were derived from it for practical policy purposes. But the theorem in fact is hedged by so many restrictive (and therefore unrealistic) conditions that it is trivial.

If there is perfect knowledge both about the future and the (relevant activities of others in the) present, if all individuals aim to maximise their utility, if there are no external effects whatsoever, if everybody is free to adjust the amount and kind of purchases and sales (including of work) that they will make, if everybody is rational, if there is perfect competition among all buyers and sellers, if all producers are genuine cost-minimisers as well as profit maximisers and if the economy comes to an equilibrium, so that supplies and demands are equal at some stable prices—then the resulting allocation of resources will be an optimal one *according to the value judgments of Section 1*; i.e. the allocation will be an overall Paretian optimum. Depending on how the initial ownership of commodities and factors is distributed, there is an infinite number of points of equilibrium for such an economy; and therefore an infinite number of Paretian optima. Each optimum, as we have noted above, is distinguished by a different distribution of utility levels.

When there is equilibrium in a perfectly competitive economy all markets are cleared, and the price of any commodity or factor is the same for each buyer and seller. Each buyer or seller is assumed to be such a small part of the relevant market that he can take any price as a constant for his purposes. Now each individual in his capacity as a consumer will, in equilibrium, have the price ratio between any two goods, or between a good and a productive resource, equal to his subjective marginal rate of substitution between the two, if he is to maximise his utility. Since all prices are the same for all individuals under perfect competition, these rates of substitution will be the same for all of them at equilibrium:

$$\frac{P_i}{P_h} = \frac{\delta U^g/\delta x_i^g}{\delta U^g/\delta x_h^g} \quad (i, h = 1, \ldots n)\, (g = 1, \ldots s) \tag{2.27}$$

and

$$\frac{W_j}{P_i} = \frac{\delta U^g/\delta v_j^g}{\delta U^g/\delta x_i^g} \quad (i, = 1, \ldots n)\, (j = 1, \ldots m) \tag{2.28}$$

where P stands for price of a commodity and W for the price of a factor. These prices are the same for all individuals and firms.

Similarly, under perfect competition in equilibrium, the price of each good is equal to its marginal cost (M); that is

$$P_i = M_i = \frac{W_j}{\partial X_i/\partial v_{ji}} \tag{2.29a}$$

and

$$P_h = M_h = \frac{W_j}{\partial X_h/\partial v_{jh}} \tag{2.29b}$$

therefore

$$\frac{P_i}{P_h} = \frac{\partial X_h/\partial v_{jh}}{\partial X_i/\partial v_{ji}} \tag{2.30}$$

and hence

$$\frac{P_i}{P_h} = \frac{\partial U^g/\partial x_i^g}{\partial U^g/\partial x_h^g} = \frac{\partial T/\partial X_i}{\partial T/\partial X_h}$$

$$(i, h = 1, \ldots n)\, (j = 1, \ldots m)\, (g = 1, \ldots s) \tag{2.31}$$

In other words, since the price ratio between any two goods equals the inverse of the ratio of the marginal physical products for these two goods of each pair of factors of production (which equals the marginal rate of technical transformation between these two goods), this technical rate also equals the common for all individuals' marginal rate of subjective substitution between the same two goods.

Further, from equations (2.28) and (2.29), we can derive the following:

$$\frac{W_j}{P_i} = \frac{\partial T/\partial V_j}{\partial T/\partial X_i} = \frac{\partial U^g/\partial v_j^g}{\partial U^g/\partial x_i^g} \tag{2.32}$$

This shows that in equilibrium the subjective marginal rate of substitution between any productive service and any good, which is common for all individuals, is also equal to the marginal technical rate of transforming that productive service into the good in question.

Thus, given the assumptions mentioned above, when a perfectly competitive economy is at equilibrium the necessary conditions for an overall Paretian optimum are satisfied. In proving this statement, the equality of the price of each good with its marginal cost which prevails under competition at equilibrium has played a crucial role. It was once speculated whether all prices proportional to the marginal costs would also satisfy the necessary conditions for a Paretian optimum. It can easily be shown that it will not.

Assume that the prices of all goods are proportional to their marginal costs and the factor of proportionality is k. We have then:

$$P_i = k \frac{W_j}{\partial X_i / \partial v_{ji}} \quad \text{(where } k \neq 1\text{)} \tag{2.33}$$

and

$$\frac{P_i}{P_h} = \frac{\partial X_h / \partial v_{jh}}{\partial X_i / \partial v_{ji}} = \frac{\partial T / \partial X_i}{\partial T / \partial X_h} \tag{2.34}$$

We see here that even with prices only proportional to the respective marginal costs, the price ratio between any two goods is equal to the marginal rate of technical transformation between the two. Hence one of the two necessary conditions for a Paretian optimum is still satisfied. However, the other necessary condition is now violated, because with prices proportional to marginal costs a rearrangement of equation (2.33) gives us:

$$\frac{W_j}{P_i} = \frac{\partial X_i}{\partial v_{ji}} \cdot k = \frac{\partial T / \partial V_j}{\partial T / \partial X_i} \cdot k \quad (k \neq 1) \tag{2.35}$$

but

$$\frac{W_j}{P_i} = \frac{\partial U^k / \partial v_j{}^k}{\partial U^k / \partial x_i{}^k} \tag{2.36}$$

Hence

$$\frac{\partial U^q / \partial v_j{}^q}{\partial U^q / \partial x_i{}^q} \neq \frac{\partial T / \partial V_j}{\partial T / \partial X_i} \tag{2.37}$$

In other words, the price ratio between a factor of production and a commodity is no longer equal to the marginal technical rate of transformation between them. However, the individuals would still, in equilibrium, equalise this price ratio with their marginal subjective rate of substitution between the factor and the good. Hence this subjective rate of substitution between the two will no longer be equal to the technical rate and the second necessary condition for an overall Paretian optimum will not be fulfilled.[1]

Mishan [19, p. 210] has said, '. . . perfect competition is neither a necessary nor a sufficient condition for meeting . . . the optimum conditions . . .' That perfect competition is not a necessary condition is obvious when one remembers that the marginal conditions could be met by state managers taking prices as parameters and consumers being allowed to buy at uniform prices. Mishan considers that perfect competition is not a sufficient condition for meeting the marginal conditions, because 'universal perfect competition is consistent with fixed hours of work in production, [so that] each worker is subjected to a constraint which, in general, prevents his adjusting the supply of his labour to the going wage-rate' [19, pp. 210–11]. This is a refreshing intrusion of an empirical consideration into this highly abstract context of discourse, but considering all the other unlikely assumptions on which the model of perfect competition is based, perhaps not much is either lost or gained by adding the assumption that each individual is free to adjust the supply of his labour to the equilibrium wage-rate.

It is worth emphasising that the propositions about the relation between a Paretian optimum and the perfectly competitive model apply only when the system is *at equilibrium*. Nothing has been said so far about how the system comes to be in equilibrium, or the relation between such a competitive system when it is in disequilibrium and a Paretian optimum. We shall return to these questions in a later chapter.

2.7 SOME QUALIFICATIONS AND THE THEOREMS OF ACTIVITY ANALYSIS

We have so far glossed over some technical limitations of the marginal conditions for a Paretian optimum, which now it is time to mention. These necessary conditions only establish stationary values of the functions to be maximised and are therefore consistent with both maximum and minimum values of those functions. Certain second-order conditions have to be satisfied along with the necessary

[1] Kahn [11] had argued that an optimum allocation of resources is achieved even if prices everywhere are not equal to marginal costs but have the same ratio to them. Kahn's argument requires a zero elasticity of all factor supplies (which he had assumed) and the assumption that no good be both a final product and an intermediate good. See McKenzie [18]. These two assumptions make equation (2.36) irrelevant. Kahn's assumption that the distribution of economic welfare did not matter (because everybody had the same *marginal* utility of income) made his idea of the 'ideal output' similar to that of a Paretian optimum.

first-order conditions for the relevant functions to be maximised. However, with the assumption of diminishing marginal rates of substitution between any two factors in the production of every good, between any two goods for every consumer, and between any factor and any good for every individual; and the assumption of decreasing returns to scale in the production of every good, the second-order conditions necessary for a maximum will also be satisfied whenever the various first-order necessary conditions mentioned earlier are satisfied.

The traditional *a priori* welfare model explicitly rules out any indivisibilities as we noted in Section 2 above. But there are some indivisibilities to be found in real life—especially in factors of production. Indivisibilities do not make rational decisions about the allocation of an economy's resources impossible: if an explicit social welfare function is given, the values of the social welfare function in the different possible allocations of the indivisible factors and goods can be directly verified; thus a *unique* social optimum—or the single best arrangement of factors and goods—can be chosen.

But of course this is not the procedure of the *a priori* welfare theory. Here the search is for some necessary conditions which will be true of all social optima in general so long as they are in conformity with the Paretian value judgments. The starting-point is not a specific fully-defined social welfare function, but only a general *type* for the social welfare function. Because of this procedure of the traditional theory, the calculus as well as the newly developed activity analysis are incapable of either formulating any necessary general conditions for a Paretian optimum (and hence the social optimum) or proving the theorems about the correspondence between the equilibrium point of a perfectly competitive system and a Paretian optimum in the presence of indivisibilities. Indeed, the reason for the latter outcome is not difficult to appreciate. Indivisible factors are often associated with declining marginal costs up to large levels of outputs. If a firm with such a marginal cost has an infinitely elastic demand curve for its product it will soon grow so large that the market will no longer be perfectly competitive. Regarding indivisibilities, then, the conclusion is that if they are important in a system no general propositions about Paretian optimality are possible. In Chapter VII we shall consider some *ad hoc* procedures for dealing in a partial way with questions involving indivisibilities—that is dealing with one or a few sectors at a time rather than the whole economy at a time.

Even if all indivisibilities are assumed away, so that all the production and utility functions are smooth and continuous with the right kind of curvature, there remains a problem. Since the traditional analysis of allocation has relied on the calculus and theory of implicit functions, it also rests on the implicit assumptions that every factor of production is used for producing each commodity and that something is produced of each good, so that the necessary equalities will apply to all factors and goods simultaneously. The former assumption conflicts with the existence of some free goods in real life and the latter with the existence of goods whose production is physically possible but which in fact are not produced because it is not profitable for anybody to do so. In other words, an allocation which is optimal on the Paretian value judgments may well be what is sometimes called a 'corner solution'; diagrammatically it is a point which is not within a box diagram such as in fig. 2.2 but on one of its axes. Yet another problem left unsolved by the application of the calculus is that the first-order and second-order conditions are only necessary conditions for a maximum, and not both necessary and sufficient. This is because they ensure only a local maximum. They need to be supplemented by what have been called the total conditions, which ensure that no improvement (in the light of the Paretian value judgments) can be brought about by totally ceasing the production and/or consumption of some good or by introducing the production and/or consumption of some new good.

The recently developed techniques of activity analysis have proved the existence of Paretian optima in a model which does not include the assumptions that every factor of production is used for producing each commodity and that something is produced of each good. Moreover, these techniques also do away with the need to formulate second-order and total conditions. However, it is important to emphasise that though these techniques have provided more rigorous formulations of the old propositions about a perfectly competitive model in equilibrium and Paretian optima, *they have not tackled any of the problems raised by indivisibilities and possible non-market interdependencies in production and consumption*; again, just like the old analysis, *the new techniques also assume away all uncertainty or imperfections of knowledge about the relevant data for individual decision-making in production or consumption*.

Activity analysis has also needed the assumption of convexity in production and preferences. This concept of convexity is in terms of the properties of sets of points. A set is convex if all the points on a straight line joining any two points within the set are also in the set. Convex preference maps entail diminishing marginal rates of substitution between any two goods for each individual. With constant returns to scale, production is convex; with decreasing returns

33

to scale, it is strictly convex; but with strong increasing returns to scale somewhere in the economy, production as a whole may be non-convex. Based on the above-mentioned assumptions of no non-market interdependencies, indivisibilities or uncertainty, and using the properties of convex sets and the notion of a supporting plane, activity analysis has proved the following two propositions:

(i) Every competitive equilibrium is a Paretian optimum—with respect to a given pattern of distribution of utility levels.

(ii) Every Paretian optimum is a competitive equilibrium—with respect to a given pattern of distribution of utility levels.

For the first of the two propositions, the assumption of convexity in production and preferences is not strictly necessary. It is not difficult to see that even if there are some non-convexities in the system, provided a perfectly competitive model has somehow got in equilibrium, there is necessarily a Paretian optimum on the reasoning given in the last section. But the second proposition (that every Paretian optimum is a competitive equilibrium) does require the assumption of convexity, because if non-convexities (like unexhausted increasing returns) exist, then obviously some industries cannot be perfectly competitive; a Paretian optimum for such a model, requiring price to equal marginal cost, cannot be sustained by perfect competition because it would require a number of firms to make perpetual losses.[1]

Finally, we should note that when applied to a specific problem activity analysis of either the linear-programming type (when returns to scale are assumed constant) or the non-linear programming type (when returns to scale are assumed to decrease) produces through its duality properties a set of accounting prices for factors and goods which is consistent with a given objective function. Accounting prices are no more than the programming equivalents of the optimal ratios of the type given in equations (2.19) and (2.20); those ratios also imply a set of relative prices. Therefore, it needs to be remembered that activity analysis can begin to be applied in any specific situation only when the coefficients of the variables in the objective function are first given. These coefficients have to be found from a social welfare function if the problem concerns the society rather than an individual firm. Managers of firms in a completely socialised economy, or of departments within a large firm, can use accounting prices which have been calculated (a difficult task!) and handed

[1] See Koopmans [13] and [14]. A pioneering article in this field was by Arrow [1]. See also Debreu [4].

down to them by a higher authority. This process has been described as 'decentralised decision-making'. But the title is somewhat inapt; to make each manager use the specially calculated accounting prices for their production decisions is likely to require much more control and planning than the usual methods of muddling through. However, this is not meant to be a criticism of the use of accounting prices for some micro problems—or even at the national level if that were practical. In any case, they can only be calculated according to given objectives, technological conditions, and factor availabilities.

Hence though activity analysis shows that decentralised decision-makers can, working on their own, maximise the social objective function once they are given the correct accounting prices for their outputs and inputs, it does not imply that there is no longer the need in any social allocation problem to start with a given social welfare function. Activity analysis is only a new mathematical technique which is more suitable to establish some results than the calculus for the sort of reasons which were given above. Even with the old methods there are—on certain simplifying assumptions—unique marginal rates of substitution (identical in production and consumption) between every pair of goods in the equilibrium solution. But the equilibrium solution is not unique unless one distribution of utility levels is specified as the most desirable; this remains true whether the programming methods or the more traditional methods are used for analysis.

2.8 PIGOVIAN IDEAL OUTPUT

Pigou assumed the aim of social policy to be to 'promote welfare' [21, p. 10], but in order to simplify this 'task so enormous and complicated as to be quite impracticable' [21, p. 11] he chose to restrict the range of his inquiry to 'that part of social welfare that can be brought directly or indirectly into relationship with the measuring-rod of money' [21, p. 11]. He suggested: 'This part of welfare may be called economic welfare' [21, p. 11]. For an individual, Pigou identified economic welfare with satisfaction—assuming expected and realised satisfaction from economic activity to be equal except in the case of the saving decision because of the defective 'telescopic faculty' [21, pp. 23–37] of the individual.

As we shall notice in the next chapter, Pigou had assumed measurability and inter-personal comparability of utility, and had also drawn some conclusions from the premise that aggregate social utility ought to be maximised. Therefore, he could have gone on to formulate a concept of a unique social optimum where the allocation was both efficient (in some sense) and also had the right distribution of incomes. But Pigou's concept of the ideal allocation or ideal output is in fact something similar to the concept of an overall Paretian optimum. (Moreover, the underlying analytical structure of Pigou's theory was exactly similar to Pareto's; that is, the basic assumptions mentioned in Section 2 also underlie Pigou's formulation.) For Pigou, a situation 'in which each several sort of resource is allocated in such a way that the last unit of it in any one use yields a physical product of the same money value as the last unit of it in any other use' [22, p. 33] is one of ideal allocation, irrespective of the distribution of money incomes. If it is a community comprising some rich and some poor people, then 'though it is true that aggregate satisfaction can be increased by departures from this type of allocation in ways deliberately designed to benefit poor people, it is *probable* that departures taken at random, e.g. through the operation of monopoly power, would diminish aggregate satisfaction' [22, p. 35, original italics]; therefore, according to Pigou, such an allocation is properly called the ideal allocation with respect to the existing distribution of money income.

It is then not surprising that from Pigou's rule for ideal allocation, mentioned above, it is possible to derive the marginal conditions for a Paretian optimum. (In respect of the theory of allocation, the only big difference between the Paretian and the Pigovian approaches is the latter's emphasis on external economies and diseconomies, with which we shall be dealing in Chapter IV.) Pigou's allocation rule, given in words in the foregoing paragraph, can be expressed thus:

$$P_i \cdot \partial X_i/\partial v_{ji} = P_h \, \partial X_h/\partial v_{jh} \tag{2.38a}$$

where P stands for price; thus price of a commodity times the marginal product of a factor in that sector must be equal to the price of another commodity times the marginal product of the same factor in that other sector. Similarly, the allocative rule applies to any other factor too:

$$P_i \cdot \partial X_i/\partial v_{ki} = P_h \cdot \partial X_h/\partial v_{kh} \tag{2.38b}$$

If equation (2.38a) is divided by equation (2.38b) we have our equation (2.9) again. Hence the allocative rule covers the necessary conditions for production optimum (assuming, of course, that producers are genuine cost-minimisers who *know* the best-practice production functions). Since P_i has to be the same for all consumers for equations (2.38a) and (2.38b) to be meaningful, the necessary conditions for the Paretian exchange optimum are also covered by the allocative rule, provided it is also assumed that all individuals aim at maximising utility. Finally, if we divide equation (2.38a) by $P_h \cdot \partial X_i/\partial v_{ji}$ and equation (2.38b) by $P_h \cdot \partial X_i/\partial v_{ki}$ we obtain the following:

$$\frac{P_i}{P_h} = \frac{\partial X_h/\partial v_{jh}}{\partial X_i/\partial v_{ji}} = \frac{\partial X_h/\partial v_{kh}}{\partial X_i/\partial v_{ki}} \qquad (2.39)$$

or

$$\frac{P_i}{P_h} = \frac{\partial T/\partial X_i}{\partial T/\partial X_h} \qquad (2.40)$$

But the price ratios are equal to the common marginal rates of subjective substitution; hence equation (2.40) can be written out as equation (2.19). Since another part of Pigou's allocative rule laid it down that the price paid to a factor must be equal to the value of its marginal product, by similar manipulation equation (2.20) could also be derived from Pigou's rule. Hence his allocative rule for an ideal allocation and the marginal conditions for a Paretian optimum amount to the same thing.

2.9 TIME AND ALLOCATION

Various attempts have been made to introduce time and thus 'dynamise' the traditional theory of allocation. One simple way of doing this was suggested by Lange [15]: we first need to know the total period (a finite time horizon) over which total welfare is to be maximised; we can then imagine this total period to be divided into a finite number of discrete time intervals. The same physical good in different time intervals can then be considered a different commodity. Armed with these assumptions, our individual utility functions and the production functions given above can now be interpreted to cover the whole period of time. (X_1 is one good; X_2 is another physical good in the same period, or the *same* physical good in *another* period; and so on.) Our necessary conditions for a Paretian optimum, equations (2.19) and (2.20), can now be reinterpreted also to imply that for any one commodity the intertemporal marginal rate of subjective substitution between any two periods must be equal to the intertemporal marginal rate of technical substitution for the same two periods, and that these rates should be the same for all individuals. An exactly similar necessary condition for the relation between goods and factors can also be derived. Different goods may now have different marginal rates of intertemporal subjective or technical substitution for the same pair of periods, and the 'same' good may have different marginal rates of substitution for different pairs of periods. However, this approach does not tackle the problem that the requirements of goods for the *end* of a finite time horizon would help to determine the subjective and technical intertemporal rates of substitution between goods and factors. More sophisticated models have been constructed in recent years.

An interesting model of technological efficiency over time has recently been developed.[1] Technological efficiency over time may be defined as the characteristic of that path of expansion of an economy on which—with given rates of investment in each period—no increase in the consumption of any good in any period is possible without a decrease in the consumption of some other good in some period or other; or if consumption rates for different periods are taken as given, then no increase in the accumulation of any good in any period is possible without a reduction in the accumulation of some other good in some period.

For technological efficiency over time, it would not be sufficient for the output of each successive point of time to be just anywhere on the corresponding instantaneous production frontier. Assume two commodities each of which can be divided into two parts, consumption (C) and stock (S), so that we have $C_1 + S_1$ and $C_2 + S_2$. Time is counted in discrete periods $(1, 2, 3, \ldots T)$. There are constant returns to scale with diminishing marginal rate of substitution along any iso-product curve in each process. Let us now consult fig. 2.6. Assume that point P gives the initial endowments of the stocks of the two goods: $S_1(0)$ and $S_2(0)$. MN is then the instantaneous production-possibility curve for period 1. The consumption combination of the two goods prescribed by the social welfare function for period 1 is given by point R. Given this prescription, the actual combination of the two goods in period 1 should be chosen on the instantaneous production frontier from among the points on the arc xy. Different points on the arc xy—after the prescribed consumption for period 1 (as shown by point R) is subtracted—will result in different combinations of S_1 and S_2 as inputs for period 2.

Corresponding to each of these points on xy—for example, a, b, and c—there will be in fig. 2.7 a different instantaneous production-possibility curve for period 2—such as M_aN_a, M_bN_b, or M_cN_c. We can generate an envelope (the *efficiency envelope*, E^2F^2 in fig. 2.7) of all such instantaneous production-possibility curves resulting from the choice of the different points on xy in fig. 2.6.

Suppose it is prescribed that the two goods will be wanted in period 2 in the proportion shown by point e. Then technological

---

[1] See Dorfman, Samuelson, and Solow [6], especially pp. 318 ff. See also Koopmans [13]. A great deal of the work in this field is built on Malinvaud [17]. A survey section is to be found in Hahn and Mathews [9].

efficiency requires that in period 1 a *particular* point be chosen on the segment *xy*—namely point *b*. If any other point is chosen, then output of each of the two goods in the prescribed proportion in period 2 will be smaller than it need be. Choosing just any point on the instantaneous production-possibility curve is not sufficient for technological efficiency over time. For example, on the instantaneous production-possibility curve of period 1 only one particular point is relevant; but that particular point can be chosen only if the proportions for the two goods for period 2 are prescribed.

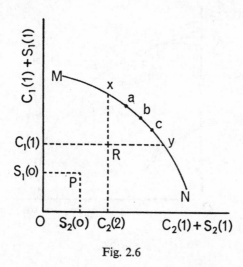

Fig. 2.6

Implicit in the foregoing discussion is the following necessary condition for technological efficiency over time: The marginal rate of substitution between any two goods regarded as outputs of the previous period must equal their marginal rate of substitution as inputs for the next period. This condition applies for any number of goods.

Let us look at fig. 2.8. Each point on E^2F^2 (which is the outer envelope of the instantaneous production-possibility curves resulting in period 2 from different stock combinations of period 1) can, in its turn, generate a production-possibility curve for period 3; the envelope of all such curves is E^3F^3. Given the relevant production functions, the time profile of consumption, and the initial stocks, it is possible to generate for the successive periods a succession of envelopes—E^2F^2, E^3F^3, E^4F^4, etc.

39

The efficient two-period path *Pbe* of fig. 2.7 stretches out into successive periods as the time horizon is extended, and appears as *Pbexyz* in fig. 2.8. Each point on any efficiency envelope is a point on one efficient path, and on only one such path if we assume diminishing marginal rates of substitution between the inputs and the outputs. Efficiency envelopes are the loci of successive terminal points on efficient paths. Given the same initial stocks (as shown by point *P*

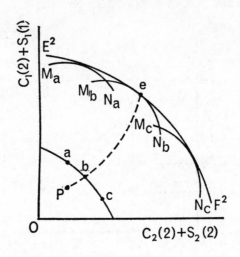

Fig. 2.7

in fig. 2.8) and the same decisions regarding consumption in each period, there are infinitely many efficient paths emanating from *P*, each distinguished by a different composition of stocks in the final period. Instead of beginning with given initial stocks (as at point *P* in fig. 2.7) and working into the future to successive efficiency envelopes, it is also possible to begin with a prescribed terminal point. In that case, there will be infinitely many efficient paths leading to the same terminal point, with each path starting from a different initial composition of stocks.

It can be shown that if each small competitor knows all the relevant current prices and their current rates of change, then perfect competition will result in a technologically efficient path of expansion over time. Of course it will be only one of the infinitely many such technologically efficient paths, so that, given the initial stocks, if the decision-makers or the comment-makers (see Chapter VI on this distinction) are not indifferent between the different compositions of stocks in the terminal period it will be necessary for the policy-makers to choose a particular terminal stock composition and to calculate corresponding relative prices for the terminal and other periods.

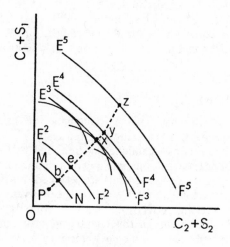

Fig. 2.8

Attempts have also been made to develop propositions about the relation between perfect competition and growth paths for the economy which are Pareto optimal. These models also assume perfect knowledge on the part of each individual and firm, and absence of any externalities. Further, to the extent that they rest on the 'widely acceptable' Paretian value judgments, their theorems are subject to the criticisms we shall develop in Chapter VI; that critique applies as much to any attempted 'dynamic', as to the standard static *a priori* welfare economics. Finally, even if the decision-makers or the comment-makers did accept the Paretian value judgments, a 'dynamic' Paretian optimal solution is no more unique than a static one: nor does the 'dynamic' solution necessarily dominate—even on the Paretian value judgments—any Paretian non-optimal 'dynamic' solution. The problem, which we shall discuss in the next chapter, of the unlikely feasibility of altering the distribution of purchasing power (or utility levels) without violating some of the necessary Paretian

D   41

conditions, exists as much at the 'dynamic' level as at the static level.

Returning to technologically efficient growth paths, we need to emphasise that just as the theorems regarding static technological efficiency cannot begin to be applied, even in a stationary economy, unless the relative amounts of goods are laid down by a social welfare function, so also the theorems of intertemporal technological efficiency cannot be applied unless the length of the time horizon, the time profile of consumption, and the initial composition of stock are specified according to a social welfare function. We shall return to these questions in Chapter VI, Section 6.2c, and again in Chapter VII.

CONCLUSIONS

We have noted the basic value judgments and assumptions on which the concept of a Paretian optimum rests. We showed that a Paretian optimum is not a unique position, and that such an optimum does not necessarily dominate any non-optimal arrangement—even if the Paretian value judgments are accepted. We introduced the concept of Scitovsky community indifference curves. We examined the relation between a perfectly competitive economy at equilibrium and a Paretian optimum. In this chapter we also came across the important concepts of technological efficiency and the production frontier which would be relevant even if we rejected some or all of the Paretian value judgments. The frame of reference of the theory outlined in this chapter has been very artificial and restricted; we have shown how qualified the results of the traditional theory are, even within such a framework; in the next two chapters we examine some further and more important qualifications of its theorems which are made necessary as some of the more unrealistic assumptions are removed.

REFERENCES FOR CHAPTER II

[1] K. J. Arrow, 'An Extension of the Basic Theorems of Welfare Economics', *Proceedings of the Second Berkeley Symposium on Mathematical Statistics and Probability*, Berkeley, California, 19

[2] F. M. Bator, 'Simple Analytics of Welfare Maximisation', *American Economic Review*, 1957

[3] A. Bergson, 'A Reformulation of Certain Aspects of Welfare Economics', *Quarterly Journal of Economics*, 1938; also reprinted in his *Essays in Normative Economics*, Cambridge, Mass., 1966

[4] G. Debreu, *Theory of Value*, New York, 1959

REFERENCES FOR CHAPTER II

[5] Maurice Dobb, 'Economic Theory and Socialist Economy: a reply', *Review of Economic Studies*, 1934–35

[6] R. Dorfman, P. A. Samuelson, and R. M. Solow, *Linear Programming and Economic Analysis*, New York, 1958

[7] W. M. Gorman, 'Community Preference Fields', *Econometrica*, 1953

[8] J. de V. Graaff, *Theoretical Welfare Economics*, Cambridge, 1957

[9] F. H. Hahn and R. C. O. Mathews, 'The Theory of Economic Growth: A Survey', *Economic Journal*, 1964

[10] J. R. Hicks, 'The Foundations of Welfare Economics', *Economic Journal*, 1939

[11] R. F. Kahn, 'Some Notes on Ideal Output', *Economic Journal*, 1935

[12] P. B. Kenen, 'On the Geometry of Welfare Economics', *Quarterly Journal of Economics*, 1957

[13] T. C. Koopmans, *Three Essays on the State of Economic Science*, New York, 1957

[14] T. C. Koopmans, 'Convexity Assumptions, Allocative Efficiency, and Competitive Equilibrium', *Journal of Political Economy*, 1961

[15] Oscar Lange, 'The Foundations of Welfare Economics', *Econometrica*, 1942

[16] I. M. D. Little, *A Critique of Welfare Economics*, 2nd edn., Oxford, 1957

[17] E. Malinvaud, 'Capital Accumulation and Efficient Allocation of Resources', *Econometrica*, 1953

[18] L. W. McKenzie, 'Ideal Output and Interdependence of Firms', *Economic Journal*, 1951

[19] E. J. Mishan, 'A Reappraisal of the Principles of Resource Allocation', *Economica*, 1957

[20] E. J. Mishan, 'A Survey of Welfare Economics, 1939–59', *Economic Journal*, 1960

[21] A. C. Pigou, *The Economics of Welfare*, 4th edn., London, 1932

[22] A. C. Pigou, *Socialism versus Capitalism*, London, 1932

[23] P. A. Samuelson, *Foundations of Economic Analysis*, Cambridge, Mass., 1947

[24] P. A. Samuelson, 'Evaluation of Real National Income', *Oxford Economic Papers*, 1950

[25] T. Scitovsky, 'A Note on Welfare Propositions in Economics', *Review of Economic Studies*, 1941–42

III

FEASIBILITY, SECOND BEST AND IMPERFECT KNOWLEDGE

This chapter is in a sense a continuation of the last, because we do not yet question the ethical presumptions of *a priori* welfare theory, but only investigate the modifications which need to be made in its theorems if some of its assumptions are relaxed. We shall remove the following three assumptions one by one in the three sections of this chapter: that lump-sum redistributions of purchasing power are possible; that all the necessary conditions for Paretian optimality can be simultaneously satisfied; and that all individuals have perfect knowledge of the circumstances they need to know for rational decisions regarding profit and utility maximisation. The consequences are serious for the traditional theory—each one of its theorems has to be qualified.

3.1 FEASIBILITY PROBLEMS

Even if the whole set of Paretian value judgments were found morally impelling (which is in fact asking for a lot), and ignoring all the special assumptions we have mentioned, the concepts of a Paretian optimum and the Paretian welfare frontier (and the corollaries derived from them concerning allocation) have relevance for policy only on the assumption that a redistribution of utility among individuals, whenever it is desired, can be brought about through a very special kind of taxation which consists of lump-sum levies and grants. Let us see why this is so.

Suppose a tax is laid on the sale of all or some goods. Irrespective of whether it is an *ad valorem* tax (i.e. per unit of price) or a specific tax (i.e. per unit of good), in general the price paid for a good by the buyers is not now exactly the price received by the sellers. Consumers, in equilibrium, will equate the ratio between prices which they pay for any two goods with their marginal rate of subjective substitution, and the producers would equate for the same two goods the ratio between their prices which they received with their marginal rate of technical substitution. Hence the subjective and technical rates of substitution between any two goods will not be equal in equilibrium, and a necessary condition for a Paretian

44

optimum will be violated. That is, we have the following situation:

$$\frac{P_i}{P_h} = \frac{\delta U^g/\delta x_i{}^g}{\delta U^g/\delta x_h{}^g} \neq \frac{\partial T/\delta X_i}{\delta T/\delta X_h} = \frac{M_i}{M_h} = \frac{P_i{}^- t}{P_h{}^- t} \qquad (3.1)$$

where P stands for price; M for marginal cost, and t for the rate of the specific tax which is the same for all goods. If we assume an *ad valorem* tax, then P_i and P_h have to be multiplied by $(1 - t)$, where t is the common *ad valorem* tax rate. Now $(1 - t)$ will cancel out from the last ratio in equation (3.1). It was therefore at one time believed that an equal rate of *ad valorem* indirect tax on all goods does not interfere with the necessary conditions for Pareto optimality. However, such a tax does affect the marginal conditions regarding substitution between a commodity and the supply of a factor. In short, we have the situation as given by equation (3.2a), where W_j is the price per unit of factor V_j.

$$\frac{W_j}{P_i} = \frac{\partial U^g/\partial v_j{}^g}{\partial U^g/\partial x_i{}^g} \neq \frac{\partial T/\partial V_j}{\partial T/\partial X_i} = \frac{W_j}{P_i(1-t)} \qquad (3.2a)$$

The situation is about the same if instead of the general *ad valorem* tax there is a general (proportional or progressive) income tax. Now the prices for the goods which the buyers pay will be the same prices as the sellers receive. However, this time the price received by the owner of a factor of production is not the same as the price paid by its buyer. Hence, in equilibrium, the marginal rate of subjective substitution between a factor of production and a good will not be equal to marginal rate of technical substitution between the same two. That is, we have the following situation:

$$\frac{W_j}{P_i} = \frac{\delta U^g/\delta v_j{}^g}{\delta U^g/\delta x_i{}^g} \neq \frac{\delta T/\delta V_{ji}}{\delta T/\delta X_i} = \frac{W_j{}^- t^*}{P_i{}^- t} \qquad (3.2b)$$

where W_j is the price per hour of labour and t^* is the rate of tax per hour.

Only such taxes as do not produce a difference between the price of anything (good or factor of production) as received by the seller and as paid by the buyer are free from this shortcoming of interfering with some necessary condition for a Paretian optimum. Only poll taxes and such like pass this test; a tax which passes this test is described as a lump-sum tax. So long as the criteria on the basis of which a tax is assessed are non-economic, it can be a lump-sum tax. However, if a tax is assessed on the basis of income (or the type of goods consumed, e.g. luxury goods)—as it must be if it is to bring about some desired change in the distribution of utility levels—then

45

the price received by the seller of the services of a factor of production (if it is an income tax) is different from the price that the buyer pays for it, or the price paid for a luxury good (if it is a sales tax) is different from the price which the buyer receives. The same applies to the subsidies on incomes or on goods.

It is possible in theory to devise a very special system of *indirect* taxes which leave each individual on a higher level of utility than if the same amount of total revenue were raised by direct taxes. It was shown by Corlett and Hague [5] that such a system would consist of unequal indirect taxes for all individuals, whereby commodities which are most complementary to leisure for an individual have the highest tax rates and the commodities which are most competitive with leisure for him have lowest rates. The exact rates would have to depend on the degree of complementarity and competitiveness; hence the system would require a detailed knowledge of the utility functions of individuals or small sub-groups. Anyway, since what is complementary to leisure for some person may be a substitute for another, the same commodity may have to be differently taxed according to who is buying it.

Any *feasible* taxes, subsidies and transfer payments, etc., will then be such as interfere with some Paretian marginal condition or other about the equality of various ratios of partial derivatives. If externalities are assumed away, non-interfering taxes and subsidies have to be lump-sum. With the assumption of externality which takes the form of uncompensated envy they need not be lump-sum in order to be non-interfering; but if they are to be non-interfering with Paretian optimal conditions when such an externality exists, then the fiscal authority must know the precise utility functions of the individuals *as judged by themselves*. Since this assumption cannot ever be satisfied, *feasible* fiscal measures even then would be such as do interfere with some of the necessary conditions for Paretian optimality. See Chapter IV, Section 2.

Suppose society is at point H on its Paretian welfare frontier in fig. 3.1. According to the given Pareto-type welfare function point L is the social optimum. If lump-sum redistribution is possible, the economy moves along the welfare frontier to point L, and the concept of the Paretian welfare frontier has proved its usefulness.

But what if the only characteristics of the individuals which could be the criteria for lump-sum transfers (such as the height, colour of the hair or the eyes, etc.) are not so distributed as to enable the decision-making authority to get the kind of redistribution that it desires? In any large community that will almost certainly be the case. Moreover, redistribution changes are seldom once-for-all. If changes in circumstances—e.g. in production possibilities—necessitate recurring redistributions, then whatever criteria are chosen for the lump-sum transfers will get known so that the transfers will no longer be lump-sum; they will necessarily violate some of the necessary conditions for a Pareto optimum.

If we admit that any redistribution has to take place as a result of 'feasible legislation', then starting from point *H* on the Paretian

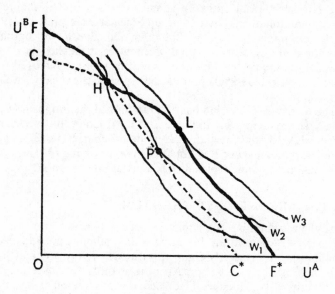

Fig. 3.1

welfare frontier, the economy has the choice of points in the utility space along a locus which necessarily lies, on both sides of *H*, inside the Paretian welfare frontier; such a locus is known as the *feasibility locus* (*CC** in fig. 3.1). For given levels of economic welfare of one person, this locus shows the maximum level of economic welfare that is administratively feasible for the other person to have.

A given welfare function, even if it is Pareto-type, may be such that the *feasible social optimum* does not lie on the Pareto welfare frontier. For example, in fig. 3.1 the feasible social optimum is at point *P*, which is inside the Paretian welfare frontier. At point *P* some of the necessary conditions for a Paretian optimum are necessarily violated; yet it is the social optimum.

47

Thus, even if the whole set of Paretian value judgments (and therefore a Pareto-type welfare function) were found to be morally impelling, the necessary conditions for a Paretian optimum may have little relevance for the social optimum once the question of feasibility is recognised, unless the economy is already at a Paretian optimum which also happens to be the social optimum according to the adopted welfare function. The relevant measures for policy are those which will take the economy from point H along the feasibility locus to the feasible social optimum at point P (in fig. 3.1). And yet, a Paretian optimum has come to occupy such an exaggerated position in the economists' thinking that often the phrase 'the optimum allocation of resources' is used when what is implied is only a *Paretian* optimum—an 'optimum' which may be far removed from what is the feasible social optimum according to the society's welfare function.

The foregoing discussion has also established the proposition that unless we are completely indifferent to distribution, it can never be worth while to attain just any Paretian optimum. In fig. 3.1, H is a Paretian optimum, but P is not. Yet even according to the Pareto-type welfare function depicted, P is a better point than H.

3.2 THE SECOND-BEST THEOREM

If all the assumptions of Chapter II, Section 6 can be granted, then the necessary conditions for a Paretian optimum are satisfied at equilibrium in a perfectly competitive model; *but* in any real situation there is likely to be some reason or other for some of those conditions to be violated. One such obvious reason is the fiscal activity of any government whenever it takes a form other than that of lump-sum transfers. We have just discussed in the last section the inevitability of non-lump-sum transfers for purposes of distributive justice. (Cf. also Chapter IV, Section 2.) Moreover, if there is any differentiation of product in an otherwise large market, if some markets are small and specialised, or if there is a degree of monopoly for some other reason, then profit-maximising behaviour will not be sufficient to equate the prices of the relevant goods to their marginal costs. Similarly, imperfections in a factor market will make the price received by the owner of the factor different from the marginal cost of employing that factor as seen by the producer. Further, for some institutional reason or other the price of the same factor may be different in different sectors of the economy.

For a long time economists had believed that if for some reason a marginal condition for a Paretian optimum is not fulfilled it still remained desirable to meet the other marginal conditions as nearly as possible. Hence in a world where there obviously existed monopolistic competition in at least some sectors, it was considered desirable (on the assumption that a Paretian optimum was desirable) that price should be made equal to marginal cost wherever a government could enforce its judgment—as in public utilities. There was an implicit belief that the greater the number of the various necessary conditions which could be satisfied in an economy, the nearer the system would be to such an optimum. This belief found application in a number of special fields like public finance and international trade theory. At the same time there were also indications of doubt about the validity of these inferences till, some years ago, Lipsey and Lancaster [10] published a paper in which they established the propositions: '. . . given that one of the Paretian optimum conditions cannot be fulfilled, then an optimum situation can be achieved only by departing from all the other Paretian conditions'. They went on: 'The optimum situation finally attained may be termed a second best optimum because it is achieved subject to a constraint which, by definition, prevents the attainment of a Paretian optimum.' However, their conclusion about the general conditions for a second-best position (which is second best in the light of the Paretian value judgments) was not encouraging: '. . . in general nothing can be said about the direction or the magnitude of the secondary departures from optimum conditions made necessary by the original non-fulfilment of one condition'.

Let us now show how Lipsey and Lancaster derive their theorem. Following their procedure, let us assume that we are interested in maximising the following utility function of one individual

$$U = U(x_1, \ldots x_n) \tag{3.3}$$

subject to the transformation function

$$t(x_1, \ldots x_n) = 0 \tag{3.4}$$

where x stands for *both* goods (1 to s) and factors of production ($s + 1$ to m). The necessary conditions for a maximum are

$$\frac{\partial U/\partial x_i}{\partial U/\partial x_n} = \frac{\partial t/\partial x_i}{\partial t/\partial x_n} \quad (i = 1, \ldots n) \tag{3.5}$$

Now assume that one of these necessary conditions cannot be fulfilled for some reason, so that we have

$$\frac{\partial U/\partial x_1}{\partial U/\partial x_n} = k \frac{\partial t/\partial x_1}{\partial t/\partial x_n} \quad \text{where } k \neq 1 \tag{3.6}$$

The utility function (3.3) now has to be maximised subject to two constraints (3.4) and (3.6). Therefore, the conditions which are *now* necessary for a second-best maximum can be written as:

$$\partial U/\partial x_i - \lambda \partial t/\partial x_i - \Pi \frac{\partial U/\partial x_n \cdot \partial^2 U/\partial x_1 \partial x_i - \partial U/\partial x_1 \cdot \partial^2 U/\partial x_n \partial x_i}{(\partial U/\partial x_n)^2} -$$

$$k \frac{\partial t/\partial x_n \cdot \partial^2 t/\partial x_1 \cdot \partial x_i - \partial t/\partial x_1 \cdot \partial^2 t/\partial x_n \partial x_i}{(\partial t/\partial x_n)^2} = 0 \quad (3.7)$$

These necessary conditions for a second-best maximum will be different from the old conditions unless the coefficient of Π is zero. (Π cannot itself be zero because that contradicts the additional constraint.) Without investigating the nature of the particular goods and factors involved in a given situation, it is impossible to lay down the conditions for the coefficient of Π to be zero. Similarly, there are no general rules about how the necessary conditions for a maximum when there is only one constraint should be modified when there is an additional constraint. Lastly, once an additional constraint has been introduced of a kind which destroys the simplicity of the necessary first-order conditions, the existence of a second-best maximum position cannot be counted upon. As in the original article, the theorem has been proved here for one person's utility function (subject to a transformation constraint); but Lipsey and Lancaster claim that the theorem also applies to the situation where the utility functions of all individuals are compared.

However, it is instructive at this stage to remind ourselves that in a sense the (overall) Paretian optimum is based on two other kinds of optima: the technological production optimum and the Paretian exchange optimum. It is possible that the additional constraint in some situation affects the necessary conditions only on the exchange side. For example, excise taxes make the prices paid by the buyers different from those received by the sellers, but they may not drive a similar wedge between the received and the paid factor prices. In such a situation the necessary conditions for technologically efficient production remain unaffected. Now, technological efficiency may be relevant to the social objectives of an economy, and will be capable of achievement, even if the ideals of consumer sovereignty and a Paretian exchange optimum are rejected. Even if the prices of some commodities are not the same for all individuals, technological efficiency in production is still possible. It is for this reason that a much-cited alleged corollary of the second-best theorem is wrong.

The alleged corollary is: '. . . there is no *a priori* way to judge as between various situations in which some of the Paretian optimum conditions are fulfilled while others are not' [10, p. 11]. This alleged corollary has recently also been used as a new *a priori* welfare criterion. (See pp. 206–208 of Chapter VIII.) In fact, though Lipsey and Lancaster asserted that this corollary followed from their theorem, they never proved that it did. The most that the theorem implies is that between *some* pairs of situations where some Paretian conditions are satisfied while others are not, it will not be possible to make any *a priori* comparisons. The theorem does *not* imply that this is true of *all* such pairs. Of course, this leaves us with the problem of having to decide which of these two categories any given pair of situations drops into. But this is not as bad as it might seem; after all, we are in any case left with the problem of having to decide if any of the necessary conditions for Paretian optimality (and if so which and how far) are violated in some given situation. Further, the blanket— and as we shall be arguing rather unattractive—concept of Paretian optimality also covers the concept of technological efficiency. Hence in any given situation if the first impression is that 'some of the necessary conditions for Paretian optimality are violated' it might make good sense for the comment-maker or the decision-maker (see Chapter VI on this distinction) to try to discover whether the violations are at the technological production frontier level or at the Paretian exchange optimum level or both; and whether the violations are more easily removable at one of these levels as compared to the other. It is information of this kind which would enable them to decide whether any *a priori* judgment can be made between the two sub-optimal situations.

As it happens, the argument is easier to grasp in a diagram rather than in algebra. Consider fig. 3.2. Assume that there is some imperfection in the factor market (e.g. different rates of pay in different sectors for exactly the same kind of labour) as well as some imperfection in the commodity market (e.g. different prices for the same product to different consumers). The first imperfection implies that the economy's production possibility frontier is not attained because the necessary conditions for technological efficiency cannot be fulfilled. The economy is stuck at a point, such as A in fig. 3.2, *within* its production frontier. The second imperfection implies that the necessary conditions for a Paretian *exchange* optimum are not satisfied; hence point A of fig. 3.2 does not lie on a Scitovsky community indifference curve.

Let us also consider another possible situation. Now assume that the necessary conditions for technological efficiency are met: each factor has the same price everywhere; and all producers are effective cost minimisers who know the economics of the best practice techniques. Hence the economy is at a point (B in fig. 3.2) on its production frontier. However, 'assume that due to some indirect taxes the marginal rate of technical substitution between goods is not equalised with their marginal rate of subjective substitution. The prices of goods might yet be the same for all individuals, so that a Paretian exchange optimum is reached. This means that the economy is on a Scitovsky community indifference curve, which cuts the production frontier at *B* in fig. 3.2.

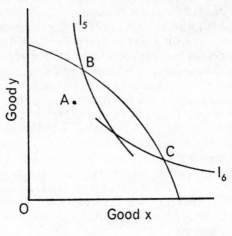

Fig. 3.2

For both the situations depicted as points *A* and *B* in fig. 3.2 some of the necessary conditions for Paretian overall optimality are violated. Now some economists would like to conclude that on the Paretian value judgments there is no *a priori* way of choosing between the two points *A* and *B*. Yet *B* lies *on* the production frontier, whereas *A* lies *within* the frontier. It may be that *B* is to the North-East of *A*, as in fact it is in fig. 3.2. In this case, since *B* has more of at least one good and no less of any other, it will pass the Samuelson comparisons when compared with *A*, and will therefore, on the Paretian value judgments, show greater *potential* welfare. (We have inevitably had to anticipate here the results of Chapter V, Section 2.) As it happens, there is neither a current-weighted nor a base-weighted quantity index which can ever unmistakably tell us that one position has more of at least one good and no less of any other. None the less, we might easily be faced with comparisons between situations in one of which all the conditions for technological efficiency are met, though some other Paretian optimal conditions are violated, while in the other, some of the necessary conditions for technological efficiency are also violated.

Suppose, now, that we have a comparison between points such as C and A in fig. 3.2. Movement along a technological production frontier is easier than along the Paretian utility frontier, because the policy measures in the former case do not have to be lump-sum. Provided the equality of prices of factors (as paid by their employers) between sectors is not affected by the administrative and/or fiscal measures to change the composition of output from a point like C (in fig. 3.2) on the production frontier to another point like B on it, we can say that any point on the production frontier—even though it does not have the properties of an overall Paretian optimum—at least potentially dominates in a technological sense any point within the production frontier. All this is on *a priori* basis. Of course comparisons based on the production frontier *alone* are not likely to be sufficient basis for *welfare* comparisons according to most social welfare functions—Paretian or non-Paretian. A larger output may possibly be unfairly distributed, for example. Hence no complete *recommendation* can be based on the basis of technological efficiency alone. However, we have proved that it is not true to say, as Lipsey and Lancaster claimed, that there is no *a priori* way to judge as between various situations in which some of the Paretian optimum conditions are fulfilled while others are not. Depending on which category of necessary conditions (technological, exchange, or overall) is involved, it is possible to make *a priori* comparisons on the Paretian value judgments. However, whether any *a priori welfare* comparisons—between optimal and/or non-optimal situations—are valid is a different and more fundamental question to which we return in Chapter VI. We shall produce reasons there to show that no *a priori welfare* comparisons are valid.

In their concluding section Lipsey and Lancaster recognise a limitation of their proof of the second-best theorem—namely that it is 'conceived in terms of single-layer optimum'. In their discussion of the more realistic multiple-layer optima, they make a remark which by implication contradicts the foregoing alleged corollary of their theorem. They say there: 'It is obvious, of course, that the second best will never be at a point which is technically inefficient (has less of one commodity and no more of the other) relative to any attainable point' [10, p. 32]. This clearly implies that if we are confronted with two attainable sub-optimal points, and if one of them (say B in our fig. 3.2) is on the production frontier to the North-East of the other

(A), then A cannot be the second-best point, whereas B might be. Hence some *a priori* comparison is already possible, even though both A and B are sub-optimal, and we are still talking in terms of global (i.e. production-cum-exchange) Paretian optimality. If we confine our attention to the technological production level, then any sub-optimal point which is on the technological production frontier (even though some of the Paretian exchange conditions are violated there) at least potentially dominates, for the reasons given above, the sub-optimal points which are also within the technological production frontier.

An incidental criticism of the use of the second-best theorem as a criterion on the strength of its alleged corollary is the following: if it is argued that of any two non-optimal situations neither can ever necessarily be the superior, it can lead one to conclude that a Pareto optimal situation will necessarily be better than either of the two non-optimal situations. But of course the proposition is false, because we showed in Chapter II that a Pareto optimum is not necessarily superior to any non-optimum (pp. 21–22). In the chapter on international trade we shall examine an example from the literature of the use of the second-best theorem as a criterion and find that as a result this false proposition has been formulated there (pp. 206–208).

Some other considerations qualify the second-best theorem. One exception arises from the possible specificity of factors (and, much less likely, of commodities). A factor of production is specific to a factory, farm, industry, or sector if it has no alternative use. Again, if a factor has different prices between some large sectors but the same price within each sector, or happens to be immobile between sectors due to some institutional reasons, then though the conditions for technologically efficient allocation for the economy as a whole are violated, it may still be possible to have technological efficiency *within* each sector.

If we could assume that each utility function (and therefore also the social welfare function) is separable, and that each transformation function is separable, then we could conclude that even if some necessary condition for a Paretian optimum were not fulfilled somewhere in the system, the rest of the necessary conditions would still be required to reach a second-best Paretian position; with separable utility and transformation functions, violation of a necessary condition affects only a part of the economy and not the rest.[1] Going back to our equation (3.7) above, the assumption of separabi-

[1] In the above argument *additive* separability is assumed; see Davis and Whinston [6]. For the definition of a function which is additive separable, see Chapter IV, Section 5, p. 83.

lity reduces each of the second-order cross partial derivatives to zero, and therefore also the coefficient of Π. Hence the rest of the necessary conditions for a Paretian second-best are the same as those for a Paretian (first-order) optimum. However, these are strong assumptions, which amount to saying that if the inter-relations between the relevant variables are weak enough for a violation of some of the necessary conditions in some parts of the economy not to affect the marginal conditions prevailing in the other parts, then the other parts will not be affected. In other words, the problem of investigating in a particular situation where some necessary conditions are violated whether the other necessary conditions need to be modified (and if so, how) still remains.

In discussions of what the necessary conditions for a second-best position are likely to be, economists have sometimes given the impression of forgetting that the Paretian second-best is as much a relative concept as the Paretian (first-best) optimum. First, it is a (second-best) optimal position only on the Paretian value judgments; it may not necessarily be optimal (any more than is a first-best Paretian optimum) on some other value judgments. Further, we have shown in Chapter II, pp. 21–22, that a first-best Paretian optimum is not necessarily superior (even according to the Paretian value judgments) to any position which is not such an optimum; similarly, a Paretian second-best position—even is the necessary conditions for it in some given context could somehow be discovered—is not necessarily superior (even according to the Paretian value judgments) to *any* position which is not a second-best position. Unless there is a specific welfare function to work with, it is no more logical (even if we are told that the welfare function will have to be Pareto-type) to recommend moving to any Paretian second-best position than it is to recommend moving to any Paretian (first-best) optimum. *If we do not accept that social welfare functions have to be Pareto-type, then of course both the Paretian first-best and second-best positions cease to have any general relevance.* But this argument is to be fully developed in Chapter VI.

3.3 IMPERFECT KNOWLEDGE

In the last chapter we noted that *if we grant many assumptions* (see p. 28) a perfectly competitive economy in equilibrium is a Paretian optimum. It is legitimate to ask how a perfectly competitive economy actually comes to be in equilibrium. The traditional answer is that in a perfectly competitive industry every firm knows the price of its output and inputs; this information then enables it to devise the profit-maximising output. This is referred to as the assumption of perfect knowledge. Let us now examine if there are likely to be situations in practice for which such an assumption is likely to be significantly untrue.

In an industry where the level of total output has varied according to a fairly regular pattern in the recent past, and where there are no strong reasons for not expecting that pattern to continue, a firm can make reasonably accurate estimates of the expected prices of its output and inputs. Provided the firms in an industry make fairly compatible estimates about the rate of change over time of these prices, none of them is likely to be seriously disappointed. Hence though the assumption of perfect knowledge about the relevant prices seems a very strong assumption, it is possible to believe that some real-world situations would approximate it sufficiently for a more or less unique equilibrium price for more or less identical products to emerge.

But it is also possible to conceive of real-world situations where the assumption of perfect knowledge is far too strong. When we have a new industry, or an industry experiencing rather rapid technological change, or an industry with marked fluctuations in demand, then there is no *necessary* reason why a number of sellers of even a homogeneous good (in a market of many buyers) should all hit on the same price either simultaneously or fairly close together in time. Unless we presume the existence of industry-wide equilibrium, with the total amounts supplied and demanded equalling each other at a given price—or unless we presume a recent history of a more or less stable price for the industry as a whole—the demand curve of each firm as visualised by it is not necessarily perfectly elastic, and there is no reason why in exploring their individual demand curves all firms should hit at the same price. When a perfectly competitive industry is not in equilibrium, since price is no longer a given parameter, marginal revenue is no longer equal to it. However, it is the marginal revenue that a profit-maximising producer equalises with marginal cost. Hence under the kind of circumstances visualised, price no longer equals marginal cost in each firm. In other words, even an economy solely consisting of perfectly competitive industries, at least some of which are *not* in equilibrium, will not have allocation which is Paretian optimal. Moreover, if perfect knowledge is not assumed there is no necessary reason why each perfectly competitive industry should be in equilibrium.

The recognition of imperfect knowledge also has the important implication that the price mechanism working on its own may not be sufficient to bring about the necessary conditions for technological efficiency—which is likely to be relevant to most kinds of social welfare functions. One important reason for this is that the recognition of the possibility of uncertainty introduces information as a good into the analysis for the first time. The marginal cost of transmitting certain kinds of information is often low or even zero. To the extent that some information (e.g. about improvements in techniques and design, etc.) is a factor of production, technological efficiency requires that its price must be the same for all producers. This requires that the information should be available to all its potential users at the very low or zero marginal cost at which it is available to its original possessor or discoverer. But if information once gained has to be transmitted so cheaply, there may be very little incentive for firms and individuals to engage in information-seeking activity, i.e. research. On the other hand, with the grant of legal rights for restricting the use of newly-discovered knowledge, the necessary conditions for reaching the economy's production frontier are violated; one might say this is because less than the 'maximum' use is made of the new knowledge. There is then a dilemma here.

Governments try to solve this dilemma to some extent by subsidising some of the more basic kinds of research on the condition that its results will be freely available. But obviously much more needs to be done in this field in most economies. Moreover, even the free or low-cost availability of information about new techniques of a kind which would pass a reasonable investment criterion sometimes does not ensure that entrepreneurs will in fact utilise that information, so that governments often give extra inducements to bring this about. (Cf. Chapter VI, Section 3 and Chapter VII, Section 3.) This may be due to 'lethargy', 'irrationality', or 'lack of drive', etc.; or due to the existence of another form of uncertainty (to be discussed below) in a rather large measure. As to the first list of causes—all put in inverted commas—they all obviously involve ethical assessments. For, if entrepreneurs prefer a 'quiet life' and, according to the adopted social welfare function of the society concerned, are entitled to follow their own judgment in such things, then technological efficiency for such an economy would have to be modified to include the constraint of a 'quiet life' among the other constraints. If we ignore this rather special possibility we have here an important reason for doubting the ability of the market mechanism working entirely on its own to take the economy to its production frontier or, consequently, its Paretian utility frontier.

Let us now examine the other way in which the existence of uncertainty might prevent the attainment of the economy's production frontier. An example may be helpful at this stage. Suppose the welfare function of some society and its economic circumstances are such that it is considered desirable to have an annual amount of a good called X_1. So far this good has been imported by some firms. Assume that X_2 is an important component of X_1. X_2 is not produced at present at home because X_1, its sole or main user, is produced abroad; and because transport costs prevent competitive sale of X_2 abroad. Hence if any firms are to undertake the manufacture of X_2 at home they must know that X_1 will also begin to be produced at home. Now it may be that it would be more profitable to manufacture X_1 at home rather than to import it if X_2 were available at home. Hence if it was known that X_2 was going to be produced at home, then X_1 would also be produced at home. If both X_2 and X_1 are produced at home, then the society would get X_1 cheaper by at least the transport costs. If there also happens to be some unemployment in the economy—structural or involuntary, whether it is disguised or not—then there is also a favourable employment effect.

The example could be slightly altered by assuming that X_1 is neither produced nor imported; but that if X_2 were produced at home, then it would become profitable for some firms to produce X_1, and that X_2 is profitable to produce only if X_1 is also being produced.

Normally when the mutual repercussions on the profitability of any two (or a group of) industries are so strong we should expect integration between them or exchange of information through trade journals (or even monopolistic collusion—if the repercussions are along a horizontal relationship rather than a vertical one as in our example). But vertical integration is sometimes uneconomical when a region is adopting a certain kind of industry for the first time: the necessary entrepreneurial and managerial skills for quite so large an enterprise may be lacking; and—to introduce an imperfection in the market—it might be difficult to raise the necessary finance for a large integrated undertaking, even though it would otherwise be economically viable. As for tacit or overt monopolistic collusion, there may be legal prohibitions to prevent that. Exchange of information is the other possibility mentioned above. Such exchange of information may actually take place. Assuming perfect knowledge implies that it must take place. But in fact there is no absolute necessity about it, and it is possible that in economies with relatively few entrepreneurs, trade journals, or clubs where businessmen might meet, such exchange of information often fails to take place. Such conditions of imperfect dissemination of commercial information then constitute another reason why the market working on its own may not be able to take the economy to its production frontier.

It is possible for someone to argue that all we have done in the last few pages is to say that if competition is imperfect, then neither the production frontier nor the Paretian utility frontier of the economy is attained, and that we have already come across this proposition. However, the consequences of assuming imperfect knowledge constitute an important category by themselves; because even if competition were almost perfect in some economy, knowledge about changes in technology and about mutual profitability relationships would not necessarily be perfect. Indeed, the newer a certain kind of industry is to a region, and the less developed a region is generally, the more important are the imperfections in business knowledge likely to be. This type of phenomena were once described as *pecuniary external economies*. But this was ambiguous and rather inapt terminology. A pecuniary external economy was assumed to exist when the profits of a firm depend not only on its own output and inputs but also on the outputs and inputs of other firms. But profits of a firm (unless it is an absolute monopoly buying and selling everything in the economy) are always affected by the outputs and inputs of other firms; that is what constitutes the price mechanism or the market. There was nothing *external* about the relationships described as pecuniary external economies. *Unless the assumption of perfect knowledge is dropped*, the ubiquitous fact of interdependence of input and output prices is trivial or—according to another way of looking at it—momentous because this ubiquitous fact in a perfectly competitive economy *at equilibrium* implies a Paretian optimum *if we also grant certain other assumptions*. Hence though there is no such thing as pecuniary external economies, recognising the possibility of imperfections in business knowledge qualifies the propositions of the traditional theory about perfect competition and a Paretian optimum or even technological efficiency.

It is worth mentioning that in situations of the kind discussed in our foregoing example, a mere provision of information about the mutual profitability relationships of X_1 and X_2 may not always be sufficient to ensure that the two industries would get started. Depending on the kind and degree of risk-aversion prevalent among the entrepreneurs, it may sometimes be necessary—provided it does not get overruled by some other considerations laid down by the social welfare function—also to provide some assurance to entrepreneurs in each industry that the other industry would also be starting. The assurance might take the form of subsidies and guarantees for the initial phase of the industries. We are not arguing that, given imperfect knowledge, technological efficiency requires that an 'outside agency' (or the Government) should review *all* investment possibilities in the light of one another; this would be a most impractical task. For small changes in output, or small incremental investments in existing type of industry, even if firms do not know the exact inter-relationships in their profits, and are not sure of each others' actions, non-synchronised adjustments by firms to each others' policies are likely to be sufficient to ensure technological efficiency. Only if some investments are large, their profitability closely inter-related, and knowledge about these relationships limited, might there be a need for interference. This interference could then take the form of government-assisted co-ordination in the interests of technological efficiency.

Not that even government-assisted co-ordination can ever abolish another kind of uncertainty—which concerns possible changes in tastes, technology, weather and so on. Uncertainty from these sources can never be abolished, no matter what amount of co-ordination takes place. This kind of uncertainty makes it impossible to be sure that any pattern of allocation which is at present considered desirable will still be considered desirable by the time it has been achieved. This is a kind of uncertainty conditioning human existence which simply has to be lived with.

Another field where there may be an important degree of un-certainty through the market interdependencies is the consumers' saving decisions. A consumer's decision regarding the form and size of his savings is likely to be affected by his estimate of the future changes in the absolute price level and in relative prices; but what these changes will be depends, to some extent, on others' saving decisions which the consumer acting on his own has no way of knowing. Once again, this is a kind of uncertainty which can be reduced by central co-ordination.

It is not impossible to construct a model in which perfect com-petition, in spite of uncertainty, will lead to an allocation of resources which is a Paretian optimum—provided some other assumptions are granted; we assume that there is a market for each kind of future good under each kind of uncertain outcome, In each such market, buyers purchase the promise of a delivery of a certain amount only if certain particular expectations come true. For each set of inputs, every firm knows the output and revenue under each kind of uncer-tain outcome; it can then easily choose the profit-maximising set of inputs. Similarly, each consumer buys that bundle of promises of future delivery which maximises his expected utility. An equilibrium exists in the market for each good under each kind of uncertainty, with all the Paretian optimality characteristics. See Debreu [7].

But markets for each good of the kind envisaged above do not exist in practice; there is some distribution of risks through insurance companies, but it is necessarily limited. The main reason for this is what has been called the 'moral factor'. In a number of insurances the event against which insurance is to be taken out is not sufficiently out of the control of the buyer of the insurance; another way of putting it is to say that the various uncertain outcomes for which a firm sells promises of delivery may not be completely out of the control of the firm. In short, even if universal perfect competition existed in some economy, once uncertainty is recognised the economy will not be at a Paretian optimum because it will not have the kind of mechanism needed to bring about a Pareto-optimal distribution of risk-bearing.

The conclusion of this section is that we must recognise the possibility of knowledge being imperfect on the part of economic agents, that some of the imperfections in knowledge can never be removed, that some others can be removed or greatly reduced, and that unless this last set of imperfections is removed the production frontier of the economy cannot be attained.[1]

CONCLUSIONS

It is not surprising that the conclusions of a theory should change if some of its basic assumptions are removed. But we have argued in this chapter that three of the basic assumptions of the traditional theory are almost always likely to be inapplicable. Practical redistributions are not likely to be lump-sum; an imperfection in some market or other is likely to exist; and some degree of imperfection in the knowledge about the latest techniques and mutual profit interdependencies may well also exist. The feasibility and second-best considerations show that it might be impossible to get the market fully to meet the purposes of even Pareto-type welfare functions. Some form of imperfection of knowledge may stand in the way of the market mechanism attaining either the Paretian utility frontier or the technological production frontier.

We shall often be referring to the results of this chapter later in the book; the discussion of uncertainty is particularly related to Chapter VII (which is about public enterprise) and Chapter IX (which is

[1] Cf. Koopmans [9, pp. 146–7]: 'To my knowledge no formal model of resource allocation through competitive markets has been developed, which recognises ignorance about decision makers' future actions, preferences, or states of technological information as the main source of uncertainty confronting each individual decision maker, and which at the same time acknowledges the fact that forward markets on which anticipations and intentions could be tested and adjusted do not exist in sufficient variety and with a sufficient span of foresight to make presently developed theory regarding the efficiency of markets applicable.'

about economic development). One other important assumption of the last chapter was that no externalities exist. We explore the consequences of removing this assumption in the next chapter.

REFERENCES FOR CHAPTER III

[1] K. J. Arrow, 'Uncertainty and Welfare Economics of Medical Care', *American Economic Review*, 1963

[2] K. J. Arrow, 'Toward a Theory of Price Adjustment', in M. Abramovitz and others, *The Allocation of Economic Resources*, California, 1959

[3] F. M. Bator, 'The Anatomy of Market Failure', *Quarterly Journal of Economics*, 1958

[4] H. B. Chenery, 'The Interdependence of Investment Decisions', in M. Abramovitz and others, *The Allocation of Resources*, Berkeley, Calif., 1959

[5] W. J. Corlett and D. C. Hague, 'Complementarity and the Burden of Taxation', *Review of Economic Studies*, 1954

[6] O. A. Davis and A. B. Whinston, 'Welfare Economics and the Theory of Second Best', *Review of Economic Studies*, 1966

[7] G. Debreu, *Theory of Value*, New York, 1959

[8] A. Fishlow and P. A. David, 'Optimal Resource Allocation in an Imperfect Market Setting', *Journal of Political Economy*, 1961

[9] T. C. Koopmans, *Three Essays on the State of Economic Science*, New York, 1957

[10] R. G. Lipsey and K. Lancaster, 'The General Theory of Second Best', *Review of Economic Studies*, 1956

[11] M. McManus, 'Comments on the General Theory of Second Best', *Review of Economic Studies*, 1959

[12] H. B. Malmgren, 'Information, Expectation and the Theory of the Firm', *Quarterly Journal of Economics*, 1961

[13] E. J. Mishan, 'Second Thoughts on Second Best', *Oxford Economic Papers*, 1962

[14] E. J. Mishan, 'Reflections on Recent Developments for the Concept of Effects', *Canadian Journal of Economics and Political Science*, 1965

[15] S. K. Nath, 'The Theory of Balanced Growth', *Oxford Economic Papers*, 1962

[16] S. A. Ozga, *Expectations in Economic Theory*, London, 1965

[17] M. W. Reder, *Studies in the Theory of Welfare Economics*, Oxford, 1947

[18] G. B. Richardson, *Information and Investment*, Oxford, 1960

[19] T. Scitovsky, 'Two Concepts of External Economies', *Journal of Political Economy*, 1954

[20] J. N. Wolfe, 'Co-ordination Assumptions and Multiple Equilibria', *Quarterly Journal of Economics*, 1961

IV

EXTERNALITIES

4.1 HISTORICAL BACKGROUND

Externalities, external effects, external economies and diseconomies
—all these terms stand for the same phenomena. The concept goes
back to Marshall, who gave more than one definition but perhaps the
following is the most representative: 'Many of those economies in the
use of specialised skill and machinery which are commonly regarded
as within the reach of the very large establishments, do not depend
on the size of the individual factories. Some depend on the aggregate
volume of production of the kind in the neighbourhood; while others
again, especially those connected with the growth of knowledge and
the progress of arts, depend chiefly on the aggregate volume of production in the whole civilised world' [15, Bk. iv, Ch ix, Sec. 7].

Pigou [22] was to base an important part of his work on such
external effects. But the concept led to a lot of controversy. The main
criticism came from Knight [13]. He argued that if a firm is able to
obtain inputs at lower prices as its output increases, it must be because its supplying firm finds its own input prices being lowered as
its output increases, which in the end must be due to unexhausted
internal economies of scale somewhere in the system. But if there are
internal economies anywhere in the system perfect competition cannot exist. Since Marshall's analysis is about perfectly competitive
situations (according to Knight and many others), the concept of
external economies is invalid.

There are two reasons for rejecting the foregoing conclusion—
reasons which seem obvious today but which have emerged slowly
over years of controversy. Some of the examples of external effects
given by Marshall and Pigou may not be compatible with the assumptions of a perfectly competitive model, but that is no reason
why they may not form an excellent hypothesis about a situation of
uncertainty and imperfect knowledge. We have already dealt with
this point in the section on imperfect knowledge[1] of Chapter III.

---

[1] The consequences for the traditional allocation theory of the imperfections in
producers' knowledge were at one time called *pecuniary external economies* [26].
Though the phenomena are real and, notwithstanding Bator [1], have significant
implications for allocation—as we argued in Chapter III, Section 3—the name
was unfortunate for the reasons already given in that chapter. This chapter is
about what used to be called *technological external effects*; they occur not only
in production but also in consumption.

The second reason why the concept does not have to be rejected is that there are some kinds of external effects which are quite compatible with the assumptions of perfect competition; since they can be present even when a perfectly competitive system is at equilibrium, they spoil to some extent whatever appeal the theorem about the Pareto optimality of perfect competition has. In fact, the implications of some of the external effects are wider than this. We now examine the different kinds of external effects which are compatible with the assumptions of perfect competition and perfect knowledge.

An external effect is assumed to exist whenever the production by a firm or the utility of an individual depends on some activity of another firm or individual *through a means which is not bought and sold; such a means is not marketable, at least at present*—though some conceivable changes in technical knowledge, laws or other social institutions might make such a means exchangeable on the market. All this can also be expressed by saying that an external effect exists whenever, due to the nature of the present economic and social institutions, costs are imposed on others which do not have to be paid for, or benefits are bestowed on others for which no payment is received. External effects can also be referred to as *untraded interdependencies* (between individuals and firms), which may be reciprocal or uni-directional.

External effects may arise in a factory, farm, or office and affect another factory, farm, or office. In this case they are called producers' externalities on producers. Or, again, there might be consumers' externalities on consumers. There are also two mixed categories: producers' externalities on consumers, and consumers' externalities on producers; though this very last category is not so important as the others. The earlier controversies about externalities and Pigou's own contributions tended to take the examples from the first or third categories; i.e. producers' externalities on producers or consumers. The more recent controversies have been largely in terms of consumers' externalities on consumers. Consumers' externalities are closely related to the concept of public goods, which will also be discussed in a later section.

Though the concept of external effects is quite old, rigorous definitions and analysis have been lacking. Buchanan and Stubblebine [4] were the first to offer rigorous definitions. We shall be showing that their definitions are illogical and inadequate. With the help of their definitions, Buchanan and Stubblebine have argued that the Pigovian remedies of a tax or a subsidy, when there are externalities, are inadequate. We shall show that this conclusion, too, is illogical, and that the Pigovian remedies are perfectly adequate in principle.

64

4.2 MARGINAL EXTERNALITIES IN CONSUMPTION

In the last section of this chapter we shall look at some of the qualifications which must be added to our—as indeed all—abstract analyses of externalities.

4.2 MARGINAL EXTERNALITIES IN CONSUMPTION

Let us consider two persons: g and r, who are members of a community consisting of s persons. The commodities and factors which are the share of an individual, say g, are represented as x_i^g and v_j^g respectively. There are n goods and m factors. Good j is the numeraire. Apart from externalities all the other assumptions of pp. 11–12 (as well as the value judgments of pp. 8–11) are retained.

Suppose we have the following ordinal utility functions for the two individuals:

$$U^r = U^r(x_i^r, v_j^r) \tag{4.1}$$

$$U^g = U^g(x_i^g, v_j^g, x_k^r) \tag{4.2}$$

$$(i = 1, \ldots j, \ldots k, \ldots n) \ \ (j = 1, \ldots m)$$

where k is a particular one of the goods 1 to n.

The commonly accepted view is that equation (4.2) establishes that there is an externality because it shows an interdependence.[1] We shall be arguing that this definition of an externality is inadequate and has been the cause of a number of erroneous conclusions. It is also commonly accepted that this externality is *marginal* if we have the following:

$$\partial U^g / \partial x_k^r \neq 0 \tag{4.3}$$

Before we develop our main critique, we should note an incidental mistake in this accepted definition of a marginal externality. Equation (4.3) slurs over the distinction between the function for a certain marginal relationship and the value of that function at a particular point. In other words, equation (4.3) may be true for some values of x_k^r and not for some others, depending on the particular point of equilibrium.

Let us now show that in some situations equations (4.2) and (4.3) may hold, and yet there may be no externality—marginal or otherwise. Assume that commodity X_k which we are considering is a course of body-building lessons that individual r undertakes.

---

[1] Equation (4.2) is the definition of an externality which Buchanan and Stubblebine [4] give; it also underlies the recent article by Dolbear [9] and would indeed appear to be the currently accepted definition. Graaff also defines external effects in this manner in his book.

Assume that r is employed as a watchman by individual g. Assume also that the utility of g is favourably affected by $x_k{}^r$; therefore we have the following equation, which is similar to (4.3):

$$\partial U^g / \partial x_k{}^r > 0 \quad \text{when} \quad x_k{}^r = \text{(say)} \ x_k{}^{r1} \qquad (4.4)$$

where $x_k{}^{r1}$ is a particular equilibrium value of $x_k{}^r$. However, the equation does not necessarily imply the existence of an externality. Since r works for g, it is conceivable that he might get g to pay him a 'bonus' for his undertaking the course of lessons. The possibilities of their both being able to gain from trading $x_k{}^r$ to mutual advantage are not exhausted until the price for X_k that r has to pay (which is a given constant for him under competitive conditions and is also equal to the marginal cost of producing X_k) has been equalised with the sum of the amounts per unit of $x_k{}^r$ that r and g are willing to pay. In other words, the possibilities of mutually beneficial trade are not exhausted until we have the following at some point:

$$\frac{\partial U^g / \partial x_k{}^r}{\partial U^g / \partial x_j{}^g} + \frac{\partial U^r / \partial x_k{}^r}{\partial U^r / \partial x_j{}^r} = \frac{\partial T / \partial X_k}{\partial T / \partial X_j} \quad \text{where} \quad x_k{}^r = \text{(say)} \ x_k{}^{r2} \quad (4.5)$$

and where $T(X_1, \ldots X_n; V_1, \ldots V_m) = 0$ is the economy's production frontier. X_j is the numeraire good; therefore $(\partial T / \partial X_k)/(\partial T / \partial X_j)$ shows the marginal cost of X_k; under competitive conditions it is equal to the market price of X_k. Equation (4.5) expresses a situation where the market price of X_k is equal to the *sum* of its direct marginal utility in money terms to r *and* the incidental marginal utility in money terms to g of r's consumption of X_k. This situation is reached because g and r are able to negotiate that g should pay r for the incidental benefit he derives from r's consumption of X_k.

It can be proved that equation (4.5) in fact is identical with the necessary condition regarding X_k for Pareto optimality under the assumed circumstances. For discovering the necessary condition for a Pareto optimal allocation of resources, we maximise the utility of one individual, say g, as given by equation (4.1), while fixing the level of utility of individual r at one of the infinite arbitrary levels:

$$U^r(x_i{}^r, v_j{}^r) = U^{r0} \qquad (4.6)$$

The other relevant constraints are the production frontier and the following equations:

$$x_i{}^g + x_i{}^r + x_i{}^p = X_i \ (p = 1, \ldots s - 2) \qquad (4.7)$$

$$v_j{}^g + v_j{}^r + v_j{}^p = V_j \ (p = 1, \ldots s - 2) \qquad (4.8)$$

4.2 MARGINAL EXTERNALITIES IN CONSUMPTION

We form the following Lagrangean function for our purpose, find its relevant first partial derivatives, and set them equal to zero.

$$L = U^g(x_i{}^g, v_j{}^g, x_k{}^r) + \lambda r[U^r(x_i{}^r, v_j{}^r) - U^{r0}] +$$
$$\mu_i[(x_i{}^g + x_i{}^r + x_i{}^p) - X_i] + \Pi_j[v_j{}^g + v_j{}^r + v_j{}^p) - V_j] +$$
$$v[T(X_1, \ldots X_n; V_1, \ldots V_m)] \tag{4.9}$$

$$\partial L/\partial x_k{}^g = \partial U^g/\partial x_k{}^g + \mu_k = 0 \tag{4.9i}$$

$$\partial L/\partial x_j{}^g = \partial U^g/\partial x_j{}^g + \mu_j = 0 \tag{4.9ii}$$

$$\partial L/\partial x_k{}^r = \partial U^g/\partial x_k{}^r + \lambda_r \, \partial U^r/\partial x_k{}^r + \mu_k = 0 \tag{4.9iii}$$

$$\partial L/\partial x_j{}^r = \lambda_r \, \partial U^r/\partial x_j{}^r + \mu_j = 0 \tag{4.9iv}$$

$$\partial L/\partial X_k = -\mu_k + v \, \partial T/\partial X_k = 0 \tag{4.9v}$$

$$\partial L/\partial X_j = -\mu_j + v \, \partial T/\partial X_j = 0 \tag{4.9vi}$$

Expressing the partial derivatives as ratios, we derive the following necessary condition for a maximum of U^g subject to the foregoing constraints:

$$\frac{\partial U^r/\partial x_k{}^r}{\partial U^r/\partial x_j{}^r} + \frac{\partial U^g/\partial x_k{}^r}{\partial U^r/\partial x_j{}^g} = \frac{\partial T/\partial X_k}{\partial T/\partial X_j} \left[= \frac{\partial U^g/\partial x_k{}^g}{\partial U^g/\partial x_j{}^g} \right] \tag{4.10}$$

The relevant part of this necessary condition[1] for Pareto optimality is identical to the condition as shown by equation (4.5), which is satisfied in the private equilibrium of individual r. Hence *if g and r are able to trade with each other*, the market brings about the situation depicted in equation (2.5); that situation is identical with the necessary condition for Paretian optimality as shown by equation (4.10). We see then that in spite of the fact which is depicted in equation (4.3) the influence of $x_k{}^r$ on U^g does *not* operate *outside* the market. In other words, *interdependence by itself does not constitute an externality*.

Let us now assume that $x_k{}^r$ is a bed of rose bushes in the front garden of r, who lives opposite g. Utility of g is assumed to be favourably affected by $x_k{}^r$. It can be proved that once again the necessary condition for Pareto optimality is that given in equation (4.10). It is hardly surprising that it should be so, since all the relevant specifications of the situation are the same as before.

Assume that *due to institutional and/or technological reasons*, g and r cannot enter into trade regarding $x_k{}^v$. Now, individual r reaches his

---

[1] The part of equation (4.10) which appears in big brackets implies that if g also consumed X_k directly, then for Pareto optimality the marginal cost of producing X_k should also be equal to its marginal utility to g from his direct consumption of it.

equilibrium in isolation, so to say. Suppose that this equilibrium value of $x_k{}^r$ is $x_k{}^{r1}$, and that for this value of $x_k{}^{r1}$ equation (4.3) holds. With individual r having reached his equilibrium, we shall then have the following situation:

$$\frac{\partial T/\partial X_k}{\partial T/\partial X_j} - \frac{\partial U^r/\partial x_k{}^r}{\partial U^r/\partial x_j{}^r} = 0 < \frac{\partial U^g/\partial x_k{}^r}{\partial U^g/\partial x_j{}^r} \quad \text{where} \quad x_k{}^r = x_k{}^{r1} \quad (4.11)$$

Clearly, now when individual r is in his private equilibrium, the necessary condition for Pareto optimality, as given by equation (4.10), is not satisfied.

The analysis of the foregoing two cases enables us to derive a rigorous definition of a marginal external economy. According to us a (uni-directional) *marginal external economy exists*

when $\qquad \dfrac{\partial U^g/\partial x_k{}^r}{\partial U^g/\partial x_j{}^g} > 0$ for $x_k{}^r = $ (say) $x_k{}^{r1}$ and $x_j{}^g = $ (say) $x_j{}^{g3}$ (4.12a)

and $\qquad \dfrac{\partial T/\partial X_k}{\partial T/\partial X_j} - \dfrac{\partial U^r/\partial x_k{}^r}{\partial U^r/\partial x_j{}^r} = 0$ *for* $x_k{}^r = x_k{}^{r1}$ (4.12b)

However, if along with (4.12a) we have

$$\frac{\partial T/\partial X_k}{\partial T/\partial X_j} - \frac{\partial U^r/\partial x_k{}^r}{\partial U^r/\partial x_j{}^r} - \frac{\partial U^g/\partial x_k{}^r}{\partial U^g/\partial x_j{}^g} = 0 \textit{ for } x_k{}^r = x_k{}^{r1} \quad (4.12c)$$

then there is *no* externality.[1] In words: a (uni-directional) marginal externality (of consumption) exists *when* the utility of g is favourably affected by any change at the margin of r's consumption of X_k, *and when* g does *not* make an appropriate payment to r for this, so that r reaches his equilibrium (which is utility-maximising for him under the circumstances) by equating the market price of X_k with *only* the marginal utility in money terms *to himself* of his consumption of it. However, if g and r are able to trade, and *do* trade with each other— so that the situation depicted in equation (4.12c) results—then there is *no* externality in spite of the information contained in equation (4.12a).

[1] We should note here that if a marginal externality—as defined by our equations (4.12a) and (4.12b)—exists, then it is both what Buchanan and Stubblebine [4] have described as 'potentially relevant' and 'Pareto-relevant'. According to them, a marginal externality can exist which is neither 'potentially relevant' nor 'Pareto-relevant' if only something like our equation (4.3) holds; but we have shown that equation (4.3) by itself does not exhibit anything which can in any logical way be described as an *external* relationship. Our first example proved that equation (4.3) is quite compatible with the price mechanism functioning properly and achieving a Pareto optimum. Correctly defined, an *externality* cannot exist without being both, in the terminology of Buchanan and Stubblebine [4], 'potentially relevant' and 'Pareto-relevant'; hence these two categories which they introduced are redundant.

4.2 MARGINAL EXTERNALITIES IN CONSUMPTION

Suppose now that an external economy does exist as shown by equations (4.12a) and (4.12b). *Would a Pigovian subsidy enable us to reach a Pareto optimum?* (Recall that Pigou [22] had argued that external economies and diseconomies call for taxes or subsidies for an 'ideal output' to be produced. Pigou had mainly production externalities in mind.) Assume that the policy-maker has some way of finding out the value of $(\partial U^g/\partial x_k{}^r)/(\partial U^g/\partial x_j{}^g)$ (i.e. the marginal utility in terms of the numeraire of $x_k{}^r$ to g) for any specific (compatible) points of equilibrium of g and of r; further suppose that these specific values of $x_k{}^r$ and $x_j{}^g$ are $x_k{}^{r1}$ and $x_j{}^{g3}$. Now, if a subsidy (S^r) is granted to individual r for the consumption of X_k such that the marginal rate of the subsidy at any point is always equal to the value of the marginal externality for that point, then the condition for the private equilibrium of individual r becomes:

$$\frac{\partial U^r/\partial x_k{}^r}{\partial U^r/\partial x_j{}^r} + \frac{\partial S^r}{\partial x_k{}^r} = \frac{\partial T/\partial X_k}{\partial T/\partial X_j} \tag{4.13a}$$

where

$$\frac{\partial S^r}{\partial x_k{}^r} = \frac{\partial U^g/\partial x_k{}^r}{\partial U^g/\partial x_j{}^g} \tag{4.13b}$$

Equations (4.13a) and (4.13b) together amount to equation (4.10) which specifies the condition for Pareto optimality. Hence, provided the Pigovian subsidy is 'correctly' calculated—i.e. it satisfies equation (4.13b)—it will bring about Pareto optimality.[1]

Our discussion over the last few pages has been in terms of marginal external *economies*. No real difference is made to the analysis if we consider marginal external *diseconomies*. According to us, *a marginal external diseconomy exists*:

when $\quad \dfrac{\partial U^g/\partial x_k{}^r}{\partial U^g/\partial x_j{}^r} < 0$ for $x_k{}^r = $ (say) $x_k{}^{r1}$ and $x_j{}^g = $ (say) $x_j{}^{g3}$ $\quad$ (4.14a)

and $\quad \dfrac{\partial T/\partial X_k}{\partial T/\partial X_j} - \dfrac{\partial U^r/\partial x_k{}^r}{\partial U^r/\partial x_j{}^r} = 0$ *for* $x_k{}^r = x_k{}^{r1}$ $\quad$ (4.14b)

The necessary condition for a Pareto optimal allocation remains the same as shown in equation (4.10); we just have to note that with a marginal external *diseconomy* $(\partial U^g/\partial x_k{}^r)/(\partial U^g/\partial x_k{}^g)$ will have a negative sign so that the social marginal cost of producing X_k (as

---

[1] Needless to say, a 'correctly' estimated subsidy (or a tax in the case of an external diseconomy) on $x_k{}^r$—though it helps to bring about a Paretian optimum—does not in general restore g to the lower or higher level of utility that he would have enjoyed in the absence of the externality; whether he should be is question about distribution, *not Paretian optimality*: it may often be an important question. If the answer to it—according to the decision-maker or the comment-maker—is positive, we shall require a payment from or to g which is equal to the value to him of the marginal external economy or diseconomy. Cf. Dolbear [9, p. 98].

shown by its market price, which is a given parameter for r) now has to be equal to the *difference* between the marginal utility of X_k to r and its marginal utility to g—both measured in terms of the numeraire.

The conditions for a Pigovian solution when there is a marginal external diseconomy are also shown by equations (4.13a) and (4.13b); the only thing to note is that both sides of equation (4.13b) are now negative so that the 'subsidy' is a *negative* subsidy (i.e. a tax). Once again the condition for a Pigovian solution, equations (4.13a) and (4.13b), are exactly the same as that for Pareto optimality, equation (4.10), when a marginal external economy is present.

Buchanan and Stubblebine [4] have argued that the Pigovian solution is not Pareto optimal. They argue thus: Even when equations (4.13a) and (4.13b) hold, we still have the following:

$$\frac{\partial U^g/\partial x_k{}^r}{\partial U^g/\partial x_j{}^g} > \frac{\partial T/\partial X_k}{\partial T/\partial X_j} - \frac{\partial U^r/\partial x_k{}^r}{\partial U^r/\partial x_j{}^r} - \frac{\partial S^r}{\partial x_k{}^r} \quad \text{when} \quad x_k{}^r = x_k{}^{r2} \quad (4.15)$$

because the right-hand side is equal to zero when equations (4.13a) and (4.13b) hold. (Our equation (4.15) is similar to their equation (9b).) They argue: '. . . these (the terms on the right-hand side) sum to zero when equilibrium is reached. So long as the left-hand term in the inequality remains non-zero, a Pareto-relevant marginal externality remains, despite the fact that full "Pigovian solution" is attained' [4, p. 382]. This is an invalid assertion. The fact that the left-hand side of our equation (4.15), and their equation (9b), is non-zero *does not by itself* constitute an externality, as we have shown above; it is an externality only if it is accompanied by our equation (4.12b). Indeed, unless the individual g is assumed to get satiated with $x_k{}^r$, the left-hand side of equation (4.15) cannot become zero. The fact that the right-hand side of our equation (4.15) sums to zero, along with our equation (4.13b), *implies* that there is no longer any violation of the necessary conditions for Pareto optimality; that the relationship expressed by equations (4.2) and (4.3) has now been accounted for; and that there is no longer an externality.

Buchanan and Stubblebine in fact offer no logical reasons why a comparison of the kind depicted in our equation (4.15), or their equation (9b), should in fact be made. That such a comparison is quite invalid is perhaps best understood by an analogy. Consider an individual a's private equilibrium between any two goods i and j; the condition for this equilibrium is the following:

$$\frac{\partial T/\partial X_i}{\partial T/\partial X_j} - \frac{\partial U^a/\partial x_i{}^a}{\partial U^a/\partial x_j{}^a} = 0 \quad (4.16)$$

70

4.2 MARGINAL EXTERNALITIES IN CONSUMPTION

By analogy with the arguments of Buchanan and Stubblebine, one would have to argue that the individual has not reached full equilibrium even when the above condition is satisfied, because we still have the following:

$$\frac{\partial T/\partial X_i}{\partial T/\partial X_j} - \frac{\partial U^a/\partial x_i{}^a}{\partial U^a/\partial x_j{}^a} = 0 < \frac{\partial U^a/\partial x_i{}^a}{\partial U^a/\partial x_j{}^a} \qquad (4.17)$$

The confusion has arisen because Buchanan and Stubblebine consider that there is an externality so long as the left-hand side of equation (4.15) is non-zero. As we have shown earlier (in the example where $x_k{}^r$ is a course of body-building training), the fact that the left-hand side is non-zero does not by itself constitute an externality.

We can now show that an important conclusion which Buchanan and Stubblebine drew from their analysis is wrong. They maintained: 'The important implication to be drawn is that full Pareto equilibrium can never be attained via the imposition of unilaterally imposed taxes and subsidies until all marginal externalities are eliminated. If a tax-subsidy method, rather than "trade", is to be introduced, it should involve bi-lateral taxes (subsidies)' [4, p. 383]. However, our equations (4.13a) and (4.13b) show that a unilateral tax or subsidy on the person whose consumption creates the externality *does* meet the necessary conditions for Pareto optimality. The 'tax-subsidy' method should not imitate the 'trade' method; and if trade does take place—so that along with equation (4.12a), equation (4.12b) holds instead of equation (4.12c)—then the conditions for Pareto optimality are already met, there is no externality, and therefore no argument for a tax or subsidy.[1]

Davis and Whinston [7] make a similar mistake. An analysis of it will incidentally help us to further elucidate our argument. Following upon the enactment of the subsidy by the Government, when our equations (4.13a) and (4.13b) hold, Davis and Whinston would argue that since the left-hand side in our equation (4.15) is still positive, 'it follows that the . . . individuals may be able to gain by bargaining between themselves thus taking the system away from the Pareto solution' [7, p. 122]. But if the individuals *gain* from bargaining, in what sense is the system going *away* from the *Pareto* solution? In fact, if the individuals *can* bargain, then the Government's giving a subsidy to individual r on the consumption of X_k has been unnecessary, and a Pareto optimum is *not* reached until the individuals *have* bargained to their mutual advantage. Given that

---

[1] The fallacy in the Buchanan and Stubblebine position can be traced to Coase [5] who regarded *any* interdependence as an externality, irrespective of whether there was trade or not.

71

EXTERNALITIES

the Government has placed its irrelevant subsidy even though the individuals can in fact bargain, the necessary condition for Pareto optimality is

$$\frac{\partial U^g/\partial x_k{}^r}{\partial U^g/\partial x_j{}^g} - P^g = \frac{\partial T/\partial X_k}{\partial T/\partial X_j} - \frac{\partial U^r/\partial x_k{}^r}{\partial U^r/\partial x_j{}^r} - \frac{\partial S^r}{\partial x_k{}^r} - P^g = 0 \quad (4.18a)$$

or

$$\frac{\partial T/\partial X_k}{\partial T/\partial X_j} = \frac{\partial U^r/\partial x_k{}^r}{\partial U^r/\partial x_k{}^r} + \frac{\partial U^g/\partial x_k{}^r}{\partial U^g/\partial x_j{}^g} + \frac{\partial S^r}{\partial x_k{}^r} \quad (4.18b)$$

where P^g is the price per unit of $x_k{}^r$ that individual g pays r to induce him to consume more X_k than he would otherwise, even in the presence of the government subsidy.

We can now reiterate that *if there is a meaningfully defined externality, then the Pigovian tax or subsidy approach (depending on whether it is an external economy or diseconomy) will bring about Paretian optimality. However, if trade does take place (which properly implies that though equations (4.2) and (4.3) hold there is no externality), then Paretian optimality is not reached till all bargaining possibilities have been exhausted; in this situation a government tax or subsidy is irrelevant—in the sense that it is not required by the needs of Paretian optimality.*

Reciprocal Marginal Externalities of Consumption

We should now show that none of our conclusions are affected if we consider reciprocal externalities, instead of the uni-directional as hitherto. Regarding our individuals r and g, let us now assume that the externality (in this case an external economy) which X_k gives rise to, is mutual, and that both the individuals g and r themselves also consume X_k directly. We have then the following ordinal utility functions for the two individuals.

$$U^r = U^r(x_i{}^r, v_j{}^r, x_k{}^g) \quad (4.19)$$

$$U^g = U^g(x_i{}^g, v_j{}^g, x_k{}^r) \quad (i = 1, \ldots j, \ldots k, \ldots n) \quad (4.20)$$

where k is a particular good and j is the numeraire.

Once again we have the equations (4.12a) and (4.12b)—showing that when $x_k{}^r = x_k{}^{r1}$ there is a marginal externality on g; we also have the following now:

$$\frac{\partial U^r/\partial x_k{}^g}{\partial U^r/\partial x_j{}^r} > 0 \text{ for } x_k{}^g = x_k{}^{g3} \text{ and } x_j{}^r = x_j{}^{r1} \quad (4.21a)$$

and

$$\frac{\partial T/\partial X_k}{\partial T/\partial X_j} - \frac{\partial U^g/\partial x_k{}^g}{\partial U^g/\partial x_j{}^g} = 0 \text{ for } x_k{}^g = x_k{}^{g3} \quad (4.21b)$$

72

4.2 MARGINAL EXTERNALITIES IN CONSUMPTION

By a method similar to the one we used above it can be shown that the necessary condition for Pareto optimality in this case is:

$$\frac{\partial T/\partial X_k}{\partial T/\partial X_j} = \frac{\partial U^g/\partial x_k{}^g}{\partial U^g/\partial x_j{}^g} + \frac{\partial U^r/\partial x_k{}^g}{\partial U^r/\partial x_j{}^r} = \frac{\partial U^r/\partial x_k{}^r}{\partial U^r/\partial x_j{}^r} + \frac{\partial U^g/\partial x_k{}^r}{\partial U^g/\partial x_j{}^g} \quad (4.22)$$

In other words, the necessary condition is that the marginal cost of producing the good X_k must be equal to the sum of its direct marginal utility to *g* *plus* the incidental marginal utility of $x_k{}^g$ to *r*, *as well as* to the sum of its direct marginal utility to *r* *plus* the incidental marginal utility of $x_k{}^r$ to *g*.

Since in the private market equilibrium the necessary condition for Pareto optimality, which is given by equation (4.22), is not brought about (a fact which is depicted in equations (4.12b) and (4.21b), and which helps to determine that there are two marginal externalities as opposed to mere interdependence), let us examine if the Pigovian measures will bring about Paretian optimality. The Pigovian measures in this situation would consist of a subsidy on the consumption of X_k to each of the two individuals. The marginal rate of subsidy to *r* will have to be as given by equation (4.13b), and the marginal rate of subsidy to *g* will have to satisfy the following relation:

$$\frac{\partial S^g}{\partial x_k{}^g} = \frac{\partial U^r/\partial x_k{}^g}{\partial U^r/\partial x_j{}^r} \quad (4.23)$$

Now if these 'correct' marginal schedules of the two subsidies come into operation each person will then consume more X_k than he would have done otherwise until the price he pays minus the marginal rate of the subsidy equals his marginal utility from X_k. Individual *r* reaches equilibrium once again when equation (4.13a) is satisfied, and individual *g* reaches equilibrium when the following equation is satisfied:

$$\frac{\partial U^g/\partial x_k{}^g}{\partial U^g/\partial x_j{}^g} + \frac{\partial S^g}{\partial x_k{}^g} = \frac{\partial T/\partial X_k}{\partial T/\partial X_j} \quad (4.24)$$

Making substitutions in equations (4.24) and (4.13a) from equations (4.23) and (4.13b) proves that the Pigovian subsidies modify the behaviour of both the individuals in such a way that the necessary condition for Pareto optimality, as shown by equation (4.20), is satisfied even when the marginal externality is reciprocal.

Needless to say, it has been assumed so far that the revenue required for any Pigovian subsidy is raised by lump-sum taxes elsewhere in the economy. Similarly, the revenue obtained from any Pigovian tax is assumed to be spent in a lump-sum way elsewhere in

F

the economy. For a discussion of these and some other underlying assumptions, see Section 7.

Envy and Compassion

We should also mention that there might exist a rather special kind of consumers' externality, which is not caused by any particular items of any persons' consumption, but instead by the relative levels of their total income and wealth. Such an externality exists when there is (untraded) envy or compassion. If envy exists, then as a person or a group of persons have more income and wealth while the others' absolute shares of these remain the same, it does not follow that the others' *utility levels* also remain the same. Since the *relative* distribution of the economic means to welfare has turned against them, if they suffer envy their utility levels would be reduced. If by a curious turn of circumstances the poorer classes could receive a price from the richer classes which was equal to the marginal disutility to them, as judged by themselves, of the increase in the relative share of the rich, then the existence of envy would not amount to an externality. But if envy remains *untraded* or uncompensated, then it constitutes an externality.

Envy might be roused not just by the *relative* distribution of wealth but also by the *absolute* size of others' wealth. In other words, even though *everybody's* wealth increased in the same proportion, everybody would feel increased envy. With this assumption it is possible to imagine an extreme situation whereby a simultaneous and proportionate increase in everybody's income of wealth would *reduce* everybody's utility level; and similarly a proportionate reduction in everybody's income and wealth would *increase* everybody's utility level. But this really is an extreme and unlikely possibility. Similarly, compassion might exist. Again, it, too, may be roused by only the relative levels of income and wealth, or both by their relative and absolute levels. The existence of compassion also constitutes an externality only if it is untraded, or uncompensated.

In modern times Duesenberry [10] has drawn attention to the possible existence of such phenomena, though he made no distinction between mere interdependence and *untraded* interdependence. However, it must be admitted that envy and compassion, if they exist on any large scale, are likely to remain largely untraded. Duesenberry discussed an interesting possibility. If individuals with lower levels of consumption and wealth suffer a disutility from the fact of the higher levels of these things with some people, then the necessary conditions for Pareto optimality (defined to include the influence of externalities) require that the prices for productive services as received by the richer groups should be lower than the market price by an amount which is equal to the money value of the marginal disutility of their income to those who are poorer. Duesenberry contends that under his assumptions these necessary conditions would require progressive income taxation. This seems reasonable because the higher the income of an individual, the greater the number of individuals who earn less than him and therefore suffer envy, and also because the envy suffered by a person from a rich person's income and wealth may rise at an increasing rate as the rich person's income increases. Duesenberry used a model where there is one good and one productive service.

Let us now look at the required modifications of the necessary conditions for Pareto optimality when *untraded* envy exists. Assume that there is a dividing line of income and wealth. Individuals in the higher sub-group are from r to s, and those in the lower sub-group are from g to $r - 1$. The utility function for the individuals belonging to the first and the second sub-group are respectively:

$$U^r = U^r(v_i{}^r, v_j{}^r) \qquad (4.1)^*$$

$$U^g = U^g(x_i{}^g, v_j{}^g, x_i{}^r, v_j{}^r) \qquad (4.25)$$

The marginal rate of technical substitution between any good X_i and any factor V_j supplied by a person g is the same at equilibrium for all individuals; hence it can be written as $(\partial T/\partial X_i)/(\partial T/\partial V_j)$. Reasoning similar to that employed above shows that this marginal rate of technical substitution needs to be equal *not* just to individual g's own marginal rate of subjective substitution between that good and that factor but rather to his own subjective rate *minus* the sum of others' subjective rates of substitution between that good and g's share of factor V_j. Hence when the income and wealth of the richer persons give rise to an externality on each of the individuals in the poorer group the necessary conditions for Pareto optimality are:

$$\frac{\partial T/\partial V_j}{\partial T/\partial X_j} = \frac{\partial U^r/\partial v_j{}^r}{\partial U^r/\partial x_i{}^r} + \sum_{g}^{r-1} \frac{\partial U^g/\partial v_j{}^r}{\partial U^g/\partial x_j{}^g} \qquad (4.26a)$$

and $\qquad \dfrac{\partial T/\partial X_i}{\partial T/\partial X_j} = \dfrac{\partial U^r/\partial x_i{}^r}{\partial U^r/\partial x_j{}^r} - \displaystyle\sum_{g}^{r-1} \dfrac{\partial U^g/\partial x_i{}^r}{\partial U^g/\partial x_j{}^g} \qquad (4.26b)$

If X_j is the numeraire these necessary conditions can be interpreted as follows: The price that r gets for *any* productive service needs to be *lower* than its market price to others by the sum of the money value of the marginal disutility to others arising from his endowment of that productive service. Similarly, the price that r pays for any commodity needs to be *higher* than its market price to

75

EXTERNALITIES

others by the sum of the money value of the marginal disutility to others arising from his consumption of that commodity.

Now if we assume that members of the group r to s are the poorer class and that the externality takes the form of *compassion*, the foregoing formulation of the necessary conditions for Pareto optimality still applies; only this time the price for a productive service that r receives would need to be subsidised. Similarly, the price he pays for any good would also need to be subsidised. This is because the ratios of partial derivatives which appear as the second element on the right-hand side of equations (4.26a) and (4.26b) will now both be positive, whereas when envy exists they are both negative.

When envy or compassion or both exist, the necessary conditions for *Paretian* optimality would require direct and indirect taxes which are progressive and which have been calculated on the basis of equations (4.26a) and (4.26b) in the light of individuals' utility functions of a type which incorporate *their own* judgments. We have here a situation where—provided Pareto optimality is defined to include the influence of *untraded* variables of individual utility functions—*redistributive* taxes and transfer payments which are *not* lump-sum in fact help to bring about Paretian optimality. However, since the utility functions of individuals as judged by themselves are never known, any taxes or transfer payments can be based only on ethical assessments of how and in what way the income and wealth levels of one group affect the utility of some other group. Since the exact information on the utility functions is not available, any income taxes or transfers may well not conform to the rates they would need to be if the necessary marginal conditions for Pareto optimality were to be fulfilled. Hence in spite of the existence of these externalities, any redistributive policy which is *feasible* would also violate the necessary conditions for Pareto optimality, so that the locus of *feasible* utility combinations for different individuals will once again fail to coincide with the locus of Paretian utility combinations; hence the considerations and propositions regarding the feasibility locus, of Chapter III, Section 1, still apply.

Further, it seems ethically rather unattractive to try to establish a case for progressive taxation or for redistributive measures in general, on the basis of the existence of untraded envy, as judged by *themselves*, on the part of those who have less income than others. One trouble with an argument of this kind is that if it were to turn out that the poorer people in some society had no envy of the higher income levels of the richer groups, there would then be no case left for redistributive measures. And it may well be that poverty limits horizons and breeds 'resignation'. Inequality of incomes and wealth

76

has to be considered bad on a variety of ethical grounds; these provide the basis for redistributive measures: these ethical grounds can perhaps be summed up as a *belief* that all persons should have equal *economic means* to welfare, just as they should have equal *political means* to welfare. (Cf. Chapter VI, Section 2b.) But if progressive taxation weakens the incentive of certain economic groups, then the 'right' degree of redistributive policy needs to be worked out for the particular economy in the light of all these ethical and other considerations by the comment-makers or the decision-makers. See the discussion of distributive judgments in Chapter VI, Section 6.2b.

We may conclude this part of our discussion thus: the possible existence of externalities which take the form of envy or compassion arising from unequal income levels implies that the allocation of resources resulting from the workings of the market on its own will be no more Pareto-optimal than it will be if there are other kinds of externalities. However, it is idle to pretend that it is easy to take corrective action (which takes the form of tax rates carefully calculated according to individuals' *known* utility functions *as judged by themselves*) to restore Pareto optimality in the light of these externalities. In any case there are other, wider, ethically more appealing reasons for a comment-maker or decision-maker to want to reduce income inequalities.

We shall be discussing some other implications of externalities of this last kind in Chapter V, Section 4, and in Chapter VI, Section 2a.

4.3 MARGINAL EXTERNALITIES IN PRODUCTION

The analyses and definitions of the last few sections apply not only to consumers' externalities on consumers, but to each of the other kinds of externalities. Producers' externalities on producers are an important category to which quite a lot of attention has been paid by some authors in the past. See Meade [16], and Ellis and Fellner [11]. Rather than evaluate the contributions of these authors individually, we proceed now to recast the main conclusions of the previous sections for producers' externalities.

Let us consider two goods X_1 and X_2 out of the set of n goods. There are m factors of production; v_{j1} represents the amount of factor V_j which goes into the production of the good X_1. Let us consider uni-directional marginal production externalities first. Assume we have the following production functions for the two goods:

$$X_1 = X_1(v_{j1}, v_{k2}) \quad (j = 1, \ldots k, \ldots m) \qquad (4.27)$$

$$X_2 = X_2(v_{j2}) \qquad (4.28)$$

and $\quad \partial X_1/\partial v_{k2} \neq 0$ for $v_{k2} = $ (say) $v_{k2}{}^1$ and $v_{j1} = $ (say) $v_{j1}{}^3$ $\qquad (4.29a)$

77

where $v_{k2}{}^1$ and $v_{j1}{}^3$ represent particular equilibrium values of the factor inputs in the two industries; k is a particular factor from 1 to m. Once again it is to be emphasised that equation (4.27) does not establish the existence of an externality from the second industry on the first; and that, similarly, equation (4.29a) does not establish the existence of a marginal externality. An externality exists only if we *also* have the following:

$$W_k - (\partial X_2/\partial v_{k2})P_2 = 0 \qquad (4.29b)$$

where W_k is the market price per unit of the factor V_k and P_2 is the market price per unit of the good X_2. Equation (4.29b) implies that in the second industry the factor V_k is employed up to the point where its market price is brought into equality with the value of its marginal product in that sector. In other words, in their decisions about how much to employ of a certain factor, producers in the second industry do not take into account any repercussions of their decisions on the first industry.

The necessary condition for Pareto optimality now is:

$$W_k = (\partial X_2/\partial v_{k2})P_2 + (\partial X_1/\partial v_{k2})P_1 \qquad (4.30)$$

If the state of affairs depicted by this last equation is brought about through private trading between the producers of the second and the first industries, so that the producers in the second industry receive a fee or pay a charge equal to the value of the marginal product of v_{k2} in the first industry—then in that case there is no externality. However, equations (4.29b) and (4.30) cannot hold simultaneously. If equation (4.29b) holds in a situation, then the condition for a Pareto optimum is not satisfied; an externality exists, and a properly calculated Pigovian tax or subsidy on the use of the relevant factor in the second industry will bring about a Pareto optimum. The suitable tax or subsidy will have to satisfy the following equation:

$$\partial S^2/\partial v_{k2} = (\partial X_1/\partial v_{k2})P_1 \qquad (4.31)$$

where S^2 represents the subsidy on v_{k2}. The marginal rate of the subsidy on the employment of the relevant factor in the second industry should be equal to the value of the *incidental* marginal product of that factor in the other industry. If the externality in question is a diseconomy, then both sides of equation (4.31) will be negative, and the 'subsidy' therefore will in fact be a tax.

Going back to equation (4.30), it is worth noting that the right-hand side there expresses what Pigou would have called the value of the *social* marginal product of the input v_{k2} in the second industry.

78

It is the *sum* of the values of the physical marginal products of a factor, no matter where the marginal product occurs, and the values are worked out according to the given market prices of the relevant products. But this is not the only possible definition of the social marginal product. The evaluating prices need to be *market-given* only if all the Paretian value judgments are accepted. If in fact we are in a situation where the evaluating prices are to be given by the political decision-makers, then P_1 and P_2 in equation (4.30) would represent these politically-given prices. The right-hand side of equation (4.30) still represents the value of the social marginal product of v_{j2}; but this need not coincide with the value of the social marginal product determined according to the market-given prices. Hence there is an ambiguity in the concept of the value of the social marginal product which should be kept in mind. It is usually believed that provided external economies and diseconomies of the use of a factor are being all added together, we shall have a unique measure of *the* social marginal product of that factor; but this is wrong; we still have to decide on the evaluating prices in the light of a given social welfare function.

Let us now briefly analyse producers' *reciprocal* marginal externalities. Assume that now we have the following production functions:

$$X_1 = X_1(v_{j1}, v_{k2}) \tag{4.32}$$

and

$$X_2 = X_2(v_{j2}, v_{k1}) \tag{4.33}$$

Now, if equations (4.27a) and (4.27b) hold, and the following two equations, then there is a reciprocal marginal externality.

$$\partial X_2/\partial v_{k1} \neq 0 \text{ for } v_{k1} = v_{k1}{}^1 \text{ and } v_{j2} = v_{j2}{}^3 \tag{4.34a}$$

and

$$W_k - (\partial X_1/\partial v_{k1}) . P_1 = 0 \tag{4.34b}$$

The necessary condition for Pareto optimality now is:

$$W_k = (\partial X_1/\partial v_{k1})P_1 + (\partial X_2/\partial v_{k1})P_2 = (\partial X_2/\partial v_{k2})P_2 + (\partial X_1/\partial v_{k2})P_1 \tag{4.35}$$

Once again properly calculated Pigovian taxes (or subsidies) on both industries would help to bring about the necessary conditions for Pareto optimality. The subsidy to the second industry will have to be according to equation (4.31) and to the first industry according to the following:

$$\partial S^1/\partial v_{k1} = (\partial X_2/\partial v_{k1})P_2 \tag{4.36}$$

It is common practice in the literature to maintain that if an external diseconomy emanates from a firm, then it is the *output* of that firm which needs to be reduced by a tax or some other means.

But usually the external diseconomy emanating from an industry is due to some particular *input* there rather than the nature of the product as such. (Indeed, when the external diseconomy is due to the nature of the output as such one can still say that it is caused by each of the factors employed there.) Whenever it is some factor which causes the externality, our foregoing analysis shows—consider equations (4.31) and (4.36)—that the subsidy or tax needs to be on the use of that factor. If an external diseconomy arises from an industry due to the use there of some particular input (such as smoke-creating fuel), then placing the tax on the output instead of the use of that input may in some special cases move the industry to a point on its production function where, though its total output is smaller, it uses more smoke-creating fuel than before because it is an 'inferior' input for the industry (in the same way that a commodity may be 'inferior' for a consumer).

In Chapter II we came across the concept of technological efficiency which requires that the marginal physical product of a factor should be the same in all its uses. When production anywhere has marginal externalities on production somewhere else the simplicity of this rule is spoilt. Assume that there is such a (uni-directional) externality as described in equations (4.27), (4.28), (4.29a), and (4.29b). The necessary condition for *technological efficiency* (i.e. for ensuring the attainment of the production frontier) is now the following:

$$\frac{W_k}{W_j} = \frac{\partial X_1/\partial v_{k1}}{\partial X_1/\partial v_{j1}} = \frac{\partial X_2/\partial v_{k2}}{\partial X_2/\partial v_{j2}} + \frac{\partial X_1/\partial v_{k2}}{\partial X_1/\partial v_{j1}} \qquad (4.37a)$$

or $\qquad W_k = \partial X_1/\partial v_{k1} . P_1 = \partial X_2/\partial v_{k2} . P_2 + \partial X_1/\partial v_{k2} . P_1 \qquad (4.37b)$

In words, the necessary condition is that the marginal rate of technical substitution between any two factors in any ordinary industry must equal the *sum* of their marginal rates of technical substitution in the externality-creating industry *and* in the industry where the externality is created. Given a suitable numeraire and a social welfare function, the condition can also be expressed thus: the price of employing an externality-creating factor to the industry that generates the externality should differ from its price to the other industries (i.e. its market price) by the value of its incidental marginal product to the other industries.

It is worth noting that if there are no externalities in production the necessary conditions for technological efficiency require the same ratio of the marginal physical products of any two factors throughout the economy; no valuation of the products is needed. However, once an externality exists, a factor's marginal physical products in *different*

80

industries arising from its employment in the externality-creating industry, have to be added together. This is not possible unless some relative weights (or prices) are used and the heterogeneous marginal physical products are expressed in some common units, as in equation (4.37b). But prices are partly determined by tastes of consumers and the distribution of incomes and/or the preferences of the policy-makers regarding the products. Hence prices of the products (and therefore also of the factors) can be given only in the light of a social welfare function.

Of course, prices are determined in the light of some sort of social welfare function in operation even when there are no externalities. But without knowing what those factor and product prices are going to be in any given situation, we can always say that so long as there are no production externalities, technological efficiency requires a uniform price for an identical factor throughout the economy. Once there is an externality arising from the employment of a factor somewhere, we cannot make such a simple statement; now technological efficiency would require that the factor creating an externality in a factory should be available to that factory at a price which is *different* from that which other 'factories' not creating any externality pay. The difference in the price per unit of the factor is to equal the Pigovian tax or subsidy per unit on its employment; this depends on the valuation of the incidental marginal products of this factor in the other factories; and the valuation depends on a social welfare function.

4.4 INFRA-MARGINAL EXTERNALITIES

We turn now to infra-marginal externalities which can belong to any of the four categories we have come across above. Let us start by considering consumers' externalities on consumers. Referring to equations (4.1) and (4.2), a uni-directional infra-marginal externality is defined to exist between two consumers when

$$\left.\begin{array}{c} \dfrac{\partial U^g/\partial x_k{}^r}{\partial U^g/\partial x_j{}^g} = 0, \text{ for } x_k{}^r = (\text{say}) \ x_k{}^{r1}; \\[2mm] but \qquad \displaystyle\int \partial U^g/\partial x_k{}^r \ \mathrm{d}x_k{}^r \neq 0 \end{array}\right\} \qquad (4.38a)$$

where the range of integration runs from 0 to $x_k{}^{r1}$.

$$and \qquad \frac{\Delta T/\Delta X_k}{\Delta T/\Delta X_j} = \frac{\Delta U^r/\Delta x_k{}^r}{\Delta U^r/\Delta x_j{}^r} \qquad (4.38b)$$

As we have noted earlier $(\partial U^g/\partial x_k{}^r)/(\partial U^g/\partial x_j{}^g)$ may equal zero for *all* values of $x_k{}^r$—in which case we could describe it as a purely infra-marginal externality; or it may equal zero only for a particular value of $x_k{}^r$. In the latter case the same externality is marginal for some other values of $x_k{}^r$. Our definition of reciprocal infra-marginal externalities in consumption can be formulated by a simple extension of the foregoing definition, and need not be given here explicitly.

Needless to say, infra-marginal externalities have common characteristics with indivisibilities, as far as the logic of a maximisation problem is concerned. Any statement about the necessary optimal conditions must now be hedged by something like the total conditions. Keeping this qualification in mind, the necessary condition for Pareto optimality when there is an infra-marginal externality in consumption, as defined by equations (4.38a) and (4.38b), can now be formulated:

$$\frac{\Delta U^r/\Delta x_k{}^r}{\Delta U^r/\Delta x_j{}^r} + \frac{\Delta U^g/\Delta x_k{}^r}{\Delta U^g/\Delta x_j{}^g} = \frac{\Delta T/\Delta X_k}{\Delta T/\Delta X_j} \qquad (4.39)$$

It can once again be shown that if enough information is available about the externalities and the individual utility functions, then Pigovian taxes or subsidies would enable the necessary condition for Pareto optimality to be met. The essential logic of the problem remains the same, though the ratios in equation (4.39) are to be interpreted to be more like consumers' and producers' surpluses and less like rates of substitution. The Pigovian subsidy (or, where appropriate, the negative subsidy) will have to be calculated according to the following formula:

$$\frac{\Delta S^r}{\Delta x_k{}^r} = \frac{\Delta U^g/\Delta x_k{}^r}{\Delta U^g/\Delta x_j{}^g} \qquad (4.40)$$

Turning now to producers' externalities, and referring to equations (4.27) and (4.28), we have a uni-directional infra-marginal externality between two industries when

$$\partial X_1/\partial v_{j2} = 0, \text{ for } v_{j2} = \text{(say)} \ v_{j2}{}^1 \qquad (4.41a)$$

but $$\int \partial X_1/\partial v_{j2} \, dv_{j2} \neq 0$$

where the range of integration runs from 0 to $v_{j2}{}^1$.

and $$W_j = \Delta X_2/\Delta v_{j2} \qquad (4.41b)$$

The necessary conditions for Pareto optimality now are:

$$W_j = (\Delta X_2/\Delta v_{j2})P_2 + (\Delta X_1/\Delta v_{j2})P_1 \qquad (4.42)$$

A suitable Pigovian subsidy in this case would be according to the following equation:

$$\frac{\Delta S^2}{\Delta v_{j2}} = (\Delta X_1/\Delta v_{j2})P_1 \qquad (4.43)$$

We do not need to give the exact definitions of infra-marginal producers' and consumers' externalities on consumers. Their definitions are similar to those for the other categories given above.

4.5 NON-SEPARABLE EXTERNALITIES

The possibility that some externalities might be non-separable was first pointed out by Davis and Whinston [6]. They made use of the concept of 'strong' or 'additive' separability; a function is separable in this sense if

$$f(x_1, x_2, \ldots x_n) = f_1(x_1) + f_2(x_2) + \ldots + f_n(x_n) \qquad (4.44)$$

Davis and Whinston discussed externalities in terms of cost functions. But that procedure leads to some ambiguities which we shall be noticing below. We define externalities in terms of utility functions and production functions. Provided then that an externality exists— as defined, for example, by our equations (4.12a) and (4.12b)—then the externality is separable only if

$$\partial^2 U^g/\partial x_k{}^r\ \partial x_i{}^g = 0 \text{ for all values of } x_k{}^r \qquad (4.45)$$

That is, an externality on g of r's consumption of X_k is separable if it does not affect the marginal utility schedule of any good to g. A purely infra-marginal externality (i.e. an externality which is infra-marginal for all values of $x_k{}^r$) is always separable; the other externalities may or may not be. We have assumed so far in our analysis that all externalities are separable. On the other hand, if an externality, as defined above, is non-separable we have the following:

$$\partial^2 U^g/\partial x_k{}^r\ \partial x_i{}^g \neq 0 \text{ for some value(s) of } x_k{}^r \qquad (4.46)$$

Since we are assuming that all individual utility functions are convex—i.e. they are based on the usual assumption of diminishing marginal rate of substitution between any two goods—no complications arise about the second-order sufficient conditions for Pareto optimality, even though separable marginal externalities are present. The second-order conditions relate to the signs of the bordered principal minors of the Hessian determinants of second partial derivatives of a Lagrangean function, such as that in equation (4.9). There is a separate such determinant for each good. It is an accepted proposition that the conditions about these signs are met if the second partial derivative of each individual's utility with respect to every good is negative, and if there are no externalities. If utility functions still remain convex, and if the externalities are all separable, then apparently no additional complications arise: we should still expect the second-order conditions to be met.

Similarly, producers' externalities on producers between any two industries are separable if we have the following:

$$\partial^2 X_1 / \partial v_{k2} \; \partial v_{j1} = 0 \text{ for all values of } v_{k2} \qquad (4.47)$$

If equation (4.47) is not true for some values of v_{k2}, then for those particular values the externality is non-separable. Since all production functions are also assumed to be convex—i.e. they also incorporate the assumption of diminishing marginal rate of substitution between any two factors—with separable producers' externalities, again no complications arise about the second-order necessary conditions for Pareto optimality or technological efficiency.

With non-separable externalities new problems can arise. If externalities are non-separable and also reciprocal, then each individual's curve of marginal utility from a certain good shifts each time the other person makes a change in his consumption of the externality-giving good. In fact, the interdependence is exactly of the same form as exists in certain forms of oligopoly and the solution is equally indeterminate. When such non-separable externalities exist between the production functions of firms the most likely outcome is a merger. Between individual utility functions, such externalities do not seem very likely. A non-separable externality which is uni-directional does not pose the same problem. Suppose again that g gets an externality from r's consumption of X_k, and that it is non-separable. Now each time x_k^r changes, g's marginal utility curve for X_k shifts; but this shift does not then go on to change the value of x_k^r through a reciprocal non-separable externality. Hence for each value of x_k^r there is a determinate value of x_k^g. Similarly, if the non-separable externality between the production functions of firms is uni-directional no indeterminancy arises.

At any rate the problems of estimating the correct Pigovian tax or subsidy, which are enormous even with separable externalities, get even more difficult with a non-separable externality. Even when a non-separable externality is uni-directional, the problem now is not only of finding (say) the curve of marginal utility of x_k^r to g, but rather of a separate curve for each equilibrium value of x_k^r. With reciprocal non-separable externalities the problem is obviously beyond the Pigovian measures.

4.5 NON-SEPARABLE EXTERNALITIES

Baumol [2] has recently shown that if there are sufficiently strong non-separable reciprocal external economies (diseconomies) in consumption—not balanced by any similar external diseconomies (economies)—then it will be impossible to locate the social optimum (i.e. the point of maximum social welfare according to a given and well-defined social welfare function) because in such a situation the second-order requirements will not be satisfied for any point. But these are very special assumptions; they do not prove that externalities (even non-separable externalities) will make it necessarily impossible to locate the maximum point of a given social welfare function.

Moreover, non-separable externalities do not seem likely to be common. It is sometimes argued that if the externality affects the marginal cost of a firm, then the externality is non-separable. Davis and Whinston [6], who introduced the idea of non-separable externalities, also originated this argument. According to them, if we have the following two total-cost equations for any two firms or industries 1 and 2 (where C represents total costs, and q represents output):

$$C_1 = f_1(q_1) \tag{4.48a}$$

$$C_2 = f_2(q_2) \cdot g_2(q_1) \tag{4.48b}$$

then since

$$\frac{\partial C_2}{\partial q_2} = g_2(q_1) \cdot \frac{\partial f_2}{\partial q_2} \tag{4.48c}$$

there is a non-separable externality from the first firm on the second firm. But this is far too ambiguous. The total *costs* in the second firm may depend on the *output* of the first firm (or industry) because as it expands the prices of some inputs which both of them use may rise. (If the first industry is rather large the effect on the input prices need not be an indication of any imperfection of the market.) In any case, this example does not represent a properly defined externality. This shows that if we use *cost* functions it is easy to be led into thinking that non-separable externalities are likely to be common. However, once they are properly defined, non-separable externalities do not seem likely.

Even with non-separable externalities, appropriate taxes or subsidies can still be devised unless they are also reciprocal; if they are, Pigovian taxes and subsidies will be extremely difficult to calculate even in theory.[1] However, direct methods (such as prohibitions,

---

[1] Wellisz [29] argued that given enough information the Pigovian measures can be devised even with reciprocal non-separable externalities; but Davis and Whinston [8] have convincingly argued that the information requirements are particularly unrealistic in this case.

zoning, rationing, etc.) could still help reach the technological production frontier or the Paretian utility frontier—if the administrative expense is not prohibitive, which it might well be in a number of cases.

4.6 EXTERNALITIES AND PUBLIC GOODS

Consumers' externalities on consumers of a marginal and separable kind are in some cases related to a special kind of good—the kind of good which Samuelson [24] has called a public good; 'each individual's consumption of such a good leads to no subtractions from any other individual's consumption of that good . . .' Since an individual cannot exclude others from full enjoyment of such a good, the market will find it impossible to produce the good for anybody. The good must be provided collectively.

If there is such a public good in the economy, then a Pareto optimum can be reached only by equating the marginal rate of transformation between the public good and any other good with the *sum* of the marginal rates of substitution between the same two goods for all the individuals, as shown by the following equation:

$$\frac{\partial T/\partial X_h}{\partial T/\partial X_j} = \sum_{g=1}^{s} \frac{\partial U^g/\partial x_h{}^g}{\partial U^g/\partial x_j{}^g} \qquad (4.48d)$$

where good j may be regarded as the numeraire.

Even with the presence of public goods in the economy, there is an infinite number of Paretian optima, and a social welfare function is needed to select one of them. Further, the formulation of the defining characteristics of a Paretian optimum in the presence of public goods does not remove the difficulties of discovering individuals' utility functions, a knowledge of which is *essential* in order to attain a Paretian optimum in the presence of such goods. (This is because different individuals' marginal rates of subjective substitution have to be added together.) But discovering individual utility functions—which is always a difficult task—would be particularly difficult in this case because some individuals may feel tempted to hide their true preferences.

The title and tenor of Samuelson's article suggested that he was contending that all public expenditure is on goods which are 'public goods' according to his definition. But, as Margolis [14] pointed out in a forceful comment, apart perhaps from national defence, hardly any other item of public expenditure in any country totally satisfies Samuelson's definition of a public good; certainly with things like education and roads, as some individual has more of them, at least after a certain limit, others must have less of them. But a much more important shortcoming of Samuelson's formulation of the problem is that it is relevant only if all public expenditure is to be governed by individuals' own preferences; yet in most democratic countries certain parts of the public expenditure are not based on the ideal of consumer sovereignty. For example, compulsory education, and compulsory unemployment and sickness insurance are based on principles other than that of consumer sovereignty. Indeed, a much more useful concept is that of a *merit good*; it is a good which according to the social welfare function of the society concerned ought to be produced on the basis of considerations other than those of consumer sovereignty. A merit good may or may not happen also to be a public good in Samuelson's sense.

It is sometimes assumed that if a merit good or public good is produced in the market sector of an economy, then less than enough inputs will be allocated to the production of that public good; the presumption being that if the State takes over the provision of that public good more factors will be allocated to it. However, this is not necessarily so in all cases. For example, state provision of police protection in all probability requires a lower quantity of inputs than the provision of the *same* degree of police protection by individuals themselves would require. However, it may well be that often, when the State takes over the provision of a public good, the total output that is considered desirable in the light of the adopted aims of social policy is greater than it would have been otherwise.

The chief and very important contribution of the concept of the public good (which is derived from the writings of Swedish economists) is that it exposes the fallacy in the very common assumption that an individual's welfare function coincides with his utility function *as revealed by his market choices*. This common assumption is also expressed by claiming that the market produces only what the consumers want and does not produce what the consumers do not want. See Chapter VI, Section 2a for further discussion of this point.

4.7 EXTERNALITIES AND PUBLIC POLICY

In a sense each one of the previous sections has been about public policy and externalities, but in a rather limited way. We pick up now some of the important considerations which have been ignored so far.

Our analysis above has shown how a Paretian optimum might be attained in the presence of externalities. But if the conclusions arrived at there are not to run into second-best problems we must assume that lump-sum taxes are used to raise the revenue required to grant any subsidies designed for modifying allocation so that externalities will be taken into account and a Paretian optimum reached. (See Chapter III, Section 1 for a definition of lump-sum measures.) Similarly, we must assume that the revenue accruing from any taxes imposed for the same purpose is used in a lump-sum way.

The foregoing analysis is also based on the unlikely assumption that the policy-maker can always discover the precise function describing a particular externality. This implies very *detailed knowledge* about the utility and production functions; it would be impossible to come by such knowledge of the utility functions. However, the underlying value judgments guiding social policy in some situations may well permit an *ethical assessment* by the political decision-makers of the utility (or, rather, welfare) functions of the individuals —ethical assessments on which political and administrative decisions can be based. In this case the utility functions like those in our equations (4.1) and (4.2) are to be interpreted as the ethical assessments of the political decision-makers, for groups of individuals; r and g could now be taken to represent two different groups of individuals. If the externality-correcting administrative measures are worked out on the basis of such *ethical assessments* of externalities, the implication is that the value judgment according to which an individual is always the best judge of his welfare has been dropped. The 'optimality' now being aimed at in the allocation of resources would *no longer* be *Paretian* optimality but a straightforward improvement in social welfare according to specified social objectives. As for externalities on the production side, some information about the more important production functions and the externalities should not be so hard to come by.

No comparisons from the public policy standpoint between different allocations can in fact be made without an explicit or implicit set of aims of public policy; in other words, a social welfare function. (We are inevitably anticipating here a great deal of the discussion of Chapter VI.) It is worth noticing that the concept of externalities is defined with the help of the idea of an existent market; externalities are those inter-relationships in production, consumption, and welfare which do not get reflected in market actions. But *it does not follow that wherever there is an externality social policy will have to be designed to modify allocation so that a Paretian optimum may be reached*. The Paretian value judgments are unlikely to be acceptable in all situations to the decision-makers of even a democracy. Let us take an extreme example. Assume that good X_k consumed by a group of individuals r (represented as $x_k{}^r$) is an addictive drug. Assume further that $x_k{}^r$ has a *favourable* external effect (which, by definition, cannot be reflected in market actions due to some barrier or other) on another group of individuals *g according to their own judgment*. Now, if a Paretian optimum is to be reached in such a situation the consumption of good X_k by group r needs to be subsidised. But it is most unlikely that in any society the policy-makers would want to subsidise $x_k{}^r$. This extreme example serves to emphasise that *any practical action needs to be related to the explicitly given social aims of a situation and that the existence of externalities is no more a sufficient argument for government intervention aimed simply at attaining any Paretian optimum than is the existence of any other circumstances which prevent any of the necessary Paretian conditions from being fulfilled.*

Moreover, the attempt to attain just any Paretian optimum ignores the fact that the distribution of incomes is relevant to social policy decisions. After all even according to a Pareto-type welfare function, all Paretian optima are not equally desirable; nor is a Paretian optimum better than each and every non-optimal allocation (see Chapter II, Section 5). But this consideration of the distribution of incomes has been ignored in the above analysis—as is indeed the usual practice in the discussions of externalities. Again, *in any practical situation policy-makers are likely also to want to take into account the distribution aspects in deciding what to do about any externality.* When an externality is infra-marginal, so that any alterations in the allocation of resources are likely to be large, the distributional aspect is likely to be particularly important.

The formal necessary conditions for the unique social optimum in the light of a given social welfare function of any type remain exactly the same as in Chapter II, Section 5. The only difference now is that the marginal social significance of the share of any commodity or factor going to an individual is to be understood to have been adjusted for any external effects.

We should note here that though externalities are a cause of what has been called the market failure—i.e. the failure of the market to reach a Paretian optimum—they are not the only or the most important cause of the market failure in spite of Bator's claims [1]. Perhaps the most important cause of market failure is imperfect knowledge (which we discussed in Chapter III, Section 3), because uncertainties on the part of economic agents of a kind which are in principle avoidable are likely to be quite common—particularly in the under-developed countries. Those effects of uncertainties are what were once rather ineptly described as pecuniary external economies, whereas the externalities we have examined in this chapter were sometimes called technological externalities.

It might be wondered why hardly any examples have been

mentioned of *actual* externalities in real life. The reason is the following: as we have shown above, an essential part of a meaningful definition of an externality describes the fact that due to institutional or technological or some other reasons some voluntary trade does not take place. Mere interdependence of production processes or utility functions does not create an externality—contrary to what Coase [5] and Buchanan and Stubblebine [4] have claimed; *there also has to be a private failure to trade*. However, for the same kind of good or service trade may take place in one city but not in another, so that what is an externality in one place may not be so in another place. That is why we concentrated on the logic of externalities and their implications rather than on their specific examples.

But let us now consider a few examples. One important example is likely to be the different firms' use of the same road. After a certain limit the use of this factor of production (i.e. the road) by any firm is likely to have an *untraded* unfavourable effect on the production of the other firms. Paretian optimality and technological efficiency demand a suitable tax on the use of such a road. Private consumers' use of certain roads furnishes a closely parallel example. The analysis of this kind of example of externality used to be shrouded in mystery generated by its involving a 'scarce resource' which is used 'freely'.[1] But these are all indirect ways of tackling the problem. The rigorous definition (divided into three parts) of an externality—whether it arises in production or consumption—which we have given will cover all these aspects.

Other phenomena which in most situations are likely to be externalities are: industrial noise, noise of consumer durables, domestic and commercial architecture, learning by doing in the process of commercial production,[2] cultivation of personal culture, education of one's children, common cold and other infectious illnesses, and so on. Finally, though the framework of the basic theory of allocation and of our foregoing analysis of externalities is static, a number of real-world externalities work out their effect over time. Therefore, to the other barriers in the way of trade (which make an externality an externality), one must add the barrier created by imperfect knowledge

[1] These are the terms in which Ellis and Fellner [11], and Mishan [17] discuss this problem.
[2] Solow [27] has argued that since labour of all kinds 'learns by doing', greater the *present* investment, the greater will be the productivity of the *future* investment. But the present investors do not get a reward for this side effect; after all, the 'labour' trained by a firm need not stay with it in the future. Hence, according to Solow, investment always creates an external economy for the future in this way. No doubt some other examples of externalities working *through* time could be thought of.

—i.e. by the inability of either the begetter or the receiver, or both, to foresee the relevant part of the future. Sometimes this imperfect prediction is based on not having the kind of information which is already known to some specialists, etc. An example perhaps is the growth of world population. Specialists know that the present rate of increase of world population cannot be maintained for more than a few more centuries without seriously overcrowding the world—unless we colonise the seas or the other planets. Yet most parents in the under-developed and developed countries are in all probability not sufficiently aware of this. (Of course, it is possible that a mere provision of information will not change their decisions about the right size for their families.) Incidentally, we are now discussing externalities between the present generation and the future generations who cannot possibly enter into trade with one another; further these are externalities at the global rather than the national level.

CONCLUSIONS

The effects of imperfect knowledge (discussed above in Chapter III, Section 3) are to be distinguished from those of externalities; though both imperfect knowledge and externalities—separately and together—constitute a market failure. We have given rigorous definitions of externalities and pointed out the mistakes in some of their recent formulations elsewhere. We have shown that, contrary to the claims made recently by some authors, there is no valid *logical* objection to the Pigovian tax or subsidy as a means of attaining a Paretian optimum (or Pigovian ideal output—see Chapter II, Section 8) in the presence of externalities. We have argued that the concept of externalities alone cannot explain all governmental activity in the economic field that takes place in a number of countries; and also that the existence of an externality does not necessarily justify governmental action aimed at restoring a Paretian optimum. We have also pointed out that because individual utility functions are never known to the policy-maker, any taxes or subsidies used to correct for the existence of externalities are more likely to be based on ethical assessments of individuals' relative deservingness, their best interests and so on by the comment-makers or decision-makers rather than on the notion of complete consumer sovereignty. In this case the 'suitable' or 'improved' allocation aimed at is not a Paretian optimum. It is obvious that the possible existence of externalities is yet another cause (along with those mentioned in Chapter III) which qualifies the traditional theorem that a perfectly competitive economy at equilibrium is a Paretian optimum.

REFERENCES FOR CHAPTER IV

[1] F. M. Bator, 'The Anatomy of Market Failure', *Quarterly Journal of Economics*, 1958

[2] W. J. Baumol, 'External Economies and Second Order Optimality Conditions', *American Economic Review*, 1964

[3] W. J. Baumol, *Welfare Economics and the Theory of the State*, 2nd edition, London, 1965

[4] J. M. Buchanan and W. C. Stubblebine, 'Externality', *Economica*, 1962

[5] R. H. Coase, 'The Problem of Social Cost', *The Journal of Law and Economics*, 1960

[6] O. A. Davis and A. Whinston, 'Externalities, Welfare and the Theory of Games', *Journal of Political Economy*, 1962

[7] O. A. Davis and A. Whinston, 'Some Notes on Equating Private and Social Cost', *Southern Economic Journal*, 1965

[8] O. A. Davis and A. Whinston, 'On Externalities, Information and the Government-Assisted Invisible Hand', *Economica*, 1966

[9] F. T. Dolbear, Jr., 'On the Theory of Optimum Externality', *American Economic Review*, 1967

[10] J. S. Duesenberry, *Income, Saving and the Theory of Consumer Behaviour*, Cambridge, Mass., 1949

[11] H. S. Ellis and W. Fellner, 'External Economies and Diseconomies', *American Economic Review*, 1943; also reprinted in G. J. Stigler in K. E. Boulding (eds.), *Readings in Price Theory*, London, 1952

[12] T. Haavelmo, 'The Notion of Involuntary Economic Decisions', *Econometrica*, 1950

[13] F. H. Knight, 'Fallacies in the Interpretation of Social Cost', *Quarterly Journal of Economics*, 1924

[14] J. Margolis, 'A Comment on the Pure Theory of Public Expenditure', *Review of Economics and Statistics*, 1955

[15] A. Marshall, *Principles of Economics*, 8th edn., London, 1920

[16] J. E. Meade, 'External Economies and Diseconomies in a Competitive Situation', *Economic Journal*, 1952

[17] E. J. Mishan, 'Reflections on Recent Developments in the Concept of External Effects', *Canadian Journal of Economics and Political Science*, 1965

[18] E. J. Mishan, 'Pareto Optimality and the Law', to appear in *Oxford Economic Papers*, 1968

[19] E. J. Mishan, *The Costs of Economic Growth*, London, 1967

[20] R. A. Musgrave, *The Theory of Public Finance*, New York, 1959

[21] S. K. Nath, 'Are Formal Welfare Criteria Required?' *Economic Journal*, 1964

[22] A. C. Pigou, *The Economics of Welfare*, 4th edn., London, 1924

[23] P. A. Samuelson, 'The Pure Theory of Public Expenditure', *Review of Economics and Statistics*, 1954

REFERENCES FOR CHAPTER IV

[24] P. A. Samuelson, 'Diagrammatic Exposition of a Pure Theory of Public Expenditure', *Review of Economics and Statistics*, 1955

[25] P. A. Samuelson, 'Aspects of Public Expenditure Theories', *Review of Economics and Statistics*, 1958

[26] T. Scitovsky, 'Two Concepts of External Economies', *Journal of Political Economy*, 1954

[27] R. M. Solow, *Capital Theory and the Rate of Return*, Amsterdam, 1963

[28] G. Tintner, 'A Note on Welfare Economics', *Econometrica*, 1946

[29] S. Wellisz, 'On External Diseconomies and the Government-Assisted Invisible Hand', *Economica*, November 1964

V

A PRIORI WELFARE CRITERIA

5.1 HISTORICAL BACKGROUND

A priori welfare criteria are, according to their authors, sufficient rules which have been formulated with the aim that every economist may use them for two closely related purposes, on the basic assumption that individual utility functions are always known.[1] First, to compare some economic situations open to a society at a point of time, in order to be able to answer questions such as: is this change desirable? This function of the welfare criteria is always illustrated in a comparative-static framework, with no time-lags. This can be described as *ex ante* ordering of points in a welfare field. The other purpose of these criteria is to form the basis of an evaluation of the yearly figures of national income of any country: this is *ex post* ordering of points in a welfare field.

Pigou had formulated the following proposition: '. . . it is evident that any transference of income from a relatively rich man to a relatively poor man of similar temperament, since it enables more intense wants to be satisfied at the expense of less intense wants, must increase the aggregate sum of satisfaction' [21, p. 89]. According to him, this proposition was based on what he considered to be the more or less factual assumptions: that utility was cardinally measurable, that all individuals had similar tastes, that marginal utility of income diminished at the same rate for everybody and that social utility which was a sum of individual utilities had to be maximised.

The assumption of similar tastes came to be known as that of equal capacity for satisfaction. Since this assumption involved inter-personal comparisons of utility, it was argued by Robbins [22] that it was a non-scientific, ethical assumption because inter-personal comparisons of utility could not be made scientifically.[2] There was

[1] An *a priori* welfare criterion might be described as 'a social welfare function', because it implies a statement of what social welfare is supposed to depend on; however, a social welfare function has come to mean *a specific statement of social objectives and their relative weights* (see Chapter VI), whereas an *a priori* welfare criterion implies a simple, *a priori* and sufficient decision-rule (supposedly valid for all kinds of occasions) for determining the social desirability of economic policies and for the welfare evaluation of national income data.

[2] It is worth noticing that two *separate* objections could be raised against Pigou's proposition: that it assumed measurable utility and that it assumed interpersonal

no commonly accepted apparatus to resolve disagreements of judgment on such comparisons. Robbins therefore concluded that Pigou's foregoing proposition was not scientific. He considered Pigou's more or less factual assumptions to be ethical, not judgments of fact but of value. Robbins' arguments sound perfectly legitimate to us today; nobody would seriously argue that Pigou's foregoing assumptions are not in fact value judgments. Yet at that time Robbins' arguments gave rise to a great deal of dismay. It was felt that if economic theory was to be useful for solving any practical economic and social problems, then some way must be found round Robbins' strictures. Economists did not seem to want to admit boldly that no application of economic theory to any practical problem was possible without presupposing some ethical premises or other.

Kaldor [10] tried to find a way round Robbins' criticisms. (See also Harrod [6] and Robbins [23].) He did not dispute that inter-personal comparisons of utility were value judgments. But he hoped to show that neither this nor any other value judgment was required for certain prescriptions. The compensation criteria were born as a result of this search for value-free prescriptions. As we shall be showing, Kaldor's, and others' who followed him, attempts were foredoomed; *no prescriptions can be derived without starting from some ethical premises.* Moreover, the propositions they formulated were not internally consistent either. We shall be concerned with this question of internal consistency of formal welfare criteria in this chapter; the more fundamental aspects will be examined in the next chapter.

5.2 COMPENSATION CRITERIA

The first of the compensation criteria has come to be known as the Kaldor–Hicks criterion. (See Hicks [7] and [8].) Kaldor argued that if as the result of some policy somebody was made economically better off and nobody else was made economically worse off, then obviously the policy was desirable: and he further proposed that if as a result of some policy some people are made economically better off while some others are made worse off than before it might still be possible for the economist to make a value-free recommendation of the policy provided the gainers were able to compensate the losers and yet be better off themselves than they had been originally. Kaldor went on to elaborate that whether the compensation was actually

---

comparisons of utility to be possible. Even if individual utility were somehow made measurable, it would still be necessary further to assume that different individuals' measures of utility were in the same or comparable units.

paid or not was a political or ethical decision. However, the possibility of adequately compensating the losers established, for him, the *potential* superiority of the policy under discussion. Further, according to Kaldor, policies which passed his criterion could be said to have increased production; thus a distinction was possible between the *production* and *distribution* aspects of such policies.

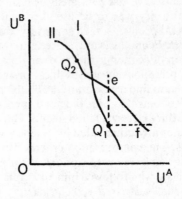

Fig. 5.1

Though Kaldor failed to point this out, a straightforward application of his criterion using *market* prices requires each of the Paretian value judgments mentioned in Chapter II, Section 1; it has to be assumed that the concern is with individual economic welfare, that individuals are the best judges of their own welfares, and that if at least one individual becomes better off without any other becoming worse off, then social welfare has increased.[1]

Assuming a community of two individuals, A and B, and that their individual preference maps are known to us, let us represent the initial position of the two individuals by the point Q_1 in fig. 5.1. (Along the horizontal and vertical axes of fig. 5.1 are measured the

[1] It is conceivable that the right amount of compensation to be paid to a person (or a group of persons) is assessed on the basis of some ethical, political, or social considerations (which include an assessment of the *relative deservingness* of that group). Though this might be an excellent procedure both in logic and in practice —if the ethical considerations were recognised and declared as such—it would have nothing in common with the *a priori* compensation criteria which we shall be criticising in this chapter and the next. *These criteria have been based on the value judgment that the (hypothetical) compensation should be based on individuals' own preferences, without any inter-personal comparisons of utility or welfare.*

ordinal utility indicators of individuals A and B respectively.) A policy measure is under discussion which when adopted will so affect the economy that the utility levels of the two individuals will then be given by point Q_2. At Q_2, B is the gainer and A is the loser. Now the Kaldor–Hicks criterion is satisfied by the point Q_2 if by *conceptually* getting B to compensate A some point in the eQf quadrant, or on its positive axes Q_1e or Q_1f, can be reached (where obviously at least one of the two individuals would be better off than at Q_1, while the other would be no worse off). In other words, the criterion is satisfied if there is a point along the utility locus of Q_2 which is Pareto-superior to Q_1. The curves I and II of fig. 5.1 can be given more than one interpretation.

(i) They can be thought of as *point* utility possibility curves (see Chapter II, Section 5). In this case each of the two curves is associated with a given fixed bundle of goods, and the different points on each curve are obtained by costless *lump-sum*[1] transfers. Neither of the two points is a Paretian optimum; i.e. neither lies on the Paretian *situation* utility possibility frontier. This is because, as we shall show later, in a comparison between any two points on the Paretian utility possibility frontier, the Kaldor–Hicks criterion can never be fulfilled.

(ii) They can also be interpreted as what Graaff [5] has called the efficiency loci; and which Little also used for propounding his criterion. Elsewhere I have called them Little-type utility possibility curves [20]. Assume that due to some imperfections in competition which cannot be eliminated the society finds itself at a point *inside* its situation utility possibility frontier. Now if redistribution of utility levels from that point is assumed to take place *once again* by means of costless *lump-sum* transfers we have *an efficiency locus*. Along it the size of non-human resources remains the same, but the amounts of goods and services produced or the amount of labour supplied can vary. Such a locus may well have no point in common with the situation utility possibility frontier. According to this interpretation, the community is at some Paretian non-optimum position Q_1; the new policy will take it to another point within the Paretian welfare frontier, Q_2; I and II are the efficiency loci of Q_1 and Q_2.

(iii) This is a somewhat problematic interpretation: curves I and II might be interpreted as feasibility curves which we have already come

---

[1] The significance of assuming lump-sum measures to raise the amount for compensation and to pay it is that in this way we are comparing two *fixed commodity bundles*—one that exists before the change in policy and the other that exists after. If the assumption of lump-sum redistributions is dropped compensation criteria can still be analysed—but now the only relevant loci are the feasibility loci; the comparison is no longer between fixed commodity bundles.

across in Chapter III, Section 1. Along a feasibility locus, the redistributions are assumed to take place by such administrative measures as are feasible and which will certainly not be lump-sum; the composition of national product alters along such a curve. Q_1 and Q_2 positions might be the results of different tariff structures; curves I and II are then the loci of feasible alternative distributions of utility levels under the two systems. As with the efficiency loci, the composition of national product is different at different points on a feasibility locus. No real difference is made to the analysis of the compensation criteria and Little's criterion (which we shall soon be discussing) by interpreting the loci in any of the three ways mentioned. This fact has not always been recognised.

It is also possible to illustrate the Kaldor–Hicks criterion with the use of the Scitovsky community indifference curves (C.I.C.s) which we have already come across in Chapter II, Section 5. In fig. 5.2 along

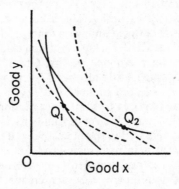

Fig. 5.2

the horizontal and vertical axes are measured x and y respectively—the only two goods the community is assumed to have. Q_1 is the original bundle of the two goods; its original distribution is shown by the solid Scitovsky C.I.C. on which it lies. Since a Scitovsky C.I.C. is assumed to pass through Q_1, it is implied that at Q_1 there is a Paretian exchange optimum; i.e. the marginal rate of subjective substitution between x and y is the same for the two individuals at Q_1 (and also at any other point on a Scitovsky C.I.C.). However, for the reason already given, Q_1 and Q_2 are not assumed to be top-level Paretian optima. Q_2 lies on a C.I.C. which intersects the C.I.C. of Q_1. Hence at Q_2 one individual is better off and the other worse off than at Q_1. If at least one of them had been better off at Q_2 without the other being any worse off than at Q_1 the Scitovsky C.I.C. through Q_2 would not have cut anywhere the C.I.C. through Q_1; and the move from Q_1 to Q_2 could have been approved on the basis of the Paretian value judgments. (See Chapter II, Section 5, to see how Scitovsky indifference curves are derived.) Now that Q_1 and Q_2 lie on intersecting curves, in order to apply the Kaldor–Hicks criterion we ask: Is it possible by lump-sum redistribution of Q_2 bundle of goods to make at least one person better off at Q_2 than at Q_1 without the other being any worse off? In order to answer this question, we draw a dotted C.I.C. through Q_2 parallel to the C.I.C. of Q_1. It happens to lie above that curve; therefore, the move from Q_1 to Q_2 satisfies the Kaldor–Hicks criterion.

Scitovsky [27] soon showed that the Kaldor–Hicks criterion was capable of contradicting itself. Referring to fig. 5.1, Q_2 is superior to Q_1 according to the Kaldor–Hicks criterion. If the change in policy under discussion is adopted and the community moves from Q_1 to Q_2 but no compensation is actually paid so that point Q_2 (rather than any other point on II) is the *actual* outcome, then applying the Kaldor–Hicks criterion again—but this time for a change back *from* Q_2 *to* Q_1—Q_1 now seems superior to Q_2. For the locus (which can be given any of the three interpretations discussed in the last section) on which Q_1 lies passes North-East of point Q_2. Using the Scitovsky C.I.C.s and referring to fig. 5.2, it is possible to draw a dotted C.I.C. through Q_2 which is parallel to the C.I.C. of Q_1, and lies above it. Hence, if we consider a move from Q_1 to Q_2 the Kaldor–Hicks criterion declares Q_2 superior to Q_1; but if we consider a move from Q_2 to Q_1 the same criterion now declares Q_1 superior[1] to Q_2.

In order to remove the possibility of this contradiction, Scitovsky suggested that a second part should be added to the Kaldor–Hicks criterion. This second part has come to be known as the Scitovsky reversal criterion; according to it the losers from an economic policy (assuming that they are not compensated) should not be able adequately to 'bribe' the gainers to oppose the change. In other words, not only should the new position meet the Kaldor–Hicks criterion but also—assuming that compensation is not to be paid— that a movement back from the new to the old position should *not*

---

[1] The basic reason for a contradiction of this kind is that the relative valuations (i.e. the commodity price ratios) of the elements of a bundle of goods differ with the way that bundle is distributed. This is true so long as tastes of the individuals are at all different. In short, the same bundle of goods will have a different value if it is differently distributed.

meet the Kaldor–Hicks criterion. In figs. 5.3 and 5.4 are illustrated a pair of points Q_1 and Q_2 which satisfy both the Kaldor–Hicks and the Scitovsky reversal criteria.

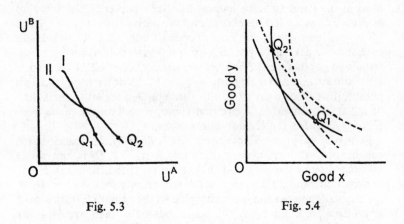

Fig. 5.3 Fig. 5.4

However, even this two-way compensation criterion can lead to contradiction if the choice of a position has to be made from among more than just two possible positions. Fig. 5.5 proves this point.

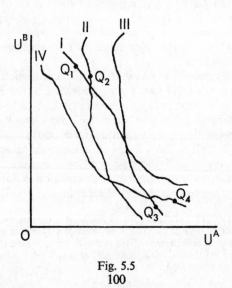

Fig. 5.5

We apply the Kaldor–Hicks and the Scitovsky reversal criterion to the comparison between Q_2 and Q_1, and find Q_2 to be superior; similarly, the two criteria declare Q_3 superior to Q_2 and Q_4 superior to Q_3. Hence Q_4 is superior to Q_1. Yet if we compare Q_4 and Q_1 directly and apply the same two criteria we find them this time evaluating Q_1 as superior to Q_4.

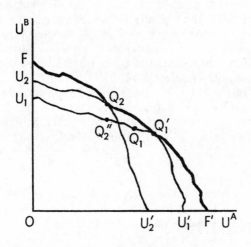

Fig. 5.6

Before concluding this section it is worth pointing out that *a Paretian top-level optimal position always satisfies the Scitovsky reversal criterion in comparison with any non-optimal position or another optimal position.* (Compare Q_2 with Q_1 and Q_1' in fig. 5.6, where FF' is the utility possibility frontier, and U_1U_1' and U_2U_2' are two point utility possibility curves.) *But the Kaldor–Hicks criterion is never satisfied in a comparison between two Paretian optima (Q_2 and Q_1'); in a comparison between a Paretian optimum and a non-optimum the criterion may be satisfied* (compare Q_2 and Q_2'') *or it may not* (compare Q_2 and Q_1).

5.3 SAMUELSON'S COMPARISONS

Samuelson [25] has criticised the two-way compensation criteria on the ground that, if the comparison between any two situations is to be *completely neutral* on the matter of distribution it is not sufficient to compare them only on the basis of the distribution of utility levels of just those two positions. Kaldor, Hicks, and Scitovsky were all looking for a criterion which would be neutral on the question of distribution of income or utility levels, and would yet be able to compare some economic situations. Samuelson pointed out that strict distributional neutrality required the new position, even if it was to be declared just *potentially* better than the old, to be Pareto-superior to the old position on each of the distributions of utility levels which could conceptually be associated with them both; in other words, potential superiority of Q_2 bundle of goods to Q_1 bundle of goods required that for every possible distribution of Q_1 there should be a distribution of Q_2 in which at least one person is better off and nobody is worse off.

In terms of the utility loci (with any of the three interpretations mentioned earlier), the Samuelson comparisons require that the utility locus of Q_2 should everywhere be outside the utility locus of Q_1—as shown in fig. 5.7. In terms of the Scitovsky community

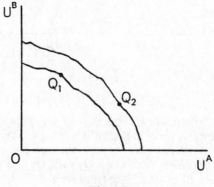

Fig. 5.7

indifference curves these comparisons require that Q_1 and Q_2 commodity bundles should be such that no Scitovsky C.I.C. through Q_1 can pass to the North-East (or, more strictly, to the North, North-East, or East) of point Q_2. As we noted in Chapter II, if individual indifference curves are assumed to be downward-sloping and convex to the origin, then so would be the Scitovsky community indifference curves—because along such a curve the marginal rate of substitution between any two goods is the same for all the individuals

in the community. With downward-sloping and convex to the origin
Scitovsky community indifference curves it is a sufficient condition
that Q_2 should have more of at least one good and no less of the
other than Q_1 for no Scitovsky C.I.C. to be able to pass to the
North-East of Q_2. That is, in terms of fig. 5.8 the sufficient condition

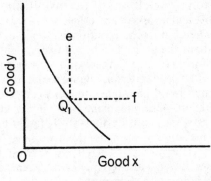

Fig. 5.8

is that Q_2 should lie within the quadrant eQ_1f. This is only a sufficient
condition and not a necessary condition, because even if Q_2 has less
of some one commodity, but more of some other, no Scitovsky
C.I.C. may be able to pass to the North-East of Q_2, provided there
is a sufficiently strong general preference in the community for the
commodity of which there is more as compared to the commodity of
which there is less in Q_2 than Q_1.[1]

However, without knowing the exact individual preference maps
in a particular situation, it would be impossible to say how much
more of some other commodity position Q_2 should have when it has
a unit less of a certain commodity for that position yet to satisfy
the requirement under discussion. Hence, we can say that, if we
are to generalise for all possible situations without requiring a
knowledge of individual preference maps, then a necessary condition
for Q_2 to pass the Samuelson comparisons against Q_1 is that it should
have more of at least one commodity and no less of the other. This is

[1] For example in fig. 5.4, if the absolute value of the common for all persons
marginal rate of subjective substitution between the two goods at Q_1—for every
possible distribution of utility levels—is greater than the absolute value of the
slope of the line joining the two points Q_1 and Q_2, then on the Samuelson comparisons Q_2 would rank as potentially better than Q_1.

one case where we can always be sure that utility possibility locus, *drawn only on the assumption of lump-sum redistribution*, of Q_2 lies outside that of Q_1, as in fig. 5.7. It *has* to be assumed that the redistributions are lump-sum even if Q_2 has more of one commodity and no less of another at a particular distribution of incomes and utility-levels; for, if the redistributions cannot be lump-sum the feasible utility locus of Q_2 might well somewhere drop inside that of Q_1. In other words, even if one of the two situations has more of some commodity and no less of any other, *and only feasible redistributions are considered*, no generalisation in terms of the Samuelson comparisons about the utility loci is possible.

It is very unfortunate that Samuelson comparisons have come to be called the 'Samuelson criterion'. Samuelson himself did not claim that these comparisons amounted to a sufficient criterion. If we accept the Paretian value judgments, and if the utility possibility curve of Q_2 lies wholly outside that of Q_1 (as in fig. 5.7)—i.e. Q_2 passes the Samuelson comparisons—then we have only established the *potential* superiority of Q_2 over Q_1; we have established nothing as regards the *actual* Q_2 and Q_1 positions, even according to the Paretian value judgments. For example, in fig. 5.9 though Q_2 is *potentially* superior to Q_1 according to the Paretian value judgments, yet even according to the Pareto-type welfare function depicted, the *actual position* Q_2 (resulting from the change in policy) is inferior to Q_1 because Q_2 lies on a lower social welfare contour than does Q_1. *This confusion between potential and actual superiority is both easy and common*. Moreover, the locus of redistributions of Q_2 as a result of *feasible* administrative measures—the only locus really relevant to any realistic discussion of economic policy—may be such that according to the given welfare function every point on it is inferior to Q_1. This is the case in fig. 5.9, when CC' is the feasibility locus of Q_2. If we consider feasible administrative measures for redistributing income and wealth resulting from the change in policy which takes the economy to the Q_2 position, then the *possible* outcomes lie on CC'. This locus lies to the South-West of the welfare contour of Q_1.

Before finishing this section we should note that in a more recent publication Samuelson [26] has suggested a new version of the basic Paretian criterion that if 'everybody' is better off, then the change is desirable. This new version takes all future time and accumulation of wealth into account. 'If the consumption prospect *over all relevant time* that every person can envisage will be deemed better after a given policy change than before, then it is a good one' [26, p. 55, original italics]. Since it is basically the Paretian criterion—mentioned as value judgment (iv) of Chapter II—its first shortcoming is that even if it could be applied, very few actual policies could ever pass it. Further, in this modified form the value judgment has no more general validity than any other formal welfare criterion. Finally, in this form the criterion has an unusually high degree of irrelevance for practical purposes—as indeed Samuelson himself recognises: 'In the absence of perfect certainty, the future prices needed for making the requisite wealth-like comparisons are simply unavailable. So it could be difficult to make operational the theorist's desired measures' [26, p. 57].

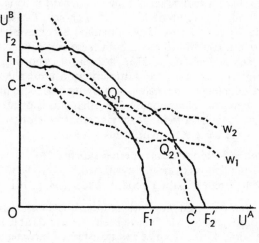

Fig. 5.9

5.4 LITTLE'S CRITERION

Little [13] put forward a criterion about the time when Samuelson's criticism of the compensation criteria was published. He considered both the Kaldor–Hicks criterion and the Scitovsky two-way criterion inadequate, because he felt that 'income distribution must . . . be admitted as an ethical variable, to which values, favourable or un-favourable, are given, and we must have a criterion which includes this variable'. Therefore he proposed combining a judgment about distributions of welfare in any two positions with the two-way Scitovsky criterion (or with the Kaldor–Hicks criterion and the Scitovsky reversal criterion). This would be a criterion for establishing actual rather than just potential superiority of a point.

Little's criterion has been the subject of much controversy in

H   105

recent years; however, it is quite unsatisfactory on any possible interpretation. There was controversy also over the nature of the utility curves employed by Little in propounding his criterion, because it was felt by some contributors that his criterion performed better on a particular interpretation of the utility curves. But we shall be showing that the criterion is unsatisfactory no matter what interpretation is given to the utility loci.

No discussion is provided by Little of the value judgments on which his criterion is based. They are mentioned in the concluding chapter: 'Two value judgments are presupposed by this criterion. The first is that an individual becomes better off if he is enabled to reach a position higher up on his order of choice. The second is that the community is better off if an individual becomes better off, and none worse off. It is thought that both these value judgments would be widely acceptable' [13, p. 276]. We shall be showing that on at least one interpretation of the Little criterion more than just these two value judgments are presupposed by it, that these presupposed value judgments are contradictory, and that this is one fundamental reason why Little's criterion can give contradictory results. The following is the basic statement of his criterion:

'(*a*) Is the Kaldor–Hicks criterion satisfied?
(*b*) Is the Scitovsky criterion satisfied?
(*c*) Is any redistribution good or bad?' [13, p. 101].

Of the answers 'yes' and 'no' to these three questions, there are eight possible combinations, which have been set out in Table II on p. 105 of Little's book. Little assumes any transfers of income, payment of compensation, etc., to be always lump-sum. With this assumption any points other than that actually attained on a utility locus are properly considered imaginary. On the other hand, if it is assumed that the redistributions along a utility locus are by feasible, and hence not necessarily lump-sum measures, then each point on a utility locus is attainable. These two possible interpretations of a utility locus correspond to Little, assumptions A and B. In other words, the utility loci of fig. 5.10 can be thought of as being either feasibility loci or one of the loci constructed on the assumption of lump-sum transfers, i.e. a point utility possibility curve or efficiency locus. In either case the Little criterion can be shown to give contradictory results; indeed, our proof of contradiction does not involve any assumptions about the nature of assumed redistributions.

Returning now to the three questions of the Little criterion, let us examine the comparisons where Little would recommend a proposed change under both his assumptions A and B. If the answer to all three questions is positive Little infers that the change should be made. (This is his case 1.) If the Kaldor–Hicks criterion is satisfied, and any redistribution will be good, then even if the Scitovsky reversal criterion is not satisfied Little infers that the change should be made. (This is his case 3.) Similarly, if the Scitovsky reversal criterion is satisfied, and any redistribution will be good, then even

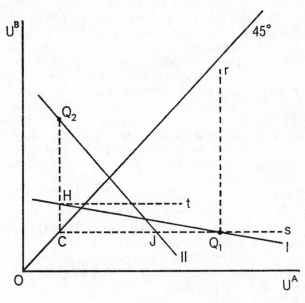

Fig. 5.10

if the Kaldor–Hicks criterion is not satisfied, Little infers that the change should be made. (This is his case 8.) The possibility of contradiction arises in each of these three cases. We shall take only Little's case 8 as an example.

We shall need to refer to fig. 5.10. Along one axis are measured ordinal indicators of A's utility, and along the other, those of B's utility. I and II are two utility loci with the possible interpretations noted above. (The 45° line in the figure is to be ignored at present.) The community is at Q_1 on the utility locus I; an economic change is being discussed which will change the utility locus to II (perhaps because the proposed change will alter the incentives, or the amounts of resources, or technology, etc.), and land the community at Q_2 on this other curve. This move from Q_1 to Q_2 makes B better off, and A worse off than before. Is the Kaldor–Hicks criterion satisfied? Can the gainer (individual B) from the move to Q_2 compensate the loser (individual A) and yet be better off somewhere along the curve II than he was on curve I at Q_1?

The farthest along II towards the South-East that B can travel in the attempt to compensate A is to the point J, because beyond that point he himself becomes worse off than he was at Q_1—so that it is not worth his while to go beyond J. But at J, A is still worse off (is at a lower level of utility) than he was at Q_1; that is, A cannot be adequately compensated; it is not possible to move from Q_2 along the utility locus II to a point which is Pareto-superior to Q_1. Hence the change to Q_2 does not satisfy the Kaldor–Hicks criterion. Similarly, the Scitovsky reversal criterion requires that along curve I by any redistribution it should *not* be possible to move to a point which is Pareto-superior to Q_2. In our example the farthest towards the North-West that it is possible to redistribute utility levels along I is H; beyond H individual A is worse off than he will be if the change to Q_2 is adopted; but at H individual B is still worse off than he will be at Q_2. Hence Q_2 is Pareto-superior to H.

Now we come to the third question. Let us quote Little on how the judgment about distribution is to be made:

> . . . if someone says that a change from Q_1 to Q_2 would be distributionally good, he means that a point which would *actually* have been reached by shifting money, and where everyone would be worse off, or everyone be better off, than at Q_2, is better than Q_1 [13, p. 103; original italics].

There can be at least three interpretations of this. The first is to take a 'distributionally good change' to mean 'a change towards a more equal distribution'. The exposition of this interpretation is made easier by assuming that though along each axis in fig. 3.10 the utility indicators are ordinal, the tastes of the two individuals are identical, so that the ordinal indicators along each axis are the same. The 45° line then is the locus of points where the distribution of utility between the two individuals is equal. Though our assumptions do not guarantee that the relative distribution of utility along any straight line from the origin other than the 45° line remains the same, by careful examination it will be possible sometimes to decide which of any two points off the 45° line has the more equal distribution of utility.[1]

[1] Quite clearly, then—since the intervals along each axis in fig. 5.10 are only ordinal and quite arbitrary—the proof of contradiction in Little's criterion that

Continuing to examine case 8, let us refer to fig. 5.10. By shifting money from A to B, we move to H on the utility curve I. H has a more equal distribution of utility than Q_1 because H is nearer a point like C than is Q_1; therefore, H is better than Q_1. At Q_2, compared to H, at least one person is better off, while the other is no worse off; therefore Q_2 is better than H. It follows from the last two results that Q_2 is better than Q_1.

But the same criterion can prove the contradictory proposition that Q_1 is better than Q_2. Suppose now that Q_2 is the initial position and that the proposed economic change will take the society to Q_1. For this change, the Kaldor–Hicks criterion is not satisfied, but the Scitovsky reversal criterion is. By making a conceptual lump-sum redistribution from Q_2, point J is reached. J has a more equal distribution than Q_2 because J is nearer a point like C than is Q_2; therefore, J is better than Q_2. At Q_1, compared to J, at least one person is better off without the other being worse off; therefore, Q_1 is better than J. It follows from these two results that Q_1 is better than Q_2. All this amounts to saying that the basic trouble with Little's criteria is that while, for example, a point like H (in fig. 5.10) is considered superior to Q_1 on *distributional* grounds, some other point, Q_2, is declared superior to H on the basis of the Paretian value judgment—namely that if at least one person is better off then the change is good—*which ignores any change in distribution*, so that finally at Q_2 we might end up with a distribution worse than at Q_1.

One way of removing the possibility of contradiction in Little's criterion would be to interpret his distribution proviso as it stands by itself—i.e. quite independently of the Scitovsky reversal and the Kaldor–Hicks criteria. In that case, provided Q_2 is judged (by 'someone') to be better than Q_1 on distributional grounds, then whether the utility curve of Q_1 passes to the right or to the left of Q_2, Q_2 is better than Q_1; in other words, irrespective of whether (in fig. 5.11) we can make everyone—or at least one person—worse off (H^*) or better off (H) than at Q_2 by any kind of transfers of income from position Q_1, Q_2 is to be accepted as better than Q_1. In this interpretation we have discarded the value judgment which established the Pareto-superiority of any point. This interpretation is in fact the one on which Kennedy [11] has been insisting for a long time. But in his first critique of these criteria he emphasised another point, namely, that if 'someone' can compare Q_2 and Q_1

---

we shall develop does not depend on the assumption of measurable utility. But the proof obviously also applies if it is assumed that utility is measurable; indeed, the interpretation of fig. 5.10 is much simpler then.

directly he gains nothing by contemplating points like *H* and *H** (fig. 5.11). Little has been able to answer that the contemplation of an intermediary point may sometimes help. But this is beside the point. If Q_2 is judged *better* than Q_1 on *distributional* grounds—on the basis of an *implicit* but necessary value judgment to the effect that certain kinds of changes in distribution are desirable and certain others are undesirable—then any further comparison between Q_2

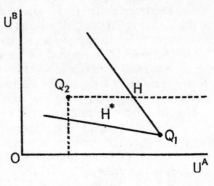

Fig. 5.11

and Q_1, through intermediary points or not, on the basis of the· *other* value judgment (i.e. the Paretian value judgment), which implies that certain changes in the economy are desirable no matter what the accompanying change in distribution, is in any case irrelevant, and can lead to contradictory results.

We come now to a second, and in fact the oldest, interpretation of Little's criterion. This was provided by Samuelson[1] in 1950. It is also the least interesting. According to this interpretation, all Little's references to 'distribution', 'distributionally better points', etc., are to be ignored. Confronted with any two points Q_1 and Q_2

[1] See Samuelson [25]. In more recent years this interpretation of Samuelson was first revived by Slasor [29] and then Sen [28] and Little himself [15]. In 1951 Arrow [1] had also suggested the same interpretation. It should be noted that both Samuelson and Arrow were quite sceptical about the usefulness of the criterion. However, Arrow immediately drew a wrong inference from his own suggested interpretation; he said, 'The possibility of moving to a situation with a very much higher real income but undesirable distribution seems to be excluded from a decision' [1, p. 932]. In fact, the trouble with this interpretation of Little's criterion is that it would approve of any degree of undesirable change in distribution provided at least one person or a group of persons is made better off.

(refer to figs. 5.12 and 5.13), we are required to inquire: (i) Does Q_2 satisfy either the Scitovsky reversal criterion or the Kaldor–Hicks criterion or both? (ii) Does the point (H) on the utility locus (constructed with lump-sum or feasible redistributions) of Q_1 which is

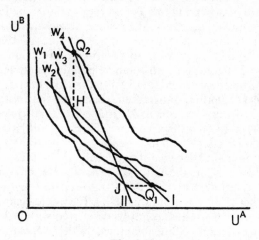

Fig. 5.12

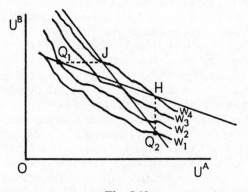

Fig. 5.13

Pareto-inferior to Q_2 (fig. 5.12) or Pareto-superior to Q_2 (fig. 5.13) seem in the light of some values, welfare weights, etc. (which, it would seem, need not be explicit) to have higher or lower social welfare than point Q_1? If Q_2 satisfies either at least the Scitovsky reversal test (his case 8, shown here in fig. 5.12) or at least the

Kaldor–Hicks test (his case 3, shown here in fig. 5.13), and if the answer to the second question is positive, Little would recommend Q_2.

As we have noted above, Little considers his criterion to be based on the Paretian value judgment, so that the comparison between H and Q_1 has to be according to a Pareto-type welfare function (which always gives welfare contours which slope downwards from left to right). Indeed, this is the distinguishing feature of this second interpretation: there is *assumed* to be a welfare function available, which *has to be* Pareto-type, to compare points like Q_1 and H. In a situation like that depicted in fig. 5.12, Q_2 (though it does not pass the Kaldor–Hicks criterion) satisfies the Scitovsky reversal criterion because Q_2 is Pareto-superior to H. H is better than Q_1 because H lies on a higher social welfare contour. Therefore Little would conclude that Q_2 is better than Q_1.

Similarly, in a situation like that depicted in fig. 5.13—where Q_2 (though it does not pass the Scitovsky reversal criterion) satisfies the Kaldor–Hicks criterion because J is Pareto-superior to Q_1—since J lies on a higher welfare contour than Q_1, Little would again conclude that Q_2 is better than Q_1. But in this case, even within the context of Pareto-type social welfare functions, Little's conclusion would be wrong. Q_2 is in fact on a lower social welfare contour than is Q_1. In other words, even if we confine ourselves to Pareto-type welfare functions, Little's case 3 can lead to a contradiction; in fig. 5.13, depending on whether we consider Q_1 or Q_2 to be the initial position, we can show both that Q_2 is better than Q_1 and that Q_1 is better than Q_2.

Under this second interpretation, whereby we are asked to compare points like Q_1 and H only according to an unspecified social welfare function of a certain type, there is no longer a Little criterion —i.e. a set of sufficient rules for comparing points in a welfare field— but only an assurance that *if* we had a social welfare function (which Little would like to be Pareto-type because it would then appear to be based on 'widely acceptable value judgments') we could compare Q_1 and H, and find H to be the superior, or the inferior point. To have called a point to be so selected a distributionally better or worse point was to give it a misleading name.

If distribution is an important enough consideration in a social welfare function, then the social welfare may not be a monotonically increasing function of individual welfare, as a Pareto-type function is. For, on a Pareto-type welfare function, by keeping the utility level of the poorer classes constant, and by arranging all economic changes to benefit only the richer classes, we can each time hit a

112

higher social welfare surface. If we, instead, assume that at least after a limit a change in distribution has a nuisance value according to the person (or persons) whose value judgments are depicted in the welfare function, then the relevant social welfare contours will turn away from the axes—as shown in fig. 5.14. With such a welfare function the Little criterion can lead to contradiction in each of its

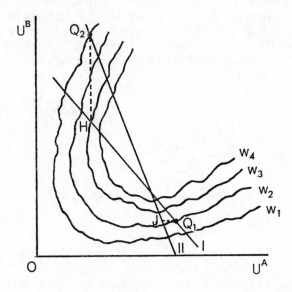

Fig. 5.14

various cases. We have depicted in fig. 5.14 his case 8 (the same as in fig. 5.12). Fig. 5.14 clearly shows that applying the kind of comparisons which the second interpretation of the Little criterion requires, we can show both that Q_1 is better than Q_2 and that Q_2 is better than Q_1. It has been thought by some defenders of the Little criterion that provided the underlying welfare function is assumed to be *transitive*, the criterion can never lead to contradictory results. But this is a wrong deduction.[1] The welfare functions of both figs. 5.13 and 5.14 are transitive—that is why the welfare contours are non-intersecting—yet the Little criterion gives contradictory results in both these examples.

[1] This wrong claim about transitivity is made by Sen [28].

We come now to a third possible interpretation of the Little criterion, which in fact constitutes a modified form of that criterion as put forward recently by Mishan [19] and Kennedy [12]. In Kennedy's words: 'There is a social improvement if the distribution is better and everyone is not made worse off.' According to this criterion, if some persons' utility levels are held constant while the utility levels of some others are reduced, *and* this *improves* the distribution of incomes, then the change is desirable. In other words, according to this criterion, social welfare is no longer a monotonic increasing function of individual utility. The Paretian value judgment (which lays down that if at least one person is better off and nobody worse off, then the change is desirable) has been discarded.

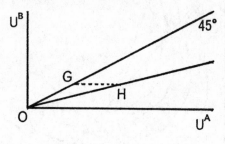

Fig. 5.15

Another way of saying this is that this reduced form of the Little criterion is not consistent with a welfare function that has contours sloping downwards from left to right (i.e. a Pareto-type welfare function) or with a welfare function that has L-shaped contours. Fig. 5.15 proves this point. Assume that the utilities of the two individuals are cardinally measurable and identical. Let us also interpret a better distribution according this criterion to mean a more equal distribution. *H* is the initial point; *G* is the new point; at *G* the distribution is better than at *H* (because it lies on the line of complete equality) and *everyone*[1] is not made worse off, though one person is made worse off. Therefore according to this reduced form of the Little criterion, *G* is better than *H*. Yet if welfare contours have only negative slope (as is the case with a Pareto-type welfare function), then the contour passing through *H* must pass

[1] 'Everyone' here does mean everyone; whereas in Little's criterion the phrase 'everyone is made better off' means 'at least one person is made better off'. This is because Little's criterion is based on the Paretian value judgments.

above G; i.e. according to such a welfare function G would in fact be worse than H. Similarly, if the contours are L-shaped G would rank at the same level as H, but not better.

Is this criterion consistent with the kind of non-Paretian welfare function depicted in fig. 5.16? Suppose again that the utilities of the two individuals are both cardinally measurable and identical; and that better distribution is to mean more equal distribution. At point K the distribution is more equal, but both individuals are worse off, than at point L. Therefore, according to the criterion under discussion, K is *not* a better point than L; nor is L better than K. Yet, according to the depicted non-Paretian welfare function, K is on a higher welfare contour than L. However, this result does not show a necessary contradiction between this 'reduced' form of the Little criterion and the type of welfare function depicted. Since the criterion is a two-part sufficient criterion (requiring that distribution should be better *and* that not everybody should be worse off), it is possible to interpret it to mean that if a point fails only one of its two parts (as does K when compared with L), that is *not* sufficient to declare the point inferior. In that case, since the criterion declares K to be neither better nor worse than L, it is consistent with a properly defined welfare function of the type that declares K to be actually better than L.

The welfare function of the type (which is non-Paretian) depicted in fig. 5.16 ranks K as better than L, because though at K each of the two persons has a lower level of utility (*which has been assumed to depend only on economic causes*, see Chapter II, Section 1), the distribution is sufficiently better than at L. In other words, though everybody has less income and wealth, social welfare rises. This does not imply that the relevant social welfare function is concerned with the welfare of some mythical entity (e.g. 'Society'); but only that though each individual in formulating his scale of preferences (or his utility function) takes into account only the commodities he consumes and the factors he supplies, the welfares of individuals are judged to be interdependent by whosoever formulated the welfare function—parliament, obversing commentator, etc. Though each person has fewer goods and has been pushed to a lower level of utility with respect to such things, the pattern of distribution of incomes and wealth has improved sufficiently for the social welfare function to give the answer that the whole change is for the better.

This kind of social welfare function implies that an individual's *general* welfare function is not to be identified with his utility function which has been so defined that it excludes any Duesenberry-like externalities arising from the relative income and wealth

115

levels of other individuals (see Chapter VI, Section 6.2a). With such a social welfare function, and the implied individual welfare functions, it is no longer correct to assume that utility and general welfare are always positively related or that non-economic causes affecting general welfare can always be taken to stay constant while we manipulate the economic causes.

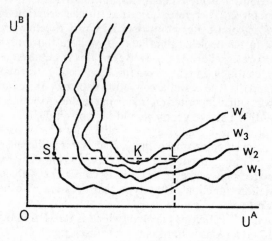

Fig. 5.16

Going back to the Mishan–Kennedy reduced form of the Little criterion, we have to note that apart from having the obvious short-coming that there are a number of points in the welfare field (such as L and K in fig. 5.16) between which this criterion cannot decide, it can also be said to be too blunt an instrument. It will approve of an individual making an indefinitely large sacrifice of utility so that another individual may make a very small gain, with only the slightest improvement in distribution. For example, the criterion would rank S as better than L in fig. 5.16, because S has a better distribution than L (the ray on which S lies is nearer the 45° ray, which has not been drawn, than is the ray on which L lies) and everybody is not worse off at S. But a properly defined welfare function of even the non-Paretian type depicted in fig. 5.16 may well rank L higher than S (as is the case in this example).

Hence we may conclude that the Little criterion is unsatisfactory on any of the three foregoing interpretations.

116

5.5 INDEX NUMBERS AND COMPENSATION CRITERIA

As we mentioned at the beginning of this chapter, one of the purposes for which the *a priori* welfare criteria were formulated was to help decide the welfare interpretation of national-income data available *ex post*. These data come only in price–quantity form. Let us now examine the relationship between compensation criteria and two kinds of index numbers of national income—the base-weighted and the current-weighted.

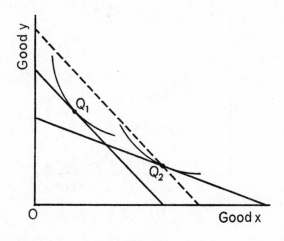

Fig. 5.17

We must first note that in this section we are out of the world of comparative static welfare comparisons, where no time is allowed to elapse. Now we compare welfare in two different years or time periods. This raises a number of new questions. Are the individual people the same in the two periods? If the people are the same, are their tastes also the same? Is the ratio of savings in the national product the same? And finally, are all the goods the same? For the present we shall assume that there is no problem arising from any of these questions: we shall return to a discussion of these questions in Chapter IX. Further, we must also note that though in our earlier analysis of the compensation criteria it was *not* necessarily implied that we were dealing with fixed totals of goods, now the implication is that the total amounts of goods do remain fixed. This is a necessary

117

assumption whenever quantity index numbers are used in an analysis.

Let us start with the Laspeyre quantity index. This involves a comparison between the national products of any two years on the basis of the prices of the base year, just as the Kaldor–Hicks criterion uses the income distribution of the base year as the basis for comparisons. However, if in a comparison between the national products of any two years the Laspeyre quantity index ranks one of them as higher, *nothing* follows about their ranking according to the Kaldor–

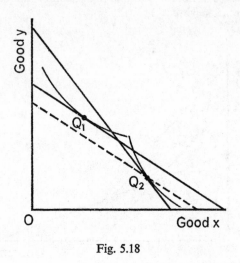

Fig. 5.18

Hicks criterion. That is, if according to the Laspeyre quantity index (say) the second year has the higher national product, then the second year as compared to the first year may yet fail to pass the Kaldor–Hicks criterion. For example, in fig. 5.17 $\Sigma P_1 Q_2 > \Sigma P_1 Q_1$, but Q_2 does not pass the Kaldor–Hicks criterion. The reason for this is easy to see from fig. 5.17. The price line on which Q_1 lies passes *under* the position Q_2. But since the Scitovsky community indifference curve on which Q_1 lies does not have to be a straight line, that curve may yet pass *over* Q_2; if it does that, then Q_2 will fail to pass the Kaldor–Hicks criterion.

However, whenever the national product of a year (say the second year) is lower than that of the first year according to the Laspeyre quantity index the second year must fail to pass the Kaldor–Hicks criterion. For example, in fig. 5.18 $\Sigma P_1 Q_2 < \Sigma P_1 Q_1$ and Q_2 *also* fails the Kaldor–Hicks criterion. The reason for this is also easy to

118

see from fig. 5.18. The price line on which Q_1 lies passes *over* Q_2. The Scitovsky community indifference curve, which is tangential to the price line of the first year at Q_1, has to be downward-sloping and convex from below; therefore it must *also* pass *over* Q_2. We should also note that no matter what the ranking between any two years according to the Laspeyre quantity index, that information implies nothing about the ranking of those two years by the Scitovsky reversal criterion.

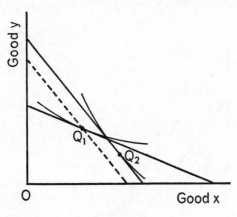

Fig. 5.19

We come now to the Paasche quantity index. This involves a comparison between the national products of any two years on the basis of the prices of the current year, just as the Scitovsky reversal criterion uses the income distribution of the current year as the basis for comparisons. Whenever the national product of a year (say the second year) is higher than that of the first year according to the Paasche quantity index the Scitovsky reversal test will *also* rank the second year as the superior year. For example, in fig. 5.19 $\Sigma P_2 Q_2 > \Sigma P_2 Q_1$ and Q_2 *also* passes the Scitovsky reversal criterion. The reason for this is also easy to see from fig. 5.19. Since the price line of Q_2 passes *over* Q_1, the Scitovsky community indifference curve must also pass over Q_2.

However, if the Paasche quantity index ranks the second year lower, then *nothing* follows about their ranking according to the Scitovsky reversal criterion. That is, if according to the Paasche quantity index the second year has the lower national product, then according to the Scitovsky reversal criterion the second year may yet be the superior year. Such a situation is depicted in fig. 5.20, where $\Sigma P_2 Q_2 < \Sigma P_2 Q_1$ but Q_2 is better than Q_1 according to the Scitovsky reversal criterion. It is easy to see from fig. 5.20 that though the price line of Q_2 passes under Q_1, this does not mean that the Scitovsky community indifference curve of Q_2 also has to pass under Q_1. We should also note that no matter what the ranking between any two years according to the Paasche quantity index, that information implies nothing about the ranking of those two years by the Kaldor–Hicks criterion.

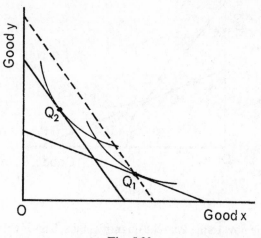

Fig. 5.20

These results imply that if we did want to use the Kaldor–Hicks *and* the Scitovsky reversal criteria together for the purposes of *ex post* welfare appraisal we should find that the criteria are in practice inapplicable, because the price–quantity data can never give sufficient information for us to be able to infer in any situation a firm conclusion about *both* the criteria. Because even if both $\Sigma P_1 Q_2 > \Sigma P_1 Q_1$ and $\Sigma P_2 Q_2 > \Sigma P_2 Q_1$, then all we can deduce is that Q_2, as compared to Q_1, passes the Scitovsky reversal criterion; as regard the Kaldor–Hicks criterion, no definite deduction is possible. In short, apart from the criticisms of compensation criteria mentioned in the previous sections, and the fundamental criticisms which will be mentioned in the next chapter, we have developed here another criticism of the compensation criteria, namely that they are impractical because price–quantity data alone can never give enough information to apply them. Needless to say, in any practical problem which is being examined (especially if the examination is *ex post*) price–quantity data are all that we are likely to have. But the criteria require full knowledge of everybody's utility function if they are to be applied consistently.

It needs to be mentioned here that the attempt to derive welfare conclusions from quantity index numbers after the fashion of the welfare criteria presupposes that we are agreed on the Paretian value judgments. Further, both Q_1 and Q_2 have been assumed to be positions where the price ratios between goods are equal to the common-for-all-people subjective rates of substitution between the same goods. In other words, the underlying assumptions are that people trade at prices which they cannot individually alter, that all markets are cleared, and that there are no externalities in production or consumption. Without assuming that the market-price ratios (on which the quantity index numbers are constructed) reflect the relative subjective evaluation of goods, one could not use the market-price ratios for *welfare* evaluation. As we shall be arguing in the next chapter, it is possible that according to some policy-makers, or some kinds of social welfare functions, prices to be used for welfare evaluations do not have to be market prices and do not have to reflect individual relative evaluations, but rather some socially approved marginal rates of substitution or marginal social welfare weights.

We showed in Section 2 that if the welfare comparisons are being made between more than two situations, then the double criterion which combines Kaldor–Hicks and the Scitovsky reversal criteria can contradict itself. Similarly, it can easily be shown that if the comparisons are between more than two situations, then a double-index-number criterion (consisting of the Laspeyre and Paasche quantity index numbers) can also contradict itself. In other words, if we were to say that we shall rank a number of years according to the order determined by the use of *both* the Laspeyre and Paasche index numbers we may find that we cannot get a consistent ranking. Consider fig. 5.21. We have there $\Sigma P_1 Q_1 > \Sigma P_1 Q_2$ and also $\Sigma P_2 Q_1 > \Sigma P_2 Q_2$. Let us therefore decide that Q_1 is better than Q_2. Similarly, Q_2 is ranked better than Q_3 and Q_3 better than Q_4 by both the Laspeyre and the Paasche quantity indices. From this we could conclude that Q_1 is better than Q_4 according to both the indices. But a direct comparison of Q_1 and Q_4 reveals that $\Sigma P_1 Q_4 > \Sigma P_1 Q_1$ and also $\Sigma P_4 Q_4 > \Sigma P_4 Q_1$; so the two indices now rank Q_1 as worse than Q_4. Hence the use of the two indices together does not lead to consistent results any more than does the use together of the Kaldor–Hicks and the Scitovsky reversal criteria. Finally, it is obvious that neither a current-weighted nor a base-weighted quantity index ever tells us enough for us to say that the Samuelson comparisons would be met by one of the positions; as we showed above, a sufficient condition for those comparisons to be met is that one of the positions should have more of at least one good and no less of any other.

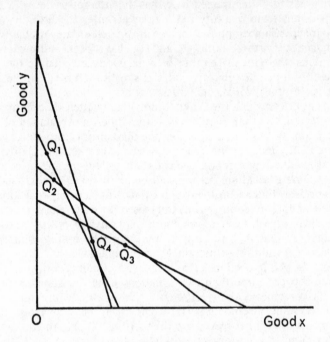

Fig. 5.21

CONCLUSIONS

The first thing to note is that our appraisal of the *a priori* welfare criteria in this chapter has been strictly on their own terms regarding the basic value judgments and assumptions—just as our appraisal of the allocation theorems of Paretian welfare theory of Chapter II was. The only *a priori* welfare criterion (i.e. the Little criterion) which had survived critical scrutiny until recently has been shown to be capable of three major interpretations: on the first, it leads to contradictions; on the second, it is nothing else but a tacit inducement to find a Pareto-type welfare function for the society in question; on the third, the underlying value judgments are no longer Paretian, but the criterion is capable of giving some rather crude rankings. We have also investigated what light quantity index numbers shed on the fulfilment of the compensation tests—such as they are. (An alleged corollary of the second-best theorem has recently emerged as a new *a priori* welfare criterion: we have already shown in Chapter III that the alleged corollary does not always follow.) In the next chapter we shall develop a critique of the ethical presumptions of *a priori* welfare criteria (and the welfare theory of allocation). By the end of that chapter the outline of a realistic approach to the problem of welfare evaluation should emerge. Our negative findings regarding the *a priori* welfare criteria are *not* meant to imply that there cannot be (or should not be—this would be a value judgment) any meaningful welfare evaluation of economic policies. The alternative procedure we propose is to be found in Section 2 of the next chapter.

REFERENCES FOR CHAPTER V

[1] K. J. Arrow, 'Little's Critique of Welfare Economics', *American Economic Review*, 1951
[2] M. J. Bailey, 'The Interpretation and Application of the Compensation Principle', *Economic Journal*, 1954
[3] R. E. Baldwin, 'A Comparison of Welfare Criteria', *Review of Economic Studies*, 1954
[4] Maurice Dobb, 'A Further Comment on the Discussion of Welfare Criteria', *Economic Journal*, 1963
[5] J. de V. Graaff, *Theoretical Welfare Economics*, Cambridge, 1957
[6] R. H. Harrod, 'Scope and Method of Economics', *Economic Journal*, 1938
[7] J. R. Hicks, 'The Foundations of Welfare Economics', *Economic Journal*, 1939
[8] J. R. Hicks, 'The Valuation of Social Income', *Economica*, 1940
[9] J. R. Hicks, 'The Measurement of Real Income', *Oxford Economic Papers*, 1958
[10] N. Kaldor, 'Welfare Comparisons of Economics and Interpersonal Comparisons of Utility', *Economic Journal*, 1939
[11] C. F. Kennedy, 'Economic Welfare Function and Dr. Little's Criterion', *Review of Economic Studies*, 1953
[12] C. F. Kennedy, 'Welfare Criterion—A Further Note', *Economic Journal*, 1963
[13] I. M. D. Little, *A Critique of Welfare Economics*, 2nd edn., Oxford, 1957
[14] I. M. D. Little, 'Welfare Criteria: An Exchange of Notes; A Comment', *Economic Journal*, 1962

[15] I. M. D. Little, 'Two Comments I', *Economic Journal*, 1963
[16] J. E. Meade, Review of Little's *Critique of Welfare Economics*, in *Economic Journal*, 1959
[17] J. E. Meade, 'Welfare Criteria: An Exchange of Notes; A Comment', *Economic Journal*, 1962
[18] E. J. Mishan, 'Welfare Criteria: An Exchange of Notes; A Comment', *Economic Journal*, 1962
[19] E. J. Mishan, 'Welfare Criteria: Are Compensation Tests Necessary?', *Economic Journal*, 1962
[20] S. K. Nath, 'Are Formal Welfare Criteria Required?', *Economic Journal*, 1964
[21] A. C. Pigou, *Economics of Welfare*, 4th edn., London, 1932
[22] L. C. Robbins, *An Essay on the Nature and Significance of Economic Science*, 2nd edn., London, 1935
[23] L. C. Robbins, 'Interpersonal Comparisons of Utility: A Comment', *Economic Journal*, 1938
[24] D. H. Robertson, 'Welfare Criteria: An Exchange of Notes; A Comment', *Economic Journal*, 1962
[25] P. A. Samuelson, 'Evaluation of Real National Income', *Oxford Economic Papers*, 1950
[26] P. A. Samuelson, 'Evaluation of Social Income, Capital Formation and Wealth', in F. A. Lutz (ed.), *The Theory of Capital*, London, 1961
[27] T. Scitovsky, 'A Note on Welfare Propositions in Economics', *Review of Economic Studies*, 1941
[28] A. K. Sen, 'Distribution, Transitivity and Little's Welfare Criteria', *Economic Journal*, 1963
[29] G. Slasor, 'A Note on Compensation Tests', *Economica*, 1961

VI

A PRIORI V *AD HOC* WELFARE ECONOMICS

'Far from decreasing the attraction of economics, the growing realism of our approach should enhance it, lifting it above the scholastic disputes about *a priori* tenets.' T. Balogh [3, p. 81].

This chapter is the core of our critique of *a priori* welfare economics. It could also have been put at the beginning or at the end of the book but we have put it in the middle because we felt that we must first evaluate *a priori* welfare economics on its own terms before developing our fundamental critique. This we now proceed to do in this chapter. (The next few chapters then will be discussions of some of the applications of *a priori* welfare economics, where we shall be able to take into account some of the conclusions which will be established in this chapter.)

Our main purpose here is to expose the illogical status of *a priori* welfare propositions and the danger of political bias in them. This is followed by a critique of Arrow's theorem. These two parts of our discussion can be said to be about the *sources* of a social welfare function. We shall then go on to discuss the *form* of a social welfare function, and note that a great deal of the question-begging procedure in welfare economics and of the consequent pessimism about its usefulness have been due to wrongly interpreting the form that a social welfare function needs to take. At the next stage we shall examine the implications of our discussions for the concepts of 'efficiency' and 'optimal allocation', and try to sort out the valid propositions from the invalid in the theory of resource allocation. Through this chapter an outline of a more realistic and logically sound welfare economics should emerge.

6.1 SOURCES OF SOCIAL WELFARE FUNCTIONS

Our critique under this heading will be divided into two parts: the first will examine the formal, logical basis of the theorems and prescriptions of *a priori* welfare economics, and the second will deal with Arrow's theorem about the social welfare function.

6.1a 'Widely Acceptable Value Judgments'

What is the formal basis of the Paretian economic welfare theory of allocation, the Pareto-type economic welfare functions and the formal welfare criteria? Since they are all about suitable, desirable, or optimum economic policies, they must necessarily depend on some considerations regarding 'suitability' or 'desirability'. Suitability of any social policy needs to be judged everywhere according to what it does to social welfare. It is possible in principle that in some particular situations social welfare may be irrelevant; the paramount consideration may be (say) the interests of a particular sub-group. But we want to leave these special and peculiar cases out. And this is the first *value judgment* at the basis of any kind of *welfare* economics, and of any *part* of it; we assert that social desirability is to be judged according to what happens to social welfare.

But *a priori* welfare economics goes much further; *it presumes that we know what will be the constituents of the aim to promote social welfare*, and some broad principles about the relative weights of these constituents. This is done by trying to discover something called 'widely acceptable value judgments'. The Paretian value judgments, which were detailed in Chapter II, are identified as these 'widely acceptable value judgments'. On the basis of these, concepts of a 'suitable' or an 'optimum' allocation of resources and of sufficient, *a priori* welfare criteria are built up. We have already critically evaluated in the last four chapters these concepts *on their own terms*; that is, so far we have ignored the formal basis of the value judgments they are based on, but now we shall be examining *a priori* welfare economics at this fundamental level.

The first question that arises is: *where* are the value judgments supposed to be widely acceptable? For it is very likely that the value judgments that are likely to be widely acceptable differ from one society to another. Some writers would like to believe that a common set of value judgments would be acceptable in what have been described as the countries of the West. But this is too sanguine. The different histories of social-security measures alone (with the greatest contrast being provided perhaps by Britain and the United States) are ample refutation of any such presumption.

The second question is: has it ever been established that the particular set of value judgments which underlie Paretian welfare economics would *truly* be widely acceptable in any society? At least a great deal of legislative measures of as obviously democratic countries as any the world has known in recent centuries can be justified only if we accept that an individual is not always the best judge of his own welfare. Compulsory education, compulsory national insurance, tax on tobacco and alcohol, subsidised milk, libraries, national parks and concert halls, to mention only the more obvious examples, are all based on the value judgment, presumably

126

widely acceptable in a country where these measures have been adopted, that in some matters an individual is not the best judge of his own welfare. Further, the most important of the Paretian value judgments is that social welfare is to be considered a monotonic increasing function of individual welfare, that if one person's income and leisure increase while those of others remain the same, then social welfare increases. As we showed in Chapter V, this value judgment would imply the approval of a series of economic policies which raised the standards of living of a group or two but left those of the others unaltered. Yet the relative distribution of incomes and wealth would be changing unfavourably in most individuals' opinion. Therefore it is too much to expect that such a value judgment is likely to be widely acceptable anywhere. Fisher [12] has argued a defence of this particular Paretian value judgment on the ground that the gaining group does not gain at the expense of the group whose absolute share remains the same. But surely to the extent that an economy uses its scarce resources in order to move in one direction, it has less of them left, in the short-run at least, to move in another direction. Therefore, as only the rich gain from a long succession of economic measures, it is in a real sense at the expense of the poor. Moreover, as we have argued above, the relative distribution alters in any case, and this might be very important according to a lot of people in some particular situation.

Suppose for a moment that we have chosen a particular country and discovered somehow its 'widely acceptable' value judgments regarding what might be broadly described as economic affairs. We would still not be justified in deducing from them a sufficient welfare criterion or a welfare function type by which all economists were meant to order the different economic policies open to that country. From the fact that most people are agreed on some value judgment, it cannot logically be deduced that the value judgment should be adopted as the norm in personal behaviour or in one's comments on a society. As David Hume argued some centuries ago, it is impossible to deduce a proposition containing the verb 'ought' from propositions which only contain the verb 'is'. The basis of this argument is the following logical rule:

No imperative conclusion can be validly drawn from a set of premises which does not contain at least one imperative.[1]

---

[1] See Hare [18]. The argument in the text does not imply that norms have nothing to do with facts or that norms cannot be influenced by facts. Norms and social ends change over time in response to the empirical study of facts. Cf. Myrdal [29].

In recent times this argument has been advanced most forcefully by Popper. To quote:

> The making of decision, the adoption of a norm or of a standard, is a fact. But the norm or standard which has been adopted is not a fact. That most people agree with the norm 'Thou shalt not steal' is a sociological fact. But the norm 'Thou shalt not steal' is not a fact, and can never be inferred from sentences describing facts. This will be seen most clearly when we remember that there are always various and even opposite decisions possible with respect to a certain relevant fact. For instance, in face of the sociological fact that most people adopt the norm 'Thou shalt not steal', it is still possible to decide either to adopt this norm, or to oppose its adoption; it is possible to encourage those who have adopted the norm, or to discourage them, and to persuade them to adopt another norm. To sum up, *it is impossible to derive a sentence stating a norm or a decision or, say, a proposal for a policy from a sentence stating a fact*; this is only another way of saying that it is impossible to derive norms or decisions *or proposals* from facts' [32, vol. I, ch. 5, original italics].

In addition to the foregoing logical flaw in the procedure, a practical point is that though most people agree on a value judgment, there might still be some who disagree with it. If the country in question is a democracy, then the political, administrative, or government *decisions* have to be taken on the basis of majority approval, but there is no compelling moral or logical need for *all comments and recommendations* also to be based on what is 'widely acceptable'. Otherwise there will never be a chance for individuals who are in some respects in disagreement with the majority's value judgments to change the majority's opinion one day. For example, most people in a certain country may be agreed (as they often are) that there should be capital punishment for certain crimes. What shall we think of the sociologists in that country if they were *all* to adopt for that reason the retention of capital punishment as a basic-value judgment—as a norm—in their comments on that society? Again, suppose that we discover that most people in a certain country consider any reduction in the inequality (somehow measured) of the distribution of money incomes a bad thing; should all economists in that country then adopt that value judgment as the basis of a criterion or a welfare-function *type* by which to judge the welfare significance of different economic policies?

Thus there are serious objections to the procedure of *a priori* welfare economics, even if it is argued that the welfare criteria and the

Pareto-type welfare function are *not deduced* from some alleged facts describing the wide acceptance of certain value judgments but are formulated to incorporate apparently 'widely acceptable value judgments' on practical grounds. However, welfare criteria and the Paretian optimum conditions aspire to be the guiding principles of social action about certain aspects of welfare called economic (which it may or may not be possible to delimit); therefore, irrespective of whether they are or are not based on 'widely acceptable value judgments', any such principles cannot be above politics, because they constitute a social policy, and any social policy is a matter of politics. Moreover, starting with the 'most widely acceptable value judgments' or the 'prevailing values' and building a system of *a priori* welfare evaluations and recommendations runs a high risk of introducing a bias in favour of things as they are into the customary evaluations of economic policies.

To sum up, the basic procedure of *a priori* welfare economics is based on a confusion between *decisions* and *recommendations or comments*. In a democratic country the former have to be based on value judgments which are at any moment widely acceptable to the delegates of the individual citizens. But there is no necessary logical or moral reason why the individual citizen's comments or recommendations, in his capacity as a labourer, engineer, or professional economist, should be based on widely acceptable value judgments. Some of the individuals may want to do so, while others do not. In short, there is no logical warrant for economists in a democratic society to choose some value judgments and make them into basic norms in their professional evaluative work *because* they are widely acceptable. Any proposed welfare criterion and *type* of welfare functions are no more than *personal* opinions of the particular economists, which the public and the other economists may accept or reject, depending on how much moral appeal those criteria make to them and quite irrespective of how widely their basic value judgments might be accepted. Norms, welfare criteria, value judgments, etc., have to be chosen by each individual for himself; if an economist wants others to adopt a particular norm he must *persuade* others to see that the norm he suggests is morally impelling.

We may note that our arguments go against the position adopted in a recent contribution by Rothenberg [37]. According to him, the task of the economist is to discover somehow the 'prevailing values' of the society and then to formulate standards of judgment in conformity with them so that they will be relevant. But this procedure is open to all the foregoing logical and other objections. Rothenberg is aware of one of them, because he says: 'Our criterion of relevance is based on generalisation of *currently* prevailing values. But we are none of us entirely satisfied with where our own or our neighbour's pathways have led us. The search for a useful welfare economics should nowhere criticise the far more urgent search for better paths' [37, p. 331; original italics]. Here Rothenberg shows keen awareness of the possible role of *comments and recommendations* by economists and others in changing the 'prevailing values' which nevertheless determine *decisions* on behalf of the society at any given time. Yet this awareness is only transitory and is not allowed to affect the rest of the argument of the book. Indeed, the following is soon added in a footnote: 'Anyone is free to criticize currently prevailing values. The welfare economist is neither uniquely nor even especially qualified for such a task. Ethical criticism is an attempt to persuade individuals to *change* their values and their institutions. If it succeeds, the welfare economist's competence is called on only to help reconstruct institutions in accordance with the newly formed values or to evaluate how well newly fashioned institutions accord with the new values. The welfare economist, qua welfare economist, is not concerned with criticizing either the old or the new values themselves' [37, p. 331; original italics].

It is totally unacceptable to us that 'the welfare economist, qua welfare economist, is not concerned with criticising either the old or the new values themselves'; according to us, it is the right, if not the responsibility, of every economist, qua economist or welfare economist, *and* of every other adult, to enter into such a criticism. Further, in our opinion, 'to help reconstruct institutions in accordance with the newly formed values' is exactly the task of applied economics.

The range of what is at present designated welfare economics has come to be restricted to the problem of making a choice from among the various combinations of outputs that an economy can produce with a given amount of resources. But this problem is of exactly the same type as the other problems of applied economics, for example, the choice among various possible levels of employment or the various possible ways of achieving and maintaining a certain level of employment. With each of these choices, different courses of action differently affect, among other important things, the availability of goods and services to individuals. There is no logical reason to put the former kind of choice into a separate category (called welfare economics) from the latter two kinds of choice. Whenever an economic theory is being applied to a practical problem, and the outcome is to be judged from the standpoint of social welfare (according to some considerations which remain to be discussed), we have a problem in welfare economics. In short, according to our arguments, welfare economics, applied economics, economic policy, and applied welfare economics—all these names describe the same field of study; there is no such thing as theoretical (or *a priori*) welfare economics.

6.1b Arrow's Theorem

This subsection in fact is very much a continuation of the last one, because Arrow's work represents a systematic effort to see if there is a way of *deriving* a welfare criterion or a social welfare function (which could then be used by all economists in the society concerned) *from* the individuals' opinions, values, and orderings of different social states. We have already argued in the last section that any such attempt is founded on doubtful logic; this indeed will be our final comment on Arrow's work in this field. However, his theorem is of interest in suggesting a possibility of more or less involuntary social inaction in a democracy.

Arrow uses the concept of a social welfare function in two senses: first, a rule or process by which a master-plan for ordering social states could be derived from the individual orderings; and secondly, the master-plan which has been so derived. The first meaning is quite unusual; due to that reason some critics have argued that Arrow's work does not belong to welfare economics. But such a point is rather uninteresting; we still need to examine the significance of Arrow's work.

Arrow defines a social state thus: 'The most precise definition of a social state would be a complete description of each type of commodity in the hands of each individual, the amount of labour to be supplied by each individual, the amount of each productive resource invested in each type of productive activity, and the amounts of various types of collective activity. . . .' The definition of a social state specifies a set of particular values of the group of variables on which social welfare is supposed to depend. This group of variables is broader than what is usually presumed to be included in the social welfare function in *a priori* economics. This is because Arrow is prepared to include variables like collective activity, and indeed even the individuals' opinion of the state of relative distribution of welfare. Therefore Arrow's conception is of a social welfare function aggregated from individuals' values rather than tastes. But as he himself shows, no difference is made to his theorem whether tastes or values are included. Though this is a most important distinction and we shall be returning to a discussion of it in the next section, it is of no relevance in analysing the significance of Arrow's theorem—contrary to what some other critics have thought.

Arrow sets out to explore if there is some non-contradictory method of aggregating individual preferences—a method which would be consistent with what he described as some 'natural conditions', but some of which are in fact so artificial and unnecessary that they mar the relevance of his exercise to any *practical* standpoint. We shall be returning to this question. However, the degree of relevance, or lack of relevance, of Arrow's theorem cannot be appreciated without considering his conditions; hence though it is a bit tedious, his conditions are reproduced below, but without the symbols he employs.

1. . . . we are requiring, for some sufficiently wide range of individual orderings, the social welfare function give rise to a true social ordering [1, p. 25].

2. '. . . the social welfare function is such that the social ordering responds positively to alterations in individual values, or at least not negatively'. This is the condition of 'positive association of social and individual values' [1, p. 25].[1]

3. . . . we may require of our social welfare functions that the choice made by society from a given environment depend only on the orderings of individuals among the alternatives in that environment [1, p. 26].

4. . . . the individuals in our society are free to choose, by varying their values, among the alternatives available [1, p. 26].

In other words, the social welfare function is not to be imposed; '. . . when the social welfare function is imposed, there is some pair of alternatives *r* and *y* such that the community can never express a preference for *y* over *r* no matter what the tastes of all individuals are, even if all individuals prefer *y* to *r*; some preferences are taboo'. This is the condition of 'citizens' sovereignty' [1, p. 28].

5. The final condition is that the social welfare function is not to be dictatorial. In other words, the social orderings are not to be determined solely by the orderings of an individual, irrespective of the orderings of the rest of the individuals.

[1] This second condition has only a superficial resemblance to the Pareto-type social welfare functions—contrary to what a number of writers have thought. Arrow does not assume that an individual's values are determined only by his own income and wealth; he assumes more than just the ordinary externalities in consumption; indeed, he considers that the social distribution of real income and wealth, as seen by the individual, is a good which enters an individual's values on par with other commodities. In other words, Arrow assumes the existence of Duesenberry-type externalities in consumption. See Chapter IV, Section 2.

In addition to these, Arrow has two obvious axioms or assumptions. Firstly, any two social states must be comparable in some way or other (preference or indifference); and secondly, the social orderings must be transitive or consistent. These two constitute Arrow's Axioms I and II.

Arrow then develops the implications of these five conditions. Assume that there are m separate social states, that there are n different ways of ordering them, and that different individuals choose different orderings from among the n orderings. Is it then always possible by methods which are in agreement with the five foregoing conditions to derive from the individual orderings of the m social states a consistent master ordering of the m social states? Arrow's answer, reached with the help of symbolic logic, is that 'if the total number of alternatives is two, the method of majority decision is a social welfare function which satisfies conditions 2–5 and yields a social ordering of the two alternatives for every set of individual orderings' [1, p. 48]. However, 'if there are at least three alternatives which the members of the society are free to order in any way, then every social welfare function satisfying Axioms I and II must be either imposed or dictatorial' [1, p. 59]. Given Arrow's conditions and a range of more than two social states, there is no method of voting which can remove the possibility of contradiction mentioned at the beginning of this section.

It has been necessary to reproduce Arrow's findings in his own words because it is particularly important to understand how much or how little significance they have. We want to argue that his theorem has very little significance. It is to be noted that his theorem is true only if none of his conditions are to be violated. Therefore we must now examine the importance of some of these conditions.

The most controversial condition is the third, which is about the independence of irrelevant alternatives. This condition implies that any ordering by the master plan of any two social states must be determined by how the individuals rank just those two social states, and not be affected at all by how the $(m - 2)$ other possible social states are ranked by them.[1] This amounts to saying that the ordering by the master plan must ignore the intensity of individuals' preferences

[1] Coleman [8] argues that the third condition is inconsistent with both collective and individual rationality, because both individual and collective decisions have to be taken under uncertainty which 'opens the possibility of expression of intensity of preference'. Hildrith [22] was one of the first to show that if the third condition is dropped, consistent aggregation of individual orderings into a social ordering will be possible. For a discussion of other contributions of this kind see Rothenberg [37].

among social states. If two social states, *a* and *b*, are being compared, then only the numbers of those who prefer *a* to *b*, and *b* to *a*, are to be considered, and no further inquiry is needed, such as whether those who prefer *a* consider it one of the most important of the *m* social states. If the intensity of preferences is sometimes considered relevant in determining the master plan, then we shall sometimes have to employ a system of weighting the individual votes. In other words, now we have to admit the possibility of interpersonal comparisons of intensities of preferences, i.e. of utilities. Such comparisons can be regarded as comparisons of *facts* (for the measurement of which there is no apparatus yet) or as value judgments or what Robbins [36] called 'conventions'. If the interpersonal comparisons of utility are to be regarded as factual comparisons, then until some apparatus for measuring utility has been invented, no help can be given to policy formulation. However, even if some such apparatus were to be invented, there would still be need for some value judgments. A value judgment would be needed to devise a formula for making the utility measures of different individuals similar in terms of their units of measurement; i.e. a value judgment would be needed to make the utilities of different individuals dimensionally comparable. This value judgment could take the form that the same apparatus is to measure everybody's utility in the same way. A further value judgment would be required to devise a formula for some method of aggregating different persons' utilities.

Anyway, no objective way of measuring utility is available, or is likely ever to be available. And since some value judgments would be required even then to proceed to policy-making, there is no reason why we should not admit the need for, and *the possibility of*, interpersonal comparisons of utility *as ethical comparisons*. We are not arguing that any part of economic theory be based on the assumption that interpersonal comparisons of utility are possible, but that since, as we saw in the last section, no *policy* discussions can be conducted without some value judgments being made, there seems no logical or other reason for refusing to admit that in real life policy discussions and recommendations might sometimes if not often be based on some ethical considerations which can be interpreted as interpersonal comparisons of utility. Moreover, we shall be arguing in the next section that detailed interpersonal comparisons of utility (even simply as *ethical* comparisons) are seldom required, because most democratic policy-making proceeds on the ethical premise that individuals should be treated *as if* they had the same degree of sensitivity and the capacity to enjoy life and, secondly, *as if* they had more or less similar tastes unless there is some special evidence to the

134

contrary in particular cases. Once these somewhat fundamental *ethical* premises (which presuppose *ethical and subjective* interpersonal comparisons) are adopted, there is seldom any need for any further interpersonal comparison of utilities.

In a new chapter in the second edition of his book, Arrow has argued that 'if there is no empirical way of comparing two states (say, indifference curves of two different individuals), there can be no ethical way of distinguishing them. Value judgments may equate empirically distinguishable phenomena but they cannot differentiate empirically indistinguishable states'. Here measurability and distinguishability have been mixed up: phenomena do not have to be objectively *measurable* to be empirically distinguishable or recognisable. Utility, welfare, beauty, and affection are not objectively measurable, but does it mean that they cannot be recognised? Of course, it is true that different individuals may not agree on the existence of beauty or its 'degree' in an object; that in fact is the meaning of saying that beauty is *not* objectively measurable. Yet each man who wants to choose the flowers for his garden according to their beauty is able to do so. Thus, though objective measures of utility and welfare may not be possible, yet *ethical* judgments about different persons' utility and welfare are not thereby precluded. If interpersonal ethical comparisons of utility or of preferences are permitted, then Arrow's theorem does not follow.

We should now look at the basic purpose of Arrow's exercise. What is it supposed to be relevant to? To the extent that it argues that majority voting can lead to intransitive decisions, we can readily accept this finding and its significance.[1] One part of its significance is that it shows up the possibility of the majority rule leading 'to a deadlock and therefore a socially undesired inaction'; and, as

---

[1] Suppose there are three individuals, *A*, *B*, and *C* who are asked to rank three possible social positions to be called *x*, *y*, and *z*, by giving them numbers from 1 to 3; the largest number for an outcome implies that it is the most preferred, and so on. Suppose we get the following data:

	x	y	z
A	3	2	1
B	2	1	3
C	1	3	2

Now two individuals (*A* and *B*) prefer *x* to *y*; similarly, two prefer *y* to *z*. Hence we might derive the master plan: $x > y > z$. But if we examine the data again we find that they also tell us that two individuals (*B* and *C*) also prefer *z* to *x*, so that on the majority rule the master plan should say: $z > x$. This illustrates the paradox of the majority rule. Incidentally, if we adopt the rather unnatural assumption that all individual orderings are single-peaked, then the paradox of the majority rule cannot arise. See Rothenberg [37].

Arrow goes on to point out, there is need for further empirical as well as theoretical study of 'the notion of a "democratic paralysis", a failure to act due not to a desire for inaction but an inability to agree on the proper action . . .' [1, p. 120]. Having said this, one must also note that it might suit the true purposes of a democracy if some social issues do not get majority approval permanently; for it strengthens the stability of a democracy if a minority of today can hope to get alternative policies to some of the current ones approved by the majority one day. Hence the possibility of intransitivity in the majority rule need not always be an unmixed misfortune, though probably in some specific empirical situations it does much more mischief than any possible good.

This is about all that can be allowed by way of the significance of Arrow's theorem. His theorem seemed unduly startling when it first appeared due to his unusual use of the phrase 'a social welfare function'. As we noted at the beginning of this section, Arrow uses the concept 'a social welfare function' to describe both the master-ordering and the process or rule by which individual orderings are to be aggregated into that master-ordering. But the common meaning of a social welfare function in the economic literature is taken to be just an ordering of social states, which may be of any individual or expert for the purposes of comment and recommendation, or which may be the adopted ordering of the decision-makers for taking *decisions* on behalf of the society. What Arrow proved was that *on his conditions* there is *no general rule* for aggregating individual orderings to reach a master-ordering which will always be consistent; it might *yet* be possible some time to reach a consistent master-ordering even on his conditions. In any case, Arrow had not proved that no master-ordering for taking decisions in a democracy can ever exist in principle.

Further, it is doubtful if it is either relevant or ever likely to be fruitful to look for a few simple rules which might describe how the master-ordering or the decision-giving social welfare function is born in a democracy. The process is necessarily complex: individuals—economic, legal, medical, and other experts, journalists, politicians, and other citizens—express their values not just as orderings to be quietly digested by a master-order-giving computer but rather as means of influencing other citizens' values so that a consensus would emerge of the kind they favour for selfish, altruistic, or mixed reasons; further, individuals' values tend to be influenced by the kind of decision-making process the society has had, and this process itself is subject to change or at least a gradual evolution according to the changing individual values. Hence a suitable study of the

136

decision-making mechanism under a democracy needs to be broader than Arrow's.

Our foregoing discussion gives us the following three possible interpretations of the concept of a social welfare function:

1. The rule or process according to which individual orderings of social states are aggregated into a master-ordering.

2. An ordering of social states that any individual, group or organisation may express for the purposes of *comments and recommendations*. It may or may not coincide with the ordering accepted by the decision-makers for making decisions.

3. An ordering of social states on which *decisions* are taken and which, of course, can *also* be used for comments and recommendations. It could also be called a rule for social decision-making.

These three interpretations need to be kept distinct in any meaningful discussion. The failure to recognise the distinction between the second and third interpretations was at the basis of the pseudo rationale for *a priori* welfare economics. As we noted in the last section, though *decisions* are taken in a democracy *because* they are widely acceptable, it does not follow that *comments and recommendations* that are based on 'widely acceptable' value judgments are in any sense non-controversial, non-partisan, or above politics. Similarly, though the processes through which democratic decisions are made (and any possible irrationalities in them) are a highly interesting field of study, any finding that those processes are in some sense 'imperfect' *does not* imply that it is useless or illogical for an economist to apply economics to any practical economic problems in the fields of resource allocation, employment, economic development, regional distribution of economic activity, investment allocation, and so on, and *evaluate* their results, and make recommendations and propaganda, in the light of *explicit ethical* considerations of a kind which appeal to him and which he persuades others to accept.

Though a social decision-making mechanism or process is needed in any society to evaluate different policies so that social *decisions* may be taken, such a decision-making process is *not* required to give the economist *once-for-all* a *social* (in the sense that it has been accepted by the society) ordering of economic states by which he may rank alternative social states in order to take decisions on behalf of the society. Indeed, there is no necessary reason why an economist or a labourer should look to the decision-making mechanism to give him a lead in forming his comments and recommendations. Where ethics are concerned, an individual has to make up his own mind. If an individual (an economist, an engineer, or a labourer) chooses to think that decisions taken by the social decision-making mechanism are *right* decisions—that whatever is approved by that mechanism is *ethically* desirable—then though for that individual the social decision-making mechanism becomes his social welfare function (his criterion of desirability), it still remains his personal choice to take this attitude. He could have taken the attitude that some decisions taken by the mechanism may be morally wrong decisions. We are in fact back with Popper's argument that ethical judgments are personal judgments.

Our conclusions regarding Arrow's theorem then are: first, his theorem is not true if interpersonal comparisons of utility as *ethical* statements are allowed; and there seems no reason why they should not be. Secondly, the theorem has relevance only to how decisions might be formed and not to how welfare assessments by any individual or group might be made. Thirdly, even to the decision-making process Arrow's theorem has only limited relevance because of the reasons which were given above. However, he has dramatically called attention to the possibility of social inaction on certain issues in a democracy, which must be kept in mind.

6.2 FORMS OF SOCIAL WELFARE FUNCTIONS

6.2a General Welfare v 'Economic Welfare'

As we noted in the first chapter, the concept of a social welfare function was first introduced by Bergson [5]. He started by formulating it as an undefined function, stating a relation between social (general) welfare and all possibly relevant variables, such as work and consumption of each individual, as well as any more economic variables. He went on to say that 'for relatively small changes in these economic variables, other elements in welfare, I believe, will not be significantly affected'. This was the origin of the concept of *economic* welfare function, commonly referred to as the (social) welfare function. Since social welfare has been taken to depend on each individual's income and wealth, and since each individual's utility is assumed to depend on his income and wealth, the social welfare function can be reformulated as a function of individual utilities. This is the common practice in welfare economics, and it is in this form that we came across it in Chapter II. In this form the social welfare function then looks like the following:

$$W = W(U^1, U^2, \ldots U^s) \tag{6.1}$$

where W is the social economic welfare and $U^1, \ldots U^s$ are the levels of utility of the s individuals. This, of course, is an undefined form of the social-economic-welfare function.

It is possible, though curious, to *imagine* that we *actually* have the *fully defined* (ordinal) utility functions of all individuals and a set of precise rules about their relative weights from the point of view of social welfare; in other words, that we have a *fully defined* social welfare function in terms of individual utility indicators. We can then construct a series of parallel and well-behaved social indifference curves which have commodities measured along the axes; each of these curves then shows different distributions of utility among individuals for which the level of social welfare is the same. One type of such curves are known as Bergson curves or frontiers. See Samuelson [40] and Gorman [14]. However, since individual utility functions can never be known, such curves (or surfaces or equations) must remain completely imaginary. True, this applies to the Scitovsky indifference curves also; but whereas Scitovsky indifference curves serve to bring out the relativity of the welfare evaluation (on the Paretian value judgments) of different commodity bundles, these other social indifference curves can be misused to give the appearance to some welfare propositions of being generally true when in fact they are true only of the particular set of non-intersecting 'social indifference curves' (with their particular curvature) which has been assumed. Examples of this kind abound in the theory of international trade. We consider as most unfortunate and misleading the use of such social indifference curves (which, incidentally, invariably pertain to Pareto-type social-welfare functions) for deriving *a priori* welfare propositions. That is why apart from the Scitovsky community indifference curves we have not dwelt on any of the other types of social or community indifference curves.

Any social welfare function specifies the aim of social policy; this is shown by what the dependent variable is meant to be. Similarly, it also contains the independent variables and their relative weights; in other words, a list of evaluative rules. This is true of both a social welfare function (which is *meant to be* a fully defined function) and of the *a priori* welfare criteria (which can be regarded as examples of social welfare functions which are at best incompletely defined). In Chapter V we have already critically examined for their internal consistency the criteria for *a priori* evaluation which various authors have suggested. Let us here examine the nature of the implied aim of social policy and the nature of the independent variables.

The typical social welfare function in welfare economics is an economic welfare function; similarly, all the so-called welfare criteria relate to economic welfare. Pigou thought of 'economic welfare' as being a part of general welfare. It is now generally recognised by economists that this is not permissible because welfare is an indivisible feeling. However, they will not, when discussing economic problems, concern themselves with general welfare but only with an *aspect* of welfare—the economic aspect which is said to depend on 'those things and services which the individual consumes or enjoys, and which could be exchanged for money, and the work done by each individual' [28, p. 6]. Likening the mind to a well of unknown depth, partly filled with water, and admitting the 'once the water is in the well there is no way of saying which tap it came from', and that 'it is impossible to say how much water there is in the well', Little goes on: '. . . but one can say that the level of the water has risen or fallen as the result of turning the economic tap, *if the other taps are not touched*, i.e. one can say that economic welfare increased or decreased' [28, p. 51; my italics]. But the other taps often do get turned as the economic tap is turned. One can still make judgments about the rising or falling level of water in the well, but there is no definite part or aspect of it which can be attributed to economic causes alone. Either, as we manipulate the economic tap, we watch out for any unfavourable turning of the non-economic taps also, and judge the level of general welfare, or we mislead others and ourselves by continuing to speak of 'economic welfare'.

Moreover, the concern with 'economic welfare' has produced a fundamental confusion, and has encouraged the neglect of the possibility that in real life there are likely to be important *non-market* interdependencies in individual welfares. There can be little doubt that in any society there are some interdependencies in individual welfares which are too varied, complex, and subtle to affect individual decisions regarding earning and spending in such a way that in making these decisions an individual can adequately allow for them. Some of these direct interdependencies are such as vaguely or clearly felt envy, compassion, guilt, and so on.

For example, an individual who experiences a rise in his income and is enabled to afford greater luxuries may also have a sense of guilt about those who are still poor. This individual would like to give up some of his own income and wealth in order to increase the share of the poor, but feels that his efforts *on his own* will be ineffective in achieving what he would like to see brought about—a better share for the poor. This amounts to 'non-marketability' of the commodity he would like, namely a better share for the poor.[1]

[1] Phenomena of this kind were first emphasised by Duesenberry (see our Chapter IV, Section 2); see also Haavelmo [16] and Baumol [4].

This, then, is another example of an externality which can be put into the category of 'external effects of consumption on consumption'. (See the paragraphs headed Envy and Compassion in Chapter IV, Section 2.) It is also possible to interpret this externality along the 'public goods' line, as we have already indicated in Chapter IV. Suppose each person wants the transference of 10% of the national income to the poorest section of the population, just as each person may want a defence programme of a certain size. No single person is able to buy the defence programme; similarly, no single person is able to buy the rise in the absolute (and the relative) standard of living of the poorest. If either of these services is provided for one person, then it is simultaneously also provided for everybody else, whether they pay for the service or not. Therefore some individuals, or nearly all individuals, may be tempted to hide the true value of such services to them. Hence the need arises to provide some goods and services collectively. Hence also the fallacy in the assumption that an individual's welfare function coincides with his utility function *as revealed by his market choices. This is a very common fallacy in economic writings.*

It is also possible that an individual anticipates important economies of scale in certain actions. How many people would be ready to fight an enemy country's forces if they had no assurance that there would be other compatriots fighting with them? Fighting an enemy on one's own, or fighting poverty on one's own, is not expected by the individual to bring much return for the community (and therefore not much welfare for himself), but if he can be sure that there will be many others doing the same the expected effectiveness increases more than in proportion with the numbers, and hence the willingness to undertake the action (or the *degree* to which a certain action will be taken).

Provided, then, that an individual can be sure that by giving up some of his goods and services he is ensuring that all the poor of his society will be looked after better, his *welfare* will be greater with fewer goods and services (and less inequality) than with more goods and services (and greater inequality). But if 'economic welfare' has by definition been linked with a preference map drawn with reference to the goods and services exchanged in the market, what shall we say about the direction of change in economic welfare in this case? Has it increased or decreased?

The 'other factors' affecting welfare do not, in general, stay constant as the economic factors (goods bought and sold) change, so that the distinction between 'economic welfare' and 'welfare' of a community is about as logical in principle or useful in practice as

141

would be the distinction between its 'literary culture' and 'general culture' on the assumption that the 'literary culture' is a function of the number of books bought per head per period.

Finally, 'economic welfare' is by now—whatever may have been the case at one time—an ethical term; it carries an implication of approval and recommendation. Hence an economist's arguments are not necessarily raised above any possible political or ethical controversy because he chooses to be concerned only with something called 'economic welfare'.[1]

6.2b Distributive Judgments

We have noted in the last sub-section how Bergson's concept of social welfare function came to be reformulated as a function of individual welfares. This led to statements of the following kind: '... it must never be forgotten that from a consistent ethical point of view decisions should be made concerning the welfare function itself. Beliefs concerning the distribution of income are derivative rather than fundamental. Except in the admittedly unrealistic case where all tastes are identical, setting up such beliefs as goals is equivalent to accepting a "shibboleth" and to embracing an ambiguous, undefinable welfare function' [39, p. 248].

But are the beliefs concerning the distribution of income derivative? Surely, people do not argue about the need for greater or less equality of distribution of *welfare*? The arguments of real life seem to be conducted in terms of the distribution of the *means* to welfare. For example, people argue about the varying degrees of equality of the *means* to education and not about those of *education* itself; and about the varying degrees of equality of the political *means* to welfare (such as the right to vote and to criticise, etc.) but not about those of 'political welfare' or of welfare itself. And there is no reason to suppose that instead of arguing about the varying degrees of equality of the *economic means* to welfare, people argue about those of 'economic welfare', or of welfare.

It may be asked here, what are the *economic means* to welfare? We take the view that the only practical concept of the economic means to welfare is that of money income, leisure and wealth, or rather, money income, leisure and wealth per head in the family. But it is usually argued that since individual tastes differ, every time relative prices change, money incomes must also change; otherwise 'such a procedure [of thinking of distribution in terms of money incomes] involves making a shibboleth of the existing distribution of relative technological scarcities of goods' [39, p. 249].

[1] Cf. the Manifesto in Hicks [21].

6.2 FORMS OF SOCIAL WELFARE FUNCTIONS

Is this a convincing argument? For example, in a democracy there is supposed to be an equal distribution of the *political means* to welfare. Now, the distribution of political rights and obligations remaining the same, if the political party in power changes, we should perhaps argue that the distribution of the political means to welfare has changed. But nobody seriously makes this argument; it is assumed that if an individual feels strongly against the political party in power his political rights and obligations permit him to make propaganda to change the party in power.

Of course, this would involve the individual extra expense of energy, but it is commonly felt that that is the cost he must pay for feeling as strongly as he does about which party is in power. Given the ethical faith in democracy, it is never considered necessary that because a man feels extra strongly against the party in power, he should have extra political rights or political means to his welfare.

Similarly, given an approved (by the decision-making mechanism) distribution of money income, if relative prices change—say because of the uneven incidence of technological progress—it need not cause the decision-making mechanism to want to change its idea of the desirable pattern of distribution in terms of money incomes.

The only exceptions need be special cases of hardship. For example, if a community living in a remote locality has to rely largely on canned foods and if the prices of such things rise markedly in comparison with other prices, the decision-making mechanism may well—without revealing any inconsistency—decide that the money incomes of that community should be made bigger or that canned foods for them should be subsidised. This is similar to the decision sometimes to give special help to the infirm at the time of an election in order to facilitate their enjoyment of political rights.

What if only a certain sub-group has a taste for a special kind of wine in the making of which so much time and skill are spent that it will be produced only if a high price could be paid for it and which that sub-group cannot afford to pay? The answer depends on the adopted social welfare function of the community for taking decisions. The same community might decide against any special assistance for this group, as decides in favour of free hearing aids for the deaf or free musical concerts. And yet there is no reason why according to the *individual* social welfare function (of some person or persons) these might not be wrong decisions.

Our arguments amount to asserting that it is a logically tenable position for a 'parliament' to say that its ethical belief is that individuals should be treated *as if* they had similar tastes, unless there is some special evidence to the contrary about a certain sub-group, and that what importance it would give to that special evidence would depend on the general ethical considerations guiding the parliament. As we argued in Section 1b of this chapter, there is no reason why the decision-makers should not adopt as an *ethical* premise what Pigou would have liked the *economist* to adopt as a more or less *factual* assumption. The famous criticism by Robbins of Pigou's work was directed against the use of a factual assumption which could not be tested or verified. In his later writings, Robbins [36] has clearly indicated that he was not arguing against the use of 'similar tastes' as an *ethical* assumption or as a 'convention' to be introduced from outside of economics.[1]

Finally, we should note a practical difficulty connected with the view that distributive judgments have to be about *welfare*. *A priori* welfare economics has been based on the Paretian value judgments, one of which lays it down that an individual is always to be considered the best judge of his own welfare. Now if distributive judgments are to be made in terms of the distribution of *welfare* and not *the means* to welfare, then no progress can be made until each individual's welfare function has been discovered. Such a thing is impossible in practice. Indeed, to the extent that any policy evaluation has to be done *ex ante*, even the individual himself may not be able always to foresee his exact tastes in the future. This difficulty is usually slurred over by assuming consistency in consumer behaviour, which amounts to assuming constant tastes and perfect foresight on the part of the individual.[2]

6.2c Social Objectives

A rather obvious fact of which little appreciation is shown in the literature of *a priori* welfare economics is that no executive in the real world either needs or expects to have a detailed social welfare function, referring to each separate individual. In any large community it is quite unrealistic to expect the decision-making mechanism to make welfare judgments in terms of all the individuals; such judgments have to be in terms of sub-groups marked out by characteristics like age, money income, marital status, the state of unemployment and so on. What seems to be required is that the executive should have (through the decision-making mechanism) a list of the

[1] Cf. Harsanyi's discussion of interpersonal comparisons of utility [19].
[2] Fisher [12] and [24] conceived of each distribution of income as a matrix expressing the fraction of each commodity going to each individual. But since all the Paretian value judgments were considered relevant, this feature did not do away with the need to know each individual's utility function. In any case, it is doubtful if either the comment-maker or the decision-maker can ever have the kind of information necessary for such a matrix.

most important social objectives for some time into the future with an indication of their relative importance. One of these objectives is likely to be about the distribution of money incomes, from which may be deduced the welfare weights to be attached to changes in money incomes (with some eye on prices) of different groups. At the same time, from those objectives could be derived a system of relative social-welfare weights to be given to changes in each of those spheres of social life.[1]

In an interesting recent book, Braybrooke and Lindblom [7] sketch a somewhat similar outline of how the executive compares different policies. (They call it 'the strategy of disjointed incrementalism'.) However, a great deal of emphasis is placed on a contrast between a strategy of using 'trading ratios at the margin between pairs of values' relating to increments in the achievement of various objectives and 'a priorities list' of social objectives. But of course the trading ratios of the margin have to be derived from some such explicit (or more likely implicit) priorities list. Having said this, it should also be admitted that for the actual decision-making by the executive the relative valuations at the margin may often be more relevant than the priorities list. Again, Braybrooke and Lindblom try to make a marked distinction between the kind of process we have been outlining and the idea of a social welfare function. But there is no logical reason whatever why the term a 'social welfare function' should be made to relate to either the kind of general statement in an undefined function that Bergson first put forward or to the special interpretations of it by Arrow. The term simply implies any statement (by the decision-making mechanism of a society, or by any individual) about some relationship between society's welfare and the things considered relevant to it. On this interpretation an executive using the kind of 'trading ratios at the margin between pairs of values' that Braybrooke and Lindblom envisage is using a social welfare function. However, their discussion rightly emphasises the point we have made above in Section 1b—that it is unrealistic and unnecessary to expect the executive to visualise all possible social states in advance.[2]

The last point to note is that though the static framework of welfare economics has tended to imprint in our minds the image of

[1] Our discussion of how policies are compared by the executive is based on the assumption that the aim of the executive is to promote welfare of the individuals; otherwise the relative weights might, for example, be 'military potential' weights, etc.

[2] However, I see no reason to go along with Braybrooke and Lindblom when they seem to imply that all social-policy evaluation has to be just marginal—that no big changes can ever be considered. See [7, pp. 99–102].

the social optimum chosen once-for-all according to a social welfare function given once-for-all, this is of course not how things happen in real life. The social welfare function chosen by the decision-making mechanism of a society is something which usually changes with time, as there are changes in the distribution of incomes, the state of employment, the balance-of-payments situation or the pattern of family obligations (e.g. customs about looking after aged relatives), etc. Indeed, it is this fact which causes us not to worry about the possibility of majority-voting leading to intransitivity.

Let us now consider a few examples of what might be described as realistic social welfare functions. We have argued that such welfare functions will not be in terms of individual utility indicators and that the dependent variable will not be something called 'economic welfare' but general welfare. The variables on which general welfare is taken to depend in any particular social welfare function can be called objectives, because though promoting welfare is the ultimate aim, it is achieved through pursuing objectives like full employment, economic growth, improvement in the distribution of incomes, etc. Some general classificatory remarks about the objectives (which are also called targets) are possible. Some of the objectives will be variables expressed in absolute terms; some others might be expressed as given rates of change. Another class of objectives might be variables expressing the degree of stability over time of some magnitudes, e.g. employment or national income, etc.

An example of a very simple social welfare function is the following:

$$W = W(E, \sigma^1, \sigma^2, R, B, G) \qquad (6.2)$$

This is an undefined function where the coefficients of the variables have not been specified; E is employment level; σ^1 and σ^2 are respectively the coefficients of equality of distribution of money incomes and of wealth; R is rate of growth of national product; B is the balance of payments; and G is the general factor to represent the non-economic variables affecting welfare. Tinbergen [44] has been a pioneer in this field of formal discussions of policy objectives, instruments and their inter-relationships. Objectives are attained through policy instruments such as taxes, subsidies, direct public investment, pricing policy of public enterprises, and so on. Often an instrument would affect more than one objective; for example, direct public investment in sluggish export industries is likely to influence the balance of payments, rate of growth and the distribution of incomes. Similarly, an objective may be affected by more than one instrument.

146

Objectives might be fixed or flexible. Fixed objectives are those for which certain fixed magnitudes have been specified and which must be attained. When all objectives are fixed the main problem is to examine the compatibility of the fixed targets with the instruments. Compatibility will not be achieved if there are fewer instruments than targets; in this case either the number of instruments must be increased or the number of targets reduced till they are equal. However, even when this is so, so that a unique solution is possible, incompatibility might arise if some boundary condition on the values of the instrument variables has been violated. If it is assumed that the targets are flexible, then the instruments will have to be so selected as to maximise the total value of the targets. The targets may also be random, or indeed mixed—i.e. some fixed, some flexible, and some random. With random targets, a magnitude like the probability that the social welfare function will attain a certain value might be maximised. When the value of a well-defined social welfare function is maximised it is said to be *the optimum solution*. But this need have very little in common with a Paretian optimum, because the social welfare function need not comply with all the Paretian value judgments. This optimum solution is more properly described as *the social optimum* as determined by a well-defined social welfare function and the empirical conditions surrounding the instruments for achieving the objectives.

Of course, some decision has to be taken about the time horizon. In this connection, an interesting approach has been suggested by Stone [42], whereby the time horizon is divided into two parts: short-run and long-run; the former relating to what may be called a transitional period and the latter to the period after that. It is assumed that welfare functions for the short-run and the long-run have been specified. From the long-run objectives can be deduced the composition of the stock of capital required at the beginning of the long-run period or, which is the same thing, at the end of the short-run period. With given initial amounts of capital and the specified required composition of capital at the end of the short-run, the problem is then to find an optimal path over the transitional period in the light of the short-run objectives. If no such path exists there will have to be a revision of the long-run objectives. This iterative process will continue till an optimal path consistent with the short-run and the long-run objectives has been discovered.

However, the search for an optimal (according to a given social welfare function) time path for all sectors of the economy is likely to prove far too ambitious; the computational and fact-gathering problems are likely to be so enormous that a rational decision is likely to be to concentrate on only a few objectives or sectors. To the extent that resources used up in this way are specific to these sectors, this concern with only a part of the economy might yet be consistent with overall optimality. But often this is not so; practical problems then rule out the pursuit of any global optimality in the economy. Economic policy then, in practice, tends to be concerned with a few broad sectors at a time. (This is perhaps true of even the Communist countries.) A special case of this kind of study is the examination of individual large projects of public investment; we shall return to this aspect of economic policy in the next chapter. Let us here briefly explain a model of economic policy, developed by Theil and others [43], which deals with more than just one sector but not at the cost of realism or practicality. In this respect it is similar to Tinbergen's policy models, but the difference is that the fact of uncertain knowledge about the relations between instruments and objectives is recognised.

Theil also recognises the need for starting with a given social welfare function (or, as it is sometimes called, a social preference function) which need not conform with the Paretian value judgments. The other essential part is an econometric model of the relations between the instrument variables and the objective variables of the social welfare function; this econometric model is then the constraint subject to which the social preference function (or, rather, its expectation) is to be maximised. In order to be able to handle uncertainty and some dynamic features and yet keep the analysis manageable, Theil assumes that the social welfare function is quadratic but that the constraints are linear. Uncertainty is taken into account by assuming that the constraints are subject to random shifts; thus the analysis of economic policy is now stochastic. It is visualised that the social welfare function takes the form of some 'desired' (by the decision-maker or the comment-maker) values for both the instrument variables and the objective variables. These two sets of values are almost certain to be inconsistent with the constraints. If this is so, the deviations between the desired values of the instrument and objective variables and their corresponding stochastic values as given by the constraints are calculated.

The problem is then finally posed as that of maximising the negative of the weighted sum of the squares of those deviations subject to the stochastic constraints. In other words, it is no longer a question of trying to maximise the social welfare function subject to the constraints of the economic relationships, but rather a question of maximising the *expectation* of the social welfare function subject to those constraints. The result of the exercise would be a maximising formula (obtained with the use of the 'certainty equivalence theorem') which would combine the coefficients of the constraint and preference functions; this indeed is a distinguishing feature of Theil's approach. The expectation-maximising formula would give the 'optimal'— according to the given social welfare function and the constraints— values for instrument variables; these values might or might not coincide with the values which were initially specified as desirable in the social welfare function.

Time can also be introduced into the model. One procedure is to visualise a succession of equal time periods such as years. Time introduces the possibility of a learning process through which targets may be modified at the beginning of a new period as more information becomes available about the instruments and their relationships with the objectives. Some methods have been devised which deal with these problems under certain simplifying assumptions—e.g. that the social welfare function does not contain any cross-products of variables belonging to different years—otherwise the successive time periods cannot be studied as separate periods one at a time. The assumption of linearity in the constraints function may sometimes be far from true. Our purpose has not been to claim that perfectly satisfactory methods are available for the realistic *ad hoc* welfare analysis of a number of sectors of an economy at a time, but to give some idea of the progress already made in the direction of such *ad hoc* analysis and of the kinds of methods used. It would seem that in the kind of approach we have just outlined the non-economic aspects of welfare would be allowed to make their impact on the choice of the objectives and of their desired values.

However, one cannot deny that the discussion of some issues of economic policy (e.g. the question of the desirability of Britain's entry into the European Common Market) is seldom conducted— even by professional economists—with reference to an explicit social welfare function coupled with an explicit model of the economic relationships between the objectives and the instruments. This points to the need for some discussion of why economists disagree so often on a practical policy issue.

Suppose we are examining the advisability of placing a protective tariff on the imports of some country. What is the necessary material for reaching a decision? We shall need to know the effects on prices, incomes, employment, health, international relations, and so on of the new policy during a specified period. For this purpose we shall need two things: a general, positive (as opposed to normative) *theory* of the effects of tariffs on the various parts of the national economy and the world economy; and, secondly, *factual knowledge* of the kind of tariff to be imposed as well as the circumstances under which it is to be imposed. In Popper's [35] words, we need a 'universal statement' and the 'initial conditions'.

While the economist is trying to predict the effects, expressed in non-emotive words, of an economic measure in a given situation, his pronouncements are scientific (or objective), because his predictions could conceivably be refuted by experience, observation, or experiment, in which case the economist would be bound to admit (provided the observation has been honest and technically competent) that his theory is wrong.

Given now the effects of the economic measure (protective tariffs) the advisability or otherwise of adopting them cannot be decided unless some aims of social policy and their relative importance are brought into the discussion. If protecting infant industries in some situations means a relatively greater scarcity of the product in the country for the next five years, extra income for a certain group, more employment, and savings in foreign exchange after five years, but greater expenditure of foreign exchange during the first three years, etc., then some social, political, or ethical judgments are needed to compare these effects and reach a net verdict on the tariffs.

There is one other aspect of the problem: the *practicability* of introducing any economic measure. If an economist *knows* what the effects of a certain system of tariffs will be, and also considers these effects desirable (in the light of his own value judgments or those of a political body), there might still be very little point in recommending the tariffs if the economy does not have adequate administrative machinery to work the tariffs effectively. Yet, the practicability or otherwise of an economic measure cannot always be decided *a priori*; whenever there is serious disagreement about the practicability of a measure the issue can be decided only by putting the measure into effect and watching its consequences. *A priori* reasoning about the practicability of changes in policy can easily be made to lend undue support to conservatism—undue in the sense that some measures may in this way be decided impracticable, even though an attempt to put them into practice would have been successful. Indeed, we can see that an argument about 'practicability' of a measure is nothing else but an argument about whether the necessary *initial conditions*—under which an outcome of that measure predicted by a certain theory has proved to be true—prevail in a given situation or not. Such an argument can never be settled except by introducing the measure and observing the consequences.[1]

Yet, there are some basic difficulties hidden in this question of

[1] See Section 25 on 'Variability of Experimental Conditions' in Popper [35].

practicability. For the truth seems to be that there are few economic theories which are 'well tested', and the 'necessary conditions' for whose predictions are fully known. To a great extent, this is due to the difficulties of 'holding experiments' for economic theories. However, this is a limitation of economic theories which the advance of quantitative studies is helping to reduce, and can be expected to go on reducing.

In the analysis of economic problems since often a theory has to be used which has not been sufficiently tested, and since often the factual knowledge of the relevant conditions is not complete either, there is necessarily a subjective element in the prediction of effects of a measure by different economists. These two difficulties, along with the differences in the conscious or unconscious political or ethical biases of different economists, lead to controversies. In principle then, the difference in the policy proposals of different economists can arise from three separate sources: (i) a different theory, often coupled with a different assessment of facts; (ii) different uncertainty discounts or allowances for the possible effects of the measure; there are likely to be differences among economists on whether to prepare for the worst or gamble on the best; and (iii) different criteria of desirability. The first two reasons apply to differences in the econometric models, and the last to differences in comment-making social welfare functions. Because these three reasons for disagreement are difficult to keep openly separate in debate, and usually are not kept separate, some economists have argued that there can be no distinction between objectives and analysis or between programmes and prognoses. But the distinctions do exist in principle, and to the extent that they are made explicit in practice, the discussion of economic problems becomes more meaningful. Though the distinction between analysis and objectives is difficult to make, if it is argued that the distinction need not be made or should not be made, then, in the words of Tawney, 'It is like using the impossibility of absolute cleanliness as a pretext for rolling in a manure heap'.[1]

An important aspect has been ignored in the foregoing discussion. The question 'Should a protective tariff be placed on imports?' is not really equivalent to asking 'Would the resulting state with such a tariff be better than the present state?' For, supposing the answer to the second question is 'yes'—according to some specific social welfare function—it would not yet be established that the tariff in question should be imposed; it might be possible by adopting some other policy to arrive at a situation which is even better than that

[1] Hutchison [23, p. 192] quotes the foregoing dictum from Tawney.

with the tariff. Hence, when assessing the desirability of some policy it is necessary to discover the possible *alternative* policies, and then compare the outcomes of them all.

6.3 CONCEPTS OF EFFICIENCY

Our arguments in Section 2 of this chapter have certain implications for the concept of 'economic efficiency'. Taking the Paretian value judgments to be 'widely acceptable' and therefore non-contro-versial, economists have tacitly assumed that all welfare functions of all societies are Pareto-type; they have therefore inferred from that type of functions some *necessary* though not sufficient conditions for the social optimum—the very best allocation of resources. These necessary conditions for the social optimum (which are also the necessary conditions for a Paretian optimum) have come to be known as the conditions necessary for '*economic efficiency*'; an overall Paretian optimum has come to be known as an 'economically efficient' allocation of resources. It is not rare for economists to suggest that this concept of 'economic efficiency' is an objective concept which requires no, or only 'minimal' value judgments.[1]

However, as we have already argued in Section 2 of this chapter, no closely reasoned case has ever been presented to show that the underlying value judgments would really be widely acceptable in any modern democratic society. As we noted earlier, these value judg-ments imply welfare functions of a type according to which a long succession of economic measures to benefit only the rich, while the poor continue to have the same absolute share of goods and services, will be approved of. Moreover, even if the underlying value judg-ments of the concept of 'economic efficiency' were found to be widely acceptable in some society, it would be unwarranted to deduce from them necessary, much less sufficient, conditions for the social optimum and brandish them to the public as objective (or even relatively value-free) conditions for 'economic efficiency'. Since any such conditions would be recommended to be made part of social

[1] Cf. the following two quotations: 'It should not be necessary to point out that, despite its slightly misleading name, the concept of a Pareto optimum is com-pletely objective and that our discussions are thus of a positive rather than a normative nature.' Farrell [11, p. 378]. 'We notice, moreover, that the necessary condition ['maximising a market preference function'] is a condition of econo-mic efficiency whilst the additional condition for sufficiency (namely a "just" money income distribution) involves a value judgment. This suggests that we may continue to use the market preference function without inhibitions and in the usual way in discussions of such topics as "optimum tariffs", or "ideal" tax systems, provided that we bear in mind that we are concerned with questions of economic efficiency and not with questions of justice and injustice' [31, p. 132].

policy (in order to achieve certain kinds of aims of social policy), they are necessarily controversial and political. In the same society, where the Paretian value judgments seem widely acceptable, there may well be a number of individuals who have welfare functions for the society which conflict with the widely acceptable value judgments. Samuelson has said, 'It is a legitimate exercise of economic analysis to examine the consequences of various value judgments, whether or not they are shared by the theorist, just as the study of comparative ethics is itself a science like any other branch of anthropology' [39, p. 220]. If economists were *only* to work out the implications of various, i.e. *different*, sets of value judgments, my criticisms will not apply. But the fact is that *sufficient* criteria and *necessary* conditions for the social optimum have been deduced from only one set of 'widely accepted' value judgments, so that the theory of the allocation of resources has come to be identified with one particular set of value judgments.

It is worth emphasising that our fundamental objections to *a priori* welfare analysis of allocation do not apply only at the static level of analysis. It is a logically invalid procedure to derive a set of necessary conditions for the social optimum from a set of seemingly widely accepted value judgments, irrespective of whether that social optimum is conceived of as a point of equilibrium of a stationary economy or as the growth path of a changing economy. It should be obvious that our argument is *not* against deriving the necessary (and sufficient) conditions for the social optimum (thought of statically or dynamically) from a *specific* welfare function chosen by decision-makers or comment-makers in a particular society during a certain period. Indeed, as we noted in the last section, this is where the economist has to play a most important role. The arguments are against the procedure of formulating *general optimal rules*, to be used by all economists, to take an economy to a position which is an optimum only according to certain value judgments which *seem* to be 'widely acceptable'.

As we have already noted in Chapter II, an allocation which leads to a Paretian optimum is *not* superior (even according to the Paretian value judgments) to *any* other allocation which does not lead to such an optimum. This fact, combined with the unlikelihood of any society being able to effect recurring costless lump-sum redistributions, destroys whatever operational significance the concept of 'economic efficiency' might have.

Further, empirical evidence suggests that the more ordinary price distortions in the commodity market by themselves do not cause very important welfare losses. This refers to distortions which take the form of imperfect competition in the commodity markets, so that the prices are higher than the marginal costs. This means that between the product of a monopolistic industry (say industry i) and that of a competitive industry (say industry h) the marginal rate of technical substitution is not equal to the marginal rate of subjective substitution. That is, between the two goods i and h we have the following:

$$\frac{P_i}{P_h} = \frac{\partial U^q / \partial x_i^q}{\partial U^q / \partial x_h^q} \neq \frac{\partial T / \partial X_i}{\partial T / \partial X_h} = \frac{M_i}{M_h} \qquad (6.3)$$

Now if through public regulation the output of the monopolistic industry is increased, so that the price of its product drops and the marginal cost rises, those two rates will be brought closer together till they are equal. Even if this could represent a movement from within the Paretian utility frontier to a point on it, we have already shown, in Chapter II, Section 5, that there are many reasons why any *a priori* welfare evaluation of a Paretian optimum is problematic; further, if some marginal conditions are violated also in some other sectors, the second-best theorem tells us that eliminating one monopoly does not move the economy to the Paretian utility frontier. In any case, such a movement would also have brought about some changes in outputs of some other sectors due to substitution and complementary effects in the commodity and factor markets. An accurate forecast of the final array of outputs and incomes (quite ignoring the utility side) is therefore quite a complex task.

However, on some simplifying assumptions some estimates are sometimes possible. For example, it is sometimes assumed that the marginal cost in the relevant range in the monopoly is constant, that the repercussions on the rest of the economy can be ignored, and that there are no externalities. Suppose now that some estimate can be made of the amount by which the monopoly price exceeds what the competitive price would be in the industry, and of the amount by which the output would expand as the price is lowered in that industry. Consulting fig. 6.1 (where D is the monopoly demand curve and MC is the monopoly marginal-cost curve), aP is the excess of the monopoly price over marginal cost; ac is the amount by which output would increase if price were made equal to the marginal cost. The area aPc is then a very rough measure of the utility gain from eliminating monopoly, if distribution considerations are ignored. (After all, it is just possible that the monopolist producers whose monopoly profit is eliminated are among the poorest and their customers among the richest people.) The area of the right-angled triangle aPc is aP times ac times $\frac{1}{2}$. If similar calculations are made for each monopolistic industry and then added together we have a *very rough* total estimate of the 'utility gains' from the elimination of monopoly. Similar estimates can be made for the elimination of tariffs or the joining of common markets. Now, most of these estimates of 'utility gains' from the pursuit of 'economic efficiency' turn out to be very small, usually in the region of 1–2% of the national income; this seems to be particularly true of the industrially developed countries.[1]

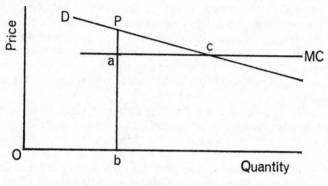

Fig. 6.1

We must admit that these estimates do not take into account any further cumulative gains from 'the increase in the value of output'. The last part of the previous sentence has been put in inverted commas because the estimates we are considering are question-begging for a number of reasons which should be familiar by now. Further, nearly all these estimates are exclusively about the commodity markets. Imperfections of competition in the *factor* markets are likely to have much greater significance, because they would prevent the attainment of the technological frontier. In the estimates discussed above it is usually taken for granted that the production frontier has been attained because factor markets are perfect and all producers are genuine cost-minimisers; the only problem is that a Scitovsky community surface is not tangential to the production frontier because of imperfections in the commodity markets. *But the belief that technological efficiency can look after itself is a very big assumption* which, as we shall be arguing, is seldom true. Indeed,

[1] See Harberger [17].

the emphasis on the question-begging concept of 'economic efficiency' has tended to lead to a neglect of the far more important concept of technological efficiency, which we have already come across in Chapters II and III.

As we have noted earlier, even the concept of technological efficiency is not entirely value free if it cannot be assumed that no welfare significance is attached, by the adopted social welfare function of the society, to the movement of workers and other factors between occupations (apart from its effect on physical productivity), and that the individuals' personal efficiency does not depend on the distribution of incomes. The second assumption may well not be true in the poorer countries. If all producers are genuine cost-minimisers who have full knowledge of the latest techniques and of the prevailing factor prices, then uniform price for each factor throughout the economy is a necessary and sufficient condition for technological efficiency—provided there are no externalities in production.

A uniform price for an identical factor is rarer than is commonly imagined. This is particularly true of the under-developed countries, where for both labour and capital there tend to be large price differentials between the traditional and the newer kind of employments for them. Again, the assumption that all producers know what are the best-practice techniques[1] is far removed from the truth even for the economically advanced countries. For example, even about the United States, Salter discovered such facts as the following: 'In the United States copper mines, electric locomotives allow a cost saving of 67%, yet, although first used in the mid-twenties, by 1940 less than a third of the locomotives in use were electric' [38, p. 98]. The argument is by no means that technological efficiency requires instantaneous replacement of plant and techniques throughout an industry on the discovery of an improvement in the production methods somewhere in it. In fact, cost-minimising behaviour requires continued use of existing plant so long as the discounted (at the socially approved rate of interest—see Chapter VII, Section 3) present value of direct costs exceeds its scrap value by a bigger margin than the discounted (at the same rate) present value

[1] Given the assumption that each producer seeks to minimise costs, full knowledge of the existing technology (including the latest advances in it) and of the relative factor prices on the part of each producer would then together determine the flow of new techniques coming into use—best-practice techniques. The best-practice technique in any period is the appropriate technique having regard to both economic and technical conditions; it is the technique which yields minimum costs in terms of the production function and relative factor prices of each period. See [39, ch. 3].

of new equipment exceeds its initial cost. The point of the foregoing example is that old techniques which do not pass such a test may well continue to be used in practice due to insufficient knowledge about the new technique, the payment of lower prices to some factors of production (e.g. the personal services supplied to a family business), and the use of a higher than usual rate of discount in assessing the profitability of the new technique.

The criterion for replacement just mentioned can also be expressed thus: Undertake replacement when the following is no longer true:

$$\sum_{t=1}^{n_1} \frac{R_{1t} - D_{1t}}{(1+r)^t} - S_1 \geqslant \sum_{t=1}^{n_2} \frac{R_{2t} - D_{2t}}{(1+r)^t} - I_2 \tag{6.4}$$

where R is revenue, D is direct costs, subscripts 1 and 2 denote the old and new plants respectively, S is site value plus working capital plus scrap value, I is initial cost, r is the rate of discount used for assessing both techniques, n is for each of the two plants the last year in which it earns a positive excess over the direct costs.

In short, though it is assumed in the traditional model of resource allocation (described in Chapter II) that each producer in a given industry has the same production function given to him by the present state of technology, in actual fact there are great differences in the technical *knowledge* of contemporary managers and entrepreneurs in the same industry, within the same country. There is no doubt that the gains in productivity from improved dissemination of existing technical knowledge, and the encouragement of its active utilisation, are tremendous. Leibenstein [26] quotes examples from several countries of increase in labour productivity of 5–500%, and similarly of both labour and capital savings of 5–83%, arising from the fuller utilisation of the existing technical knowledge.[1]

Obviously, then, the necessary conditions for technological efficiency, along with the pursuit of further innovations, constitute far more important objectives than seem to be commonly recognised by economists in discussions of allocation problems. The two objectives can be respectively interpreted as the attainment of a given

[1] What Leibenstein [26] calls 'X-efficiency' is in fact nothing other than technological efficiency, though he does not recognise it; it is attained when the economy's technological production frontier is reached; that requires uniform prices for identical factors, perfect knowledge of the relevant technical information and cost-minimising behaviour on the part of the managers of production. The same cost-minimising criterion needs to be applied also to a manager as a factor of production, though obviously it often is not. As Leibenstein says: 'It is conceivable that in practice a situation would arise in which managers are exceedingly poor, that is, others are available who do not obtain management posts, and who would be very much superior. Managers determine not only their own productivity but the productivity of all co-operating units in the organisation' [26, p. 397].

production frontier and as trying to push that frontier out. There is no reason why there should ever be a conflict between these two. Discussions of 'economic efficiency', on the other hand, tend to presume that the production frontier has been attained, and the problem is to ensure the tangency of a Scitovsky community surface with it; that is, to ensure the attainment of the Paretian utility frontier. But here *a priori* norms are presumed; further, even if the norms in question are granted, attaining the Paretian utility frontier is not necessarily an improvement; finally, there might well be a conflict between the aim of attaining the Paretian utility frontier and that of pushing out the technological production frontier. One special way in which this conflict could arise is that large firms may be necessary to develop innovations, but large firms may also tend to make commodity markets imperfect.[1] Further, whenever the Government forces the pace of economic development above what it would be if the individuals and the market economy were left alone, some of the necessary conditions for Paretian optimality are bound to be violated, even though the technological production frontier is pushed out.

CONCLUSIONS

We have argued in this chapter that the propositions which are based on value judgments which are presumed to be widely acceptable are not thereby made objective, but still remain ethical, and need to be assessed as such. We have argued that without starting from an implicit or explicit social welfare function, no welfare propositions are possible in principle, and that the concept of a social welfare function is often misunderstood. We discussed various interpretations of it. We also argued that Arrow's interesting theorem has not established that no social welfare function can ever emerge in a democracy. It was pointed out that realistic social welfare functions are likely to be highly aggregated statements of social objectives with some indication of their social weights. We argued that social distributive judgments are more meaningfully expressed in terms of money incomes (with some eye on prices) rather than, as is the usual practice in welfare economics, in terms of utility indicators. We also developed a critique of the concept of 'economic efficiency' and argued that technological efficiency is a much more important concept.

[1] This is a controversial point; though there have been some empirical studies, the argument has by no means been decided yet. For a brilliant original defence of large firms see Schumpeter [41].

Appendix to Chapter VI

GRAAFF ON MAKING A RECOMMENDATION
IN A DEMOCRACY

Graaff [15] has recently made some suggestions with the aim of infusing 'a little politics' into welfare economics in order to build up 'a body of doctrine' to which policy decisions may be referred. I think that Graaff's attempt has failed.

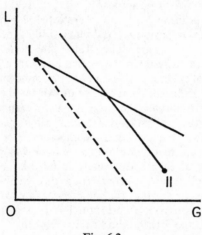

Fig. 6.2

Graaff maintains the distinction between 'economic welfare' and general welfare, and also obviously assumes that individuals' preference maps are known to the economist. He discusses four cases, but for our critique it will be sufficient to examine just one of them. Let us take his case (*b*). The figure he uses for this case is reproduced here as fig. 6.2. (Along the horizontal axis is measured a utility index which is 'any monotonically increasing function of the individual utility indicators of the gainers', and along the vertical axis is measured a similar utility index of the losers.) He does not specify which type of utility possibility curves he is using, but they can only be one of the two types: (1) The type where the redistributions are assumed to take place by imaginary lump-sum transfers—e.g. the utility possibility curve of a fixed collection of goods, or the effi-

159

ciency locus. (2) The type where the redistributions take place by feasible legislation, i.e. a feasibility locus.

In fig. 6.2 the gainers from the change from I to II could compensate the losers, while losers can also bribe the gainers to reject the change. Graaff's recommendation for this case can be divided into two parts. Here is the first part: 'If the change is popular [i.e. 'it would secure majority approval at a referendum', as discovered by 'sampling public opinion'] it can be so only on distributional grounds; therefore do not make it, but consider moving towards that distribution by transferring wealth to the gainers' [15, p. 296]. However, if Graaff's curves are of the first type, then, since lump-sum transfers are known to be impossible in practice, the utility possibility curve of position I has no operational significance. *Feasible* redistribution from position I (adopted instead of the change in policy under discussion) may take us along the dotted line in fig. 6.2. It may well be that the majority prefers position II (resulting from the change in policy) to any position to be obtained along the dotted line. Therefore, if Graaff's curves are drawn on the assumption of lump-sum redistributions, then the *economist* cannot provide any justification for the Government to take *decisions* on any basis other than that of majority approval in a democracy.

If the curves are to be interpreted as feasibility curves, then all points on both of them are equally attainable. Now it may be possible to reach some position along the feasibility curve of I which is superior to position II; but *superior in what sense*? If some position along the curve of position I is only Pareto-superior to position II, then the distribution at that point may well be different from the distribution at II; because at that point only a few need be better off than at II, for it to be Pareto-superior. In that case the majority may prefer position II to that Pareto-superior position along the feasibility curve of I; the economist will have no *economic* justification for advising the Government not to introduce the change in policy and move instead along the feasibility curve to the other point under discussion.

But what if the other point to be reached along the feasibility curve of position I is not just Pareto-superior to position II but has the same kind of distribution, with *every* person better off in the 'same proportion' than he would be at I? In that case the majority would presumably prefer that position to position II. The majority may prefer the new position—to be reached along the feasibility curve of I—even if it is only Pareto-superior to II. In any case, if the majority prefers some position along the feasibility curve of position I to position II, then *that* (i.e. the majority approval) is the criterion, both necessary and sufficient, for the Government's decision-making in a democracy; the economist cannot offer any alternative criterion.

Similar criticisms apply to the second part of Graaff's recommendation for case (b), and to the other three cases which he examines. In other words, Graaff's attempt to find a way of by-passing the duly elected decision-makers of a democracy has totally failed.

REFERENCES FOR CHAPTER VI

[1] K. J. Arrow, *Social Choice and Individual Values*, 2nd edn., New York, 1963

[2] K. J. Arrow, 'Little's Critique of Welfare Economics', *American Economic Review*, 1951

[3] T. Balogh, 'Welfare and Free Trade—A Reply', *Economic Journal*, 1951

[4] W. J. Baumol, *Welfare Economics and the Theory of the State*, 2nd edn., London, 1965

[5] A. Bergson, 'A Reformulation of Certain Aspects of Welfare Economics', *Quarterly Journal of Economics*, 1938; also reprinted in his *Essays in Normative Economics*, Cambridge, Mass., 1960

[6] A. Bergson, 'On the Concept of Social Welfare', *Quarterly Journal of Economics*, 1954; also reprinted in his collected essays

[7] D. Braybrooke and C. E. Lindblom, *A Strategy of Decision*, London, 1963

[8] J. S. Coleman, 'The Possibility of a Social Welfare Function', *American Economic Review*, 1966

[9] Maurice Dobb, 'A Review of the Discussion concerning Economic Calculation in a Socialist Economy (1953)', in his *On Economic Theory and Socialism*, London, 1955

[10] C. J. van Eijk and J. Sandee, 'Quantitative Determination of an Optimum Economic Policy', *Econometrica*, 1959

[11] M. J. Farrell, 'The Convexity Assumptions in the Theory of Competitive Markets', *Journal of Political Economy*, 1959

[12] F. M. Fisher, 'Income Distribution, Value Judgments and Welfare', *Quarterly Journal of Economics*, 1956

[13] Karl A. Fox, Jati K. Sengupta, and Erik Thorbecke, *The Theory of Quantitative Economic Policy*, Amsterdam, 1966

[14] W. M. Gorman, 'Are Social Indifference Curves Convex?', *Quarterly Journal of Economics*, 1964

[15] J. de V. Graaff, 'On Making a Recommendation in a Democracy', *Economic Journal*, 1962

[16] T. Haavelmo, 'The Notion of Involuntary Economic Decisions', *Econometrica*, 1950

[17] A. C. Harberger, 'Using the Resources at Hand More Effectively', *American Economic Review, Proceedings*, 1959

[18] R. M. Hare, *The Language of Morals*, Oxford, 1952

[19] J. C. Harsanyi, 'Cardinal Welfare, Individualistic Ethics, and Inter-personal Comparisons of Utility', *Journal of Political Studies*, 1955
[20] B. G. Hickman (ed.), *Quantitative Planning of Economic Policy*, Washington, D.C., 1965
[21] J. R. Hicks, *Essays in World Economics*, Oxford, 1959
[22] C. Hildrith, 'Alternative Conditions for Social Orderings', *Econometrica*, 1953
[23] T. W. Hutchison, *'Positive' Economics and Policy Objectives*, London, 1964
[24] P. B. Kenen and F. M. Fisher, 'Income Distributions, Value Judgments and Welfare: A Correction', *Quarterly Journal of Economics*, 1957
[25] E. S. Kirschen and others, *Economic Policy in Our Time*, Vol. I, General Theory, Amsterdam, 1964
[26] H. Leibenstein, 'Allocative Efficiency *vs.* "X-efficiency" ', *American Economic Review*, 1966
[27] I. M. D. Little, 'Social Choice and Individual Values', *Journal of Political Economy*, 1952
[28] I. M. D. Little, *A Critique of Welfare Economics*, 2nd edn., Oxford, 1957
[29] G. Myrdal, *The Political Element in the Development of Economic Theory*, London, 1953
[30] S. K. Nath, 'Are Formal Welfare Criteria Required?', *Economic Journal*, 1964
[31] I. F. Pearce, *A Contribution to Demand Analysis*, Oxford, 1964
[32] A. C. Pigou, 'Some Aspects of Welfare Economics', *American Economic Review*, 1951
[33] K. R. Popper, *The Open Society and Its Enemies*, 4th edn., London, 1962
[34] K. R. Popper, *Logic of Scientific Discovery*, London, 1959
[35] K. R. Popper, *The Poverty of Historicism*, 2nd edn., London, 1960
[36] L. C. Robbins, 'Robertson on Utility and Scope', *Economica*, 1953
[37] J. Rothenberg, *The Measurement of Social Welfare*, New Jersey, 1961
[38] W. E. G. Salter, *Productivity and Technical Change*, Cambridge, 1960
[39] P. A. Samuelson, *Foundations of Economic Analysis*, Cambridge, Mass., 1947
[40] P. A. Samuelson, 'Social Indifference Curves', *Quarterly Journal of Economics*, 1956
[41] J. A. Schumpeter, *Capitalism, Socialism and Democracy*, London, 1943
[42] R. Stone, 'The *a priori* and the Empirical in Economics', in his *Mathematics in the Social Sciences and other Essays*, London, 1966
[43] H. Theil, *Optimal Decision Rules for Government and Industry*, Amsterdam, 1964
[44] J. Tinbergen, *Economic Policy, Principles and Design*, Amsterdam, 1966
[45] J. Tinbergen, 'Welfare Economics and Income Distribution', *American Economic Review, Proceedings*, 1957

VII

WELFARE AND PUBLIC ENTERPRISE

If the traditional *a priori* welfare theory of allocation (of Chapter II) really were valid on logical and empirical grounds it would have obvious and incontrovertible corollaries to serve as guiding principles for the price and investment policies of all economic enterprises—including publicly owned enterprises. Though at one time some authors did hold such a belief, and even now some writers would argue that the traditional *a priori* welfare theory has workable and more or less valid implications for price and investment policies, serious objections to these implications are in fact fairly generally accepted. A great deal of what has gone before is relevant in this chapter; especially the sections on social objectives and the concepts of efficiency of Chapters VI, and parts of Chapters II, III, and IV.

7.1 REASONS FOR PUBLIC ENTERPRISE

We might consider here some of the reasons for the public ownership of enterprises. In communist countries, of course, most of the economic enterprises are State-owned. Again, in other countries some enterprises might be public-owned to avoid the concentration of wealth or of the 'power' to take rather important economic decisions. There are some other reasons which perhaps apply to most countries. First, some industries are natural monopolies; the size of their plants is indivisible and has to be so large that their marginal costs decline for appreciably high levels of outputs; these levels of outputs might well exceed the total amounts of those services usually consumed in the economy. With a marginal-cost curve that declines thus, perfect competition is impossible. The industry is bound to have only one or just a few firms. This description applies to gas, electricity, railways, and roads, etc. Such industries also tend to supply goods which are considered 'basic' or 'essential' for the smooth running of the economy. They form one group of public enterprises.

The other group of public enterprises arises due to the existence of what are called public goods—which we came across in Chapter IV, Section 5. If such a good is supplied for one person it is automatically available to everybody else. The usual example is defence. Once

163

defence is provided against foreign attack for anybody in a country, it is freely available to everybody else. But the definition roughly applies to such things as national parks, public libraries, litter bins, afforestation, and so on. Since an individual need not pay to enjoy such a good once it is made available for everybody, the market fails to supply such a good. If they are to be supplied, then the State must step in. These public goods are what Musgrave [26] has called social wants.

We come to what have been described as merit wants [26]. These are goods and services about which the comment-making or the decision-making social-welfare function implies that an individual is not necessarily the best judge of his own welfare. The list of examples here can be very long indeed; for, contrary to the pretensions of the traditional welfare economics, few societies—even democratic societies—have acted on the principle of consumer or producer sovereignty in all matters. Compulsory education, subsidised housing, and compulsory health insurance are some obvious examples. It should also be noted that public goods and merit goods are not exclusive categories; that is, a good may qualify to be a public good and may also be a merit good.

Finally, in a number of underdeveloped countries governments start and own certain public enterprises because this is the only way those enterprises would get started. Reasons for this are imperfect capital markets—especially where large sums for a new field of investment are concerned; sluggish private entrepreneurship; the need to train large numbers of staff—a task which can seldom pay a private enterprise to undertake, because it has no guarantee that the trained staff will stay with it for long enough to justify the capital cost; and so on.

7.2 PRICING POLICY

In the traditional theory of resource allocation, a private enterprise is assumed to aim at maximising profits. In a perfectly competitive market the price for the product is a parameter for an enterprise; it maximises profits by equating it with its marginal cost. If the market is imperfect the firm chooses the price of its product by equating the marginal cost with its marginal revenue. As we noted above, a public enterprise is often in a monopolistic position. Should it also maximise profits and choose a price where marginal cost equals marginal revenue, or should it be guided by some other principle?

What light can economic theory throw on the principles that should guide the pricing policy of a public enterprise? It was a widely ac-

cepted view at one time that the traditional theory of allocation had a
ready corollary for this problem. Did not that theory imply that for
Pigou's 'ideal output' of the various goods in an economy or for
Pareto's 'optimal allocation' of factors of production, price of every
good should equal its marginal cost? The precept that public utilities
should charge a price equal to marginal cost was formulated in the
thirties by a number of writers[1]—but most particularly by Hotelling.
Hotelling [13] clearly sets out the Paretian theory that the equality
of the price of each good with its marginal cost is a necessary condition for a Paretian optimum. However, a number of fundamental
points qualifying the significance of the Paretian theory were not
recognised in these early contributions. It was not recognised by all
that the definition of a Paretian optimum rested on certain value
judgments; that such an optimum is not unique but one out of an
infinite number; and that a movement from a position where some
of the necessary conditions are not fulfilled to one where they are all
fulfilled does *not* necessarily imply that any losers could be compensated—because though such a movement from a non-optimal to
an optimal position always passes the Scitovsky reversal criterion, it
does not always pass the Kaldor–Hicks criterion. See Chapter V,
Section 1, and fig. 5.6.

Before proceeding further, it may be an idea to introduce the
concept of *consumers' surplus* which was first formulated by Dupuit,
and then taken up by Marshall. Dupuit published a work in 1844 in
which he argued that the total satisfaction resulting from the con-
struction of something like a bridge or canal should not be taken to
be measured by the profit made on it, because many of the consumers
would be willing to pay more than they do rather than go without the
service. That in fact is the workaday definition of consumers' surplus;
it is the difference between what consumers pay for a good and the
maximum that they would be willing to pay rather than go without it.
According to Dupuit, the appropriate price to charge was that
which made profits *plus* consumers' surplus as large as possible;
this would happen where price equals marginal cost. Hence Dupuit
was the first man to recommend marginal-cost pricing. Fig. 7.1
explains all this. The profit-maximising price and output are P_1M_1
and OM_1; here the total profit is the area CP_1LB, the consumers'
surplus is the area ACP_1 and the two together amount to AP_1LB. If
price is made equal to marginal cost, so that now the price is P_2M_2,

[1] For a survey of the early controversy on the marginal-cost pricing idea, and
for the relevant references, see Ruggles [33]. Two more recent surveys are
Wiseman [38] and Oort [28]. Oort's work represents an attempt at a rehabilitation
of the marginal-cost principle—which is unconvincing to us.

then the total profit is DP_2B, the consumers' surplus is AP_2D, and the two together amount to AP_2B. Now AP_2B is a larger area than AP_1LB. This indicates that if profit plus consumers' surplus are to be maximised price should equal marginal cost. (What would appear in the diagram as super-normal profit per unit—i.e. the excess of price over average cost—has sometimes been called producers' surplus per unit of output.)

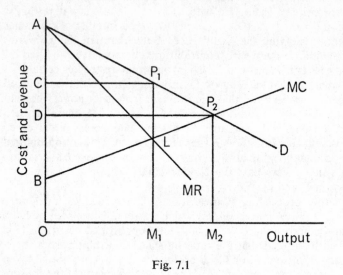

Fig. 7.1

This apparently simple and useful-looking concept of consumers' surplus is neither simple nor useful. It is not simple because there can be at least four different definitions of it—according to whether the consumer is asked what is the maximum he will pay to have the chance of buying the same amount as before *or* any other amount, *or* the minimum he will accept to forgo those chances.[1] The other serious difficulties of the concept we shall take up in the next section when we discuss investment policy. The concept is not very useful, because in the pricing-policy field its *implied* rule (that price should equal marginal cost) can be derived more directly—as we did above in Chapter II, Section 6—and in a manner which makes more sense. Though the concept is thought by some to be of use in for-

[1] For a detailed description of these four concepts of consumers' surplus, see Hicks [11]; see also the section on consumers' surplus in Mishan [24].

mulating investment policy for a public enterprise, its use there is open to serious objections as we shall see.

Returning now to the marginal-cost pricing rule, even if we ignore the qualifications we have mentioned earlier in Chapter VI, and if we also assume that there are no externalities which might spoil the need for price everywhere to equal marginal cost, there are still some further problems. For one thing, the basic concept of a Paretian optimum was developed for a timeless world (see Chapter II, Section 2); it is not clear whether the *practical* implication drawn

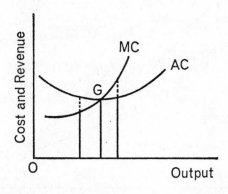

Fig. 7.2

from it is that price should equal the long-run or the short-run marginal cost. Though there has been some controversy over this point, it would seem that most of the marginal-cost pricing advocates favour the short-run marginal cost.

Under perfect competition, with all firms and industries at equilibrium, price equals not just the marginal cost but also the average cost in each firm; therefore there is no profit or loss. But a public enterprise which chooses to charge a price equal to marginal cost may make a profit or a loss. If the total cost function is cubic, so that the marginal-cost function is (as in fig. 7.2) quadratic, then unless the average revenue curve happens to cut the marginal-cost curve at precisely the output for which average-cost curve has its minimum point (point G in fig. 7.2), there will be either a profit or a loss when price equals marginal cost. Both profits and losses pose essentially the same problems, but the discussion has usually centred round the question of what to do with the losses of a public

167

enterprise if it charges a price equal to marginal cost. In some kinds of public enterprise some of the factors used are *highly* indivisible *and durable*, so that costs due to 'plant' are so much higher than those due to the variable factors that the marginal-cost curve is in fact likely to have a very long downward-sloping stretch. This is obviously true of large irrigation projects, roads, railways, and such like. These are the natural monopolies of the last section. While the marginal-cost curve

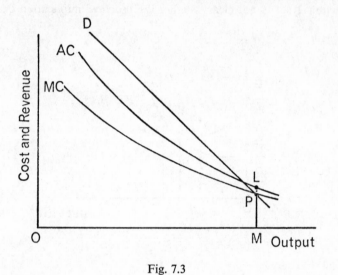

Fig. 7.3

is downward-sloping, the average-cost curve will lie above it, as in fig. 7.3. Now if price is *PM* there will be a loss per unit of *LP*. How is such a loss to be financed?

Should the loss be somehow financed by the consumers of the industry concerned, or by others? If the loss is to be financed by the revenue obtained from a tax, then the tax will have to be lump-sum. Hotelling thought that income and wealth taxes would not disturb any of the necessary marginal conditions for Paretian optimality. Though a once-for-all wealth tax may almost work out as a lump-sum tax, any recurring wealth and income taxes are bound to enter the budget constraint of the consumers as more than mere constants; therefore they are bound to violate the necessary conditions regarding the supply of factors of production (that the common for all individuals' marginal rate of subjective substitution between a

168

factor and a product must equal the common for all individuals'
marginal rate of technical substitution). See Chapter III, Section 1.

The awareness that such losses as we have been discussing of a
public enterprise which charges a price equal to marginal cost would
need to be somehow recouped dawned only slowly on the participants in the old controversy. It was also only slowly realised that if
these losses were to be recouped by a general tax on the public, then
the consumers of the product of the relevant public enterprise were
going to be subsidised at the expense of the rest of the community.
Whether such a transfer of real income was desirable or not could be
settled only by studying the class of consumers, the kind of commodity, and the nature of the relevant comment-making or decision-
making social welfare function. Is the class of consumers particularly
deserving, or the good a merit good, according to the social welfare
function?

The second-best theorem (which was analysed in Chapter III) has
obvious relevance here. We argued there that the theorem does not
necessarily imply that if in each of any two situations some necessary
conditions for Paretian optimality are violated, then there is no *a
priori* way of judging between them on Paretian or some other value
judgments; this is because it may sometimes be possible to make
evaluations about technological efficiency, even though no evaluations about Paretian optimality are possible. However, as we have
also pointed out earlier, the second-best theorem does imply that if
in a given situation a number of the necessary conditions for *Paretian*
optimality are violated, then ensuring the satisfaction of just some of
the violated conditions does not necessarily bring the economy
nearer to a *Paretian* optimum. This corollary of the second-best
theorem is relevant in the discussion of the pricing policy of state
enterprises. If all the other enterprises are charging prices equal to
the respective marginal costs, if there are no externalities or any
direct or indirect taxes which are not lump-sum, and if all the public enterprises also get their prices equal to their marginal costs, then
the necessary conditions will be simultaneously satisfied and a
Paretian optimum reached. But if in the rest of the economy prices
diverge from the respective marginal costs, or if some of the necessary conditions are violated, then the second-best theorem tells us
that equalising the prices with marginal costs in public enterprises
does not necessarily take the economy nearer Paretian optimum.

The only possibility which might qualify the force of this corollary
is that all the factors of production in some public enterprise or
group of public enterprises may be specific to that sector—with little
or no alternative use in any other sector. Now there is no determinate

rate of marginal technical substitution between the products of this sector and those of others. Hence the allocation problem is divided into two different sectors. If the prices within this special group of public enterprises are equal to the respective marginal costs we have a Paretian optimum for this sector irrespective of the situation in the rest of the economy. But such specificity of factors is a rather special assumption.

There is also the practical difficulty that if there are discontinuities in the total- and marginal-cost functions due to the lumpiness or indivisibility of factors, then in fact there is no unique marginal cost.[1] As we pointed out in Chapter II, Section 7, the traditional theory of allocation has been based on the assumption of continuous functions and divisible factors and goods; even activity analysis has to retain the assumption of divisibility in deriving the familiar theorems of the traditional theory. It is probable that in most public enterprises some factors would exhibit lumpiness; examples might be of buses, railway coaches, road-widening schemes, etc. It is also to be noted that this aspect of the problem of indivisibility is similar to but different from its other aspect, where it causes the marginal-cost curve to slope downwards up to and beyond the kind of level of output most likely to be produced; this latter aspect creates a natural monopoly.

Presuming implicitly that social-welfare functions have to be Pareto-type, economists have tended to regard the necessary conditions for a Paretian optimum as the necessary conditions for the social optimum too. We developed a fundamental critique of this procedure in Chapter VI. If our arguments presented there are accepted, then even if the economist were sure that all the necessary conditions for Pareto optimality are simultaneously fulfilled in some economy, and even if there is no ambiguity about what the marginal costs are in the public enterprises, the economist would have no logical basis to recommend marginal-cost pricing as the economists' general rule for 'efficiency' in allocation. Suppose two of the nationalised industries produce milk and education. There is no reason why the social welfare function of some economy should not ordain that milk be priced *below* marginal cost to some category of consumers (e.g. children) and that education too be priced *below* mar-

[1] For a further discussion of the difficulties of assessing marginal costs when there are discontinuities in the cost functions, see Merrett [23]; and for some attempts at estimating marginal costs under such circumstances see Beckman and others [2]. The discontinuities in the production function also raise problems for ensuring technological efficiency because rates of substitution between factors become ambiguous. To some extent the programming methods like those used in Beckman provide an answer.

ginal cost and also made compulsory.[1] Again, if the economy has marked inequalities of incomes and the 'parliament' desires redistributive measures but assesses (with the help of economists) that any further taxation of incomes of the rich would have a marked disincentive effect on the supply of effort and saving by the rich, then there is no economic reason why the 'parliament' should not choose to price well above its marginal cost some product of a nationalised industry which is consumed solely or largely by the rich and also has inelastic demand.

The equality of prices everywhere with the marginal costs does not necessarily ensure technological efficiency (the necessary conditions for which are different, as was shown in Chapter VI, Section 3), which presumably will be relevant for all kinds of social welfare functions. On the other hand, even if prices are not equal to marginal costs, there might yet prevail a technologically efficient allocation, provided the marginal rate of substitution between any two factors in one place of production is the same as the marginal rate of substitution between the same two factors in any other place of production, and the managers of production are genuine cost minimisers who know the economics of the latest techniques. (If there are production external economies the necessary conditions for technological efficiency would be more complex, as was shown in Chapter IV, Section 3.) Further, if the consumption of some goods—e.g. meat, milk, gin, tobacco, books, and holidays—has a marked effect on the efficiency of workers, and if the income-elasticities of demand for these goods are much smaller than the price-elasticities, then technological efficiency, too, *may* dictate pricing milk and meat below marginal cost and gin above it.

Apart from these necessary conditions for technological efficiency, the economist cannot offer any advice on public-utility pricing unless he has the welfare function of a particular society during a certain period; of course, he can always give his personal opinion according to his own comment-making welfare function for the society concerned (cf. Chapter VI). Though our reasons for it are more fundamental and in some respects quite different, our conclusion here is similar to Graaff's: 'I suggest that the only price a public enterprise

---

[1] It may well be that for a number of things like books, music concerts, fruit, vegetables, education, medical care, and so on, the income elasticity of demand of large numbers of persons tends to be lower than the price elasticity of demand. If according to some set of social objectives the consumption of these things needs to be greater than what it would be if price of each of these goods were equal to its marginal cost, then it would make perfect economic sense to subsidise the consumption of these goods, even though that would make their prices below their marginal costs.

WELFARE AND PUBLIC ENTERPRISE

or nationalised industry can be expected to set is what we may as well call *a just price—a price which is set with some regard for its effect on the distribution of wealth* as well as for its effect on the allocation of resources' [10, p. 155; original italics]. But Little made the following comment in his review of Graaff's book: 'The least satisfactory feature of this book is that the author shirks trying to answer the question of how much is left after all this destruction. I find it difficult to believe that he would want to say "nothing at all"— that costs and prices are no guide as to what should be produced. He very weakly concludes his chapter on public enterprise by suggesting a just price—one that *"is set with some regard for its effect on the distribution of wealth* as well as its effect on the allocation of resources". How does one have some regard for the allocation of resources? Presumably with the help of welfare theory—although the author gives no hint of *how* the theory can still be used—so the destruction has not been total' [17, pp. 263–4]. However, we would reiterate, for reasons which have already been specified in detail in Chapter VI, Section 3, that costs and prices can be guides as to what should be produced *only* in the light of the given social-welfare function of a particular society. As for having some regard for the allocation of resources, it can only be done at the technological level by an economist. Even at that level if there are significant technological externalities, he would require a social-welfare function; further, if the personal efficiency of workers is dependent on the distribution of incomes or if they (or the socially adopted welfare function) are not indifferent to the movement between occupations of individuals, the economist cannot formulate even the necessary conditions for technological efficiency unless he has given to him the relevant welfare function of the society. See Chapter VI, Section 2c, for a discussion of the concept of a social-welfare function.

The conclusion of this section, then, is that economists cannot recommend that the price of a public enterprise must equal its marginal cost or that it must equal its average cost. They can only lay down that—assuming away externalities—factors of production should be available at identical prices to all sectors, including the public enterprises; that all managers should *know* the economics of the latest techniques (see Chapter VI, Section 3); and that invention and innovation are encouraged. (In Chapter IV, Section 3, we discussed the necessary conditions for technological efficiency when there are externalities in production.) Beyond that, there can be no general principles. If the public enterprise manufactures cigarettes, then according to the relevant (decision-making or comment-making) social-welfare function the right policy may well be to

172

charge a price well above marginal costs; if it supplies electricity the right policy may be to charge a price (possibly a 'complex' price like the two-part tariff) which covers average costs and makes a little or no profit; and if it publishes textbooks, literary works, and journals the right policy may be to charge a price well below the marginal cost and/or the average cost—even though it leads to losses. It should not be an insuperable problem for industrial engineers and cost accountants to devise ways of checking the industrial efficiency (defined in terms of no wastage of raw materials and time, the maintenance of quality, and no delay in replacement once it is economic, etc.) of a public enterprise which is expected to make perpetual 'losses'. Finally, we may also note that in the case of public goods—as defined by Samuelson (see Chapter IV, Section 6)—no price can be charged to any individual, because such a good (e.g. defence) is available to an individual whether he himself buys any of it or not. Hence, such a good has to be supplied 'free' by the State, though the State would naturally cover its costs in other ways.

7.3 INVESTMENT POLICY

The other aspect of public enterprises which is important for allocation and welfare is their investment policy. This topic is also relevant to Chapter IX, which will be about economic development. We have discussed the aspects which are particularly relevant to some controversies in the literature on economic development in that chapter in Section 4. Some of the other aspects will be discussed here, but perhaps that section and this one need to be read together. Any investment decision involves a comparison between the present and future costs of the installation and running of a project, on the one hand, and the present and future returns from it, on the other. If it is a private firm's investment scheme, then the costs and returns are the straightforward commercial costs and revenue. But if it is a public investment, then perhaps some other considerations might also be relevant. What are these considerations? Further, if there are some considerations other than just the receipts and costs calculated at the market prices (i.e. the commercial considerations) should this fact be made to bear on private firms' investment policies as well? These are the questions which we shall discuss below.

When we consider investment we have to recognise the passage of time. Costs and returns of a project are necessarily spread into the future. Hence uncertainty and some rate of time discount are essential elements here. It is possible that in some particular case we might be quite certain about the time profile of costs and returns; similarly, it is possible that somebody may value £100 in any future year exactly equally with £100 today—that his rate of time discount may be zero. But these are extreme examples. We have already discussed in Chapter III how different kinds of uncertainty might arise, and their implications for public policy on some assumptions about the social aims. We should now proceed to discuss the appropriate rate of time discount before examining the other aspects of costs and returns of investments. We pick up here a thread from a previous section on allocation over time (Chapter II, Section 9). Let us first discuss how the time profile of saving (or consumption, which is its obverse) is to be chosen in an economy; this discussion would then link up with that of the appropriate rate of discount to be used in the (private and public) investment decisions of the economy.

It is sometimes argued that the choice of the time profile of saving must be based on the value judgment of complete consumer sovereignty because it is a 'widely accepted' value judgment. Even if we were to grant that it is a widely acceptable value judgment and that therefore it should be adopted as the norm by all economists (that is, even if we were to ignore the fundamental criticisms of Chapter VI), the argument still remains unsatisfactory. To the extent that the welfare of the future citizens is affected by the present saving decisions, a major portion of the relevant 'consumers' are simply not there to exercise their sovereignty.

There is another argument against letting the individuals of the present generation acting through the market decide on the rate of saving. This has to do with the possible 'public-good' character of the saving decision. It is possible that an individual would like a certain proportion of the current national income saved and invested. He knows that if such a proportion is saved and invested, then this 'service' or 'commodity' is available to any individual irrespective of what proportion of his own income he saves. Exactly like a defence programme, or a programme for the preservation of the countryside, once it is provided it is immediately available to everybody, irrespective of what they have paid. Therefore such a service or good cannot be commercially supplied; consumers will have the good available without having to pay for it. The market fails to respond to individual preferences about public goods. A certain rate of provision for the future generations might also be a public good which has to be supplied collectively (i.e. through the Government) like any other public good. Some writers have chosen to call this phenomenon 'an isolation paradox'; however, there is no paradox here, but only another instance of a public good.[1] See Chapter IV, Section 6, and Chapter VI, Section 6.2a.

In any case, we would like to argue that there is also an element of the *merit good* about the rate of savings; there is as much moral argument in favour of providing more for the future than *might* be done through the market as there is for providing more education than individuals might buy on their own. However, it does not follow that individuals' preference for the present over the future enjoyments is to be completely disregarded. For though individuals may have defective telescopic faculty as Pigou asserted, some element of preference for the near enjoyments over the distant ones is perfectly natural when one recalls the increasing uncertainty for an individual regarding the possibility of being alive as the enjoyments get more remote. In countries with low life expectancy a rather strong preference for near enjoyments would be perfectly rational. (See Eckstein [5].) Moreover, in a poor country where some rise in *per capita* income is taking place, there is another argument—based on some notion like that of the diminishing marginal utility of individual incomes—for a rather strong preference for near enjoyments. We may conclude that there is likely to be a plausible case in any economy for the rate of savings to be determined through the political decision-making process rather than for it to be determined solely by the market.

We have, then, the question: how should 'parliament' choose the right rate of saving? At one extreme there is the famous mathematical model of Ramsey [31] about maximisation of utility over an indefinitely prolonged future, and the derivation therefrom of the optimum rate of saving. He treated the question as what the mathematicians call a variational problem. But the rules he obtained for the optimum rate of saving depend on the assumption that the production function and the utility function for the society are known for all time—in other words, that the state of maximum utility (or bliss) over time is identifiable. This makes the model irrelevant for any practical use—apart from the indirect gain that may be derived from its mathematical and theoretical insights. There have been various modifications of Ramsey's model, but we do not dwell on them.

In fact, there is no reason why the rate of national savings or the social rate of discount needs to be *derived* from anything, any more than there is any reason why the social expenditure on the old-age pensioners needs to be *derived* from anything. They can be *made to appear* as though they are derived from something—e.g. on some very simplifying assumptions which are discussed in the next footnote,

[1] Sen [34] and Marglin [19] both mention this phenomenon but fail to see that it is just another instance of a public good.

the social rate of discount can appear to be derived from the postu-
lated rate of economic growth and the assumed marginal productivity
of capital—but there is always a basic-value judgment just one step
removed; in this example it is the rate of economic growth which
has been specified at a *desirable* level, and then the implied rate of
discount derived from it in the light of the given technology.[1] Hence
we must conclude that the social rate of discount and the rate of
national savings have to be directly decided upon like any other
element in a decision-making or comment-making social welfare
function.

In all economies, other than perhaps the communist ones, there
are a number of agencies—some private and some public—which
undertake investments. Moreover, there is anything but a single rate
of interest in even the private-market sector. Undoubtedly some of
the differences in the interest rates are due to different kinds of risks
involved or different kinds of credits given; therefore they are not
genuine differences. But it remains true that differences also exist
for the same kind of risk and credit; capital markets, perhaps, are
among the most imperfect markets; and economically the more
backward an economy, the greater, probably, are these imperfections. Hence, a necessary condition for technological efficiency—that
a factor should have the same price everywhere except when the
differences are due to externalities—is usually violated in most
economies.

It is quite difficult in practice to influence the rates of discount
habitually used by different businessmen. For example, recent
studies in Britain have indicated that businessmen tend to use

[1] This is the procedure adopted by Marglin [19] for deriving the social rate of
discount, and is a simple application of the Harrod–Domar model of growth.
He has to assume that output can be treated as *unidimensional* and that to *each*
rate of growth of output there corresponds a *unique* rate of investment. These are
big assumptions. The time profiles of future returns (and outputs) from different
investments may not be directly comparable without the use of a rate of discount;
some might yield a lot in near years and relatively little in later years, whereas
some others may show exactly the opposite pattern. There have also been some
other articles in which the authors give formulae for discovering the right social
rate of savings from individuals' saving decisions when there are inter-relationships in their savings functions of the kind discussed above. However, as was
pointed out in Chapter IV, when individuals' utility functions are inter-related
due to the public-goods character of a good or service it may be impossible to
discover their true preferences about goods; and if such relationships are assumed
away, then though individual preferences are in principle discoverable, they are
never known in practice. Hence these formulae must remain empty formulae.
Moreover, to the extent that there is an element of the merit good in the savings
decisions, it is not clear why individuals' own preference schedules for savings
should be the deciding factor.

rough-and-ready methods of assessing investments (one of which is the pay-back-period criterion), which in fact amount to using a very high rate of discount.[1] Moreover, various tax allowances which have been granted by the parliament to influence the size and direction of private investment fail in their purpose because businessmen tend not to take these tax allowances into account; the estimates of costs and returns they use tend to be pre-tax rather than post-tax. These facts possibly imply that less investment, and therefore also a lower rate of adoption of improved techniques (see Chapter VI, Section 3), are prevalent than the parliament would like and is trying to achieve through the tax allowances, etc.

We turn now to the question of how costs and returns are to be evaluated. We have argued at length that there may be convincing ethical reasons for rejecting the market rate of interest. Similarly, there are likely to be good reasons for not accepting the market evaluations of a number of other things. This is obviously true of the *merit goods*, and of the situations where *externalities* are present. As regards *public goods*, since it may be impossible to discover the preferences of each individual (or group) about these goods, the evaluating prices for them will have to be based on political decisions. Prices for evaluating costs and benefits are then to be decided in the light of a comment-making or decision-making social welfare function, though technological efficiency would require that price of a factor be the same wherever it is used unless there are production externalities (see Chapter IV, Section 3). These prices might well take the form of accounting prices if programming techniques have been employed.

The concept of consumers' surplus which we came across in the last section is sometimes considered to have special relevance to the choice of public investments. But the concept does not deserve any such honour. In a full-employment situation, if we want to estimate the consumers' surplus from a new investment we must also take into account the possible loss of consumers' surplus and producers' surplus in some competing industries, and possible gains in some complementary industries. Further, any estimate of consumers' surplus from a good is weighted by the accompanying distribution of incomes; with some conceptual change in incomes distribution a

---

[1] The pay-back-period criterion is also called the pay-off-period criterion, etc. No obvious rate of interest or rate of discount is used. According to this criterion, some (rather short) number of years is fixed as the period within which the sum of the net annuities from a project must cover the initial cost of the investment. Since the period fixed tends to be small, the method is equivalent to using a very high rate of interest or of discount in investment and replacement policy; the adoption of new techniques tends to get delayed. See Williams and Scott [37].

small consumers' surplus might become quite large because the relevant demand curve jumps up; and also vice versa. Hence any estimates must be qualified by this consideration. Lastly, though consumers' surplus has a nice sound to it, in fact any estimate of it—being based on the ordinary demand curve—need not take into account any external effects. By the time all these important considerations have been incorporated in any estimates of consumers' and producers' surpluses, they would begin to look rather a roundabout way of estimating costs and benefits at some socially approved relative weights or prices.[1]

Little suggests in his book a simple 'profitability criterion' for public investments. But this is altogether unsatisfactory. Of course, it is open to Little to suggest as his personal opinion that only profit-making public industries seem 'healthy' or 'efficient' to him, but there is no economic reason why some public industries should not permanently make losses if—in spite of thoroughly 'efficient' (in the industrial engineer's sense) management—that is the inevitable outcome of supplying the product in the amounts desired by the 'parliament'. Moreover, since in practice a number of nationalised industries in most countries are expected to pass on some of their profits (if they can make profits) to the consumer, any talk of recommending profitability as a criterion encourages a kind of comparison between public and private investments which is quite irrational.

Suppose that—taking all kinds of external effects and other considerations into account—the social costs and benefits over their respective lives of a group of public investments have been estimated in the light of the objectives and priorities adopted by the social decision-making mechanism and with the help of some socially approved prices; what procedure should then be adopted for choosing the best group of investments?

A number of criteria have been proposed for this purpose.[2] But they are variants of the two basic forms: the internal rate of return criterion and the *net* discounted present-value criterion. There are reasons for preferring the use of the latter, as we shall see. The two criteria are sometimes lumped together under the title of 'discounted

[1] For example, Foster [9] puts a great deal of emphasis on a consumers' surplus criterion for public investments, but we consider, for reasons given above, this approach not so useful as estimating general social costs and benefits at socially approved prices.

[2] There is by now a vast literature on criteria for public investments and cost-benefit analysis. With very few exceptions, the authors tend to borrow without any qualifications the theorems of the traditional *a priori* welfare theory—though in recent years there has been more caution, e.g. in Eckstein [5]. Another good survey is in Marglin's chapters in Maass [18].

cash flow' criterion; but they are equivalent criteria only under special conditions. Let us start by defining them precisely.

Let B stand for the private commercial revenue or the money value of the social benefit expected with certainty in a future year, C for private or social direct costs for the same future year, I for the initial cost of a new plant, n for the last year in which the investment under discussion earns a positive excess over the direct costs, and r for the rate of discount which may be the private or the social rate and which is assumed to remain constant over the relevant time horizon. Then the *net* discounted present-value criterion approves of an investment so long as the following holds:

$$\sum_{t=1}^{n} \frac{B_t - C_t}{(1 + r)^t} - I > 0 \tag{7.1}$$

At the margin the inequality sign is replaced by an equality sign. At the margin the total (gross) discounted present value of investment is equal to the initial cost:

$$\sum_{t=1}^{n} \frac{B_t - C_t}{(1 + r)^t} = I \tag{7.2}$$

This equation shows *both* the discounted present value at the margin *and* the internal rate of return (also called the Keynesian marginal efficiency of investment); because either of the latter two is that rate of discount which makes the present value of the sum of the total net yield over the life of a project equal to its initial cost. Fig. 7.4 illustrates this point. Assume some investment project whose total life and yield and direct costs over that life are known. We do not know yet what rate of discount to use for measuring the discounted present value of its net yield to be indicated along the vertical axis. Assume that the discounted present value is therefore calculated for a number of different increasing rates of discount indicated along the horizontal axis from left to right. OK is the initial cost of the investment, I. For low rates of discount the present value exceeds I, but at a certain rate of discount (which prevails at point E) the two are equal. This *particular* rate of discount is the internal rate of return of the investment in question. It is to be noted that there is a unique internal rate of return only if it is assumed, as we do here, that C does not exceed B in any year in future, that the net yield in any future year is not negative. Otherwise equation (7.2) does not give a unique r (the internal rate of return) and our curve in fig. 7.4 may cross the line KH more than once. Incidentally, this may be regarded as the first disadvantage of the internal-rate-of-return criterion as compared to the discounted present-value criterion; the latter criterion will always have a unique value provided there is a given unique rate of discount.

179

If the rate of interest, or the social rate of interest that any public department is required to use, is r^*, then the internal-rate-of-return criterion requires that investment be undertaken up to the point which makes $r = r^*$, and where r is the internal rate of return as calculated from equation (7.2). If the market for capital funds is perfect, or if it is simply assumed that each potential private or public investor has a perfectly elastic supply curve of investible capital at the rate of interest r^*, then each investment will be carried up to the

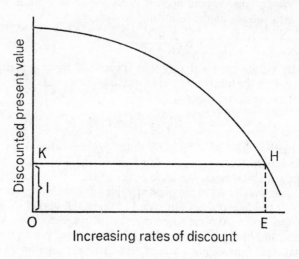

Fig. 7.4

point where the internal rate of return, r, just equals that rate of interest. In this case, though the criterion used is that of the internal rate of return—since for each project that rate is equalised with a given rate of interest—the outcome is exactly the same as it would have been if the criterion used were that of present value discounted at a rate which equals the rate of interest r^*. Provided, then, that the rate of interest used in evaluating *each* investment proposal when applying the internal-rate-of-return criterion is equal to the rate of discount used when applying the present-value criterion (and provided the net yield for any project is not negative for any future year) the two criteria would approve of the same list of investment projects; under these rather special conditions the two criteria would be equivalent.

However, as we noted above, the net yield for some future dates from a project may be negative; in this case there is no unique internal rate of return, though there is still a unique value of the discounted present value so long as there is a given rate of discount to work with. This, then, is one reason for preferring the discounted present-value criterion. It can also be argued that in any case the aim of commercial or public investment policy is to maximise the (suitably discounted) increment in future wealth—measured at commercial prices or socially adjusted evaluating ratios; the discounted present

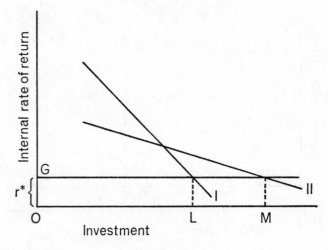

Fig. 7.5

value is a more direct, and hence more useful, measure of it than the internal rate of return. Assume that the choice is between two incompatible projects, as it is very often; now the internal-rate-of-return criterion offers no simple solution. With a perfectly elastic supply curve of capital funds at a given rate of interest the marginal internal rate of return on the two projects is equal; therefore this criterion offers no way of choosing between them. For example, in fig. 7.5, I and II are the curves of the internal rates of return (or the marginal efficiency of investment curves) of two mutually exclusive projects. *OG* is the given rate of interest. The *marginal* internal rate is the same for the two investment projects. Yet using this given rate of interest as the rate of discount, we might find that the *net* present value of one is greater than that of the other.

181

Moreover, if the amount of capital that a firm or public department can borrow at a given rate of interest is limited—as is almost invariably the case with the public departments at least—then the application of the internal-rate-of-return criterion for mutually exclusive projects becomes particularly problematic. Suppose that for any two mutually exclusive projects which are being considered by a public department the internal-rate-of-return curves and the *net* discounted present value are as shown in figs. 7.6a and 7.6b.

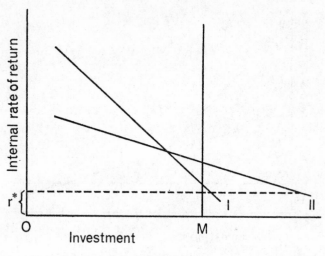

Fig. 7.6a

Assume that the department has been allocated *OM* amount of investment funds in the period under discussion; and that it has been asked to use some rate r^* as the rate of interest or of discount in its calculations. If the investing authority uses the internal rate of return as the criterion it will choose project II (see fig. 7.6a); but in doing this it would have made *no* use of the (socially) laid down rate of interest or of discount r^*. If it uses the net discounted present value as the criterion, then it straight away *has to* take the (socially) laid down rate of interest or of discount in calculating the net discounted present values. As it happens, in this example with the net-present-value criterion, project I ranks higher. (With the present-value criterion the fixed capital budget allowance would have been taken into account because it would have been subtracted from the

182

gross discounted present value of each project of a size which just exhausts the budget allowance to obtain its *net* discounted present value. We are assuming here that the investment projects are reasonably divisible.)

Hence we can conclude that the net-discounted-present-value criterion is to be preferred to the internal-rate-of-return criterion. The last, and perhaps the most important, reason for our preference that we have given is that when different government departments or

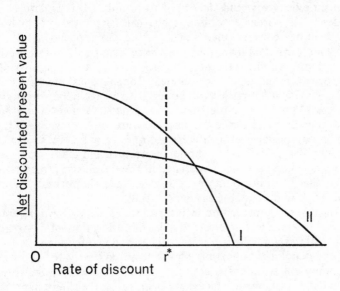

Fig. 7.6b

public investment authorities are allocated fixed capital budgets the net-discounted-present-value criterion would ensure that they all use the same (perhaps socially laid down) rate of interest or of discount, whereas the internal-rate-of-return criterion ensures no such thing. And even when capital budgets are not fixed separately for the different investing authorities, the net-discounted-present-value criterion is to be preferred for the other reasons we have given. A (present value of) benefits/(present value of) costs *ratio* criterion can also be used when costs are defined to include the initial cost of investment also. However, when the choice is between some exclusive projects the use of this criterion does not necessarily lead to the maximisation of the net present value of benefits from a given invest-ment programme, whereas the ordinary net-present-value criterion does so. See McKean [22].

Maximisation of social benefits from a given total of investible funds requires that we calculate the *net* discounted present value of the social benefits of all public and private projects (at a suitable common rate of interest), that we use a common rate of uncertainty discount for them, and that we should have used socially given common evaluating ratios to make all the benefits and costs com-mensurable. We would then need to arrange all these projects in a descending order according to the net discounted present value of their net benefits, then starting from the top choose all pro-jects until the total investible funds were exhausted. In this list only one of any two mutually exclusive projects (e.g. a swimming pool or a sports stadium) would be included. Roughly speaking, of the two mutually exclusive projects, that one is to be included which gives the greatest discounted present value of benefits for a given total cost. (For a more precise rule for this problem, see Maass (ed.) [18].) Similarly, special treatment is necessary for any two projects which are interdependent, e.g. a shopping precinct and a car park; such projects would need to be evaluated as three exclusive projects: first, when they are both built; second, when only the precinct is built; and third, when only the car park is built.

The foregoing procedure would ensure 'efficiency' (*with reference to the specified social objectives*) in the allocation of investment only within the public sector if the list included only public projects. It would not be compatible with overall efficiency for the whole economy unless the resources used in the public sector were specific to it. Otherwise, overall efficiency would require the choice of projects to be made from a single list of both private and public investment projects. Anyway, as we have already noted, in practice not even all public investments are reviewed together in this way; instead, it is usual to allocate separate sums to different departments and to ask each to make the best use of the allotted money. In this process there is necessarily some compromise with efficiency, i.e. there is neces-sarily some sub-optimisation, because some department may be able to invest in a marginal project with a lower net discounted present value of net benefits than the marginal project in some other department.

A method has been suggested of getting round this problem, as well as that of overall efficiency referred to above; it consists of finding the opportunity cost of the capital used for any project. The discounted present value (at the same social rate of discount) of the foregone flow of benefits of the next best project (which would have had the same initial cost) is the opportunity cost of an investment project. A project in any department is to be undertaken only if its discounted present value exceeds its opportunity cost. However, the same practical difficulties which prevent the simultaneous consideration of the investment projects of *all* government departments may also prevent the calculation of opportunity costs of projects, so that some sub-optimisation may be inevitable.

It is significant that Steiner [35], who was the first to emphasise the importance of taking into account the opportunity cost of a public investment, assumed as given the benefits for all possible projects. Marglin [20] has argued that if the government investment fund is raised by borrowing, then there is the opportunity cost of the foregone discounted present value of the yields from some private investments, but not if it is raised by taxation. But Mishan [25] has argued that if we assume full-employment equilibrium, then even the funds raised by taxation which reduce private consumption have a value to the individuals which is equal, *at the margin*, to the marginal efficiency of capital in the private sector, to be represented by, say, r'. For any social rate of discount r^*, the opportunity cost of a unit of public investment might be taken to be r'/r^*. Mishan also argues that, with a view to taking account of the opportunity cost of public investment the marginal efficiency of capital in the private sector may be used as the rate of discount in the public sector, so long as the chosen social rate of discount is going to be below it. But the trouble with this proposal is that while some agreement among the decision-makers or comment-makers on an appropriate social rate of discount might possibly emerge, it is likely to be more difficult for them to agree on what the marginal efficiency of capital, or the internal rate of return at the margin in the private sector is. It is worth recalling the likely imperfections of market competition. Moreover, if the marginal efficiency of capital in the private sector (assuming it has somehow been estimated) is greatly different from the socially chosen rate of time discount, there is no necessary *economic* justification for using the former instead of the latter as the rate of discount in evaluating public investments.

Needless to say, in the estimates of both future costs and benefits there is bound to be an element of uncertainty. Different analysts' forecasts of these costs and benefits (measured according to the social welfare function) may well differ. Hence, in presenting these estimates there is the need for each analyst to indicate separately what kind of uncertainty is associated with the estimates. Allowance for uncertainty might be made by adjusting the costs or benefits of a project, or the estimate of the years it will last, or the discount rate, or simply adding remarks which can be compared with the similar remarks on other projects.

There are some additional problems. To the extent that the choice of the appropriate social rate of interest is affected by the expected change in the standard of living, that choice is also affected by the size and composition of the public (and private) investment plans. Further, perhaps the most important problem in choosing public investment projects is not so much the choice of which projects to undertake but the choice of which projects to undertake *at what times*; the possible benefits of different projects are differently affected by postponement, and since often the decision on a project is not of the 'now or never' nature, the real practical problem is that of choosing a time-profile of public investments.[1] None of these problems is quite insoluble; in dealing with actual projects some fairly workable solutions can be found. Finally, programming techniques obviously have an application in this field.

7.4 CONCLUSIONS

There are no *a priori* normative principles that economic theory can offer for either pricing or investment policies of public enterprises. The principles sometimes offered are marginal-cost pricing and the consumers' surplus; we gave reasons to show that both are question-begging. The costs and benefits of a public investment need to be evaluated according to relative welfare weights derived from a comment-making or a decision-making social welfare function. The only valid principles economic theory has to offer are at the level of technological efficiency. They are that there should be no difference in the price of a factor to any of its users—unless the difference is due to an externality; and that each enterprise should decide on its production and investment policy in the light of uniform factor prices (including the rate of interest), and full knowledge of the latest techniques. A discussion of the last two points is also to be found in Chapter VI, Section 3.

[1] See the appendix on 'Importance of Time Lags for Economic Planning' in Reddaway [32]; also Nath [27]. For some algorithms designed for the problems of phasing, see Marglin [21].

REFERENCES FOR CHAPTER VII

[1] M. J. Bailey, 'Formal Criteria for Investment Decisions', *Journal of Political Economics*, 1959

[2] M. Beckman, C. B. McGuire, and C. B. Winston, *Studies in the Economics of Transportation*, New Haven, 1956

[3] H. B. Chenery, 'The Interdependence of Investment Decisions', in M. Abramovitz and others, *The Allocation of Resources*, Berkeley, Calif., 1959

[4] O. Eckstein, 'Investment Criteria for Economic Development', *Quarterly Journal of Economics*, 1957

[5] O. Eckstein, 'A Survey of Public Expenditure Criteria', in National Bureau of Economic Research, *Public Finances, Needs, Sources and Utilisation*, Princeton, 1961

[6] M. S. Feldstein, 'Net Social Benefit Calculations and the Public Investment Decision', *Oxford Economic Papers*, 1964

[7] M. S. Feldstein, 'The Social Time Preference Discount Rate in Cost Benefit Analysis', *Economic Journal*, 1964

[8] M. S. Feldstein and J. S. Fleming, 'The Problem of Time-stream Evaluation: Present value versus Internal Rate of Return', *Bulletin of Oxford University Institute of Economics and Statistics*, 1964

[9] C. D. Foster, *The Transport Problem*, London, 1963

[10] J. de V. Graaff, *Theoretical Welfare Economics*, Cambridge, 1957

[11] J. R. Hicks, *A Revision of Demand Theory*, Oxford, 1956

[12] J. Hirshleifer, 'On the Theory of Optimal Investment Decision', *Journal of Political Economy*, 1958

[13] H. Hotelling, 'The General Welfare in Relation to Problems of Taxation and of Railway and Utility Rates', *Econometrica*, 1938

[14] T. J. Koopmans, *Three Essays on the State of Economic Science*, New York, 1957

[15] J. V. Krutilla, 'Welfare Aspects of Cost–Benefit Analysis', *Journal of Political Economy*, 1961

[16] R. G. Lipsey and R. Lancaster, 'The General Theory of the Second Best', *Review of Economic Studies*, 1956

[17] I. M. D. Little, Review of Graaff's book in *Economica*, 1957

[18] A. Maass and others, *Design of Water Resource Systems*, London, 1962

[19] S. A. Marglin, 'The Social Rate of Discount and the Optimal Rate of Investment', *Quarterly Journal of Economics*, 1963

[20] S. A. Marglin, 'The Opportunity Costs of Public Investment', *Quarterly Journal of Economics*, 1963

[21] S. A. Marglin, *Approaches to Dynamic Investment Planning*, Amsterdam, 1963

[22] R. N. McKean, *Efficiency in Government Through Systems Analysis*, New York, 1958

[23] A. J. Merrett, 'A Reconsideration of Investment and Pricing Criteria

in the Nationalised Industries', *The Manchester School of Economic and Social Studies*, 1964.

[24] E. J. Mishan, 'A Survey of Welfare Economics, 1939–59', *Economic Journal*, June 1960

[25] E. J. Mishan, 'Criteria for Public Investment: Some Simplifying Suggestions', *Journal of Political Economy*, 1967

[26] R. A. Musgrave, *The Theory of Public Finance*, New York, 1959

[27] S. K. Nath, 'The Theory of Balanced Growth', *Oxford Economic Papers*, 1962

[28] C. J. Oort, *Decreasing Costs as a Problem of Welfare Economics*, Amsterdam, 1958

[29] J. D. Pitchford and A. J. Hagger, 'A Note on the Marginal Efficiency of Capital', *Economic Journal*, 1958

[30] A. R. Prest and R. Turvey, 'Cost–Benefit Analysis: A Survey', *Economic Journal*, 1965

[31] F. P. Ramsey, 'A Mathematical Theory of Saving', *Economic Journal*, 1928

[32] W. B. Reddaway, *The Development of the Indian Economy*, London, 1962

[33] Nancy Ruggles, 'Recent Developments in the Theory of Marginal Cost Pricing', *Review of Economic Studies*, 1950–51

[34] A. K. Sen, 'On Optimising the Rate of Saving', *Economic Journal*, 1961

[35] P. O. Steiner, 'Choosing Among Alternative Public Investments in the Water Resource Field', *American Economic Review*, 1959

[36] R. Turvey, 'Present Value versus Internal Rate of Return . . .' *Economic Journal*, 1963

[37] B. R. Williams and W. P. Scott, *Investment Proposals and Decisions*, London, 1965

[38] J. Wiseman, 'The Theory of Public Utility Price—An Empty Box', *Oxford Economic Papers*, 1957

VIII

INTERNATIONAL TRADE AND
A PRIORI WELFARE PROPOSITIONS

The theory of international trade is a field in which the theorems of *a priori* welfare economics abound. If we critically examine some of these theorems the purpose is not to argue against international trade but only to sort out the logical and the valid theorems from the others. We shall be examining in detail in this chapter the application of the *a priori* welfare criteria to trade theory: it may seem illogical to do so after having criticised them in previous chapters on so many grounds; however, these criteria, such as they are, have been applied to trade theory, and in some instances some propositions have been put forward which are wrong even if we ignore our fundamental objections. Hence it is necessary to review this literature.

8.1 GAINS FROM TRADE WITH PERFECT DOMESTIC MARKETS

We assume in this section that the domestic commodity and factor markets satisfy all the necessary conditions for perfect competition. However, there might yet be imperfect competition in the international market. Consequently, the analysis in this section falls into two parts. To begin with, we study the foreign trade of a country which is so small relative to the rest of the world that the world prices are not at all affected by the size of its foreign trade; the country is so small that the world prices are given parameters for it. Later in this section we shall study the gains from foreign trade of a large country.

We make the usual assumptions of diminishing marginal product for each variable factor and non-increasing returns to scale, and of the complete absence of external effects in production or consumption. The analysis is static; only a point in time is considered, and costs and tastes are assumed to remain unchanged. Let us assume that with its given resources our country can produce only two goods. In that case we have the production possibility frontier in the shape of LL' in fig. 8.1. Regarding tastes, we make all the assumptions which were mentioned in Chapter II, Section 2. Further, since we shall be using Scitovsky community indifference curves and utility possibility curves, it is also assumed that fully defined utility functions of the individual citizens of the country are also known (see Chapter II, Section 5).

Whether there is any trade or not, the economy is assumed to produce a combination of the goods x and y *on* its production frontier. This is because we are assuming that the factor markets are perfect and that all firms and farms know the economics of the best practice techniques. Let us suppose that when no trade is allowed

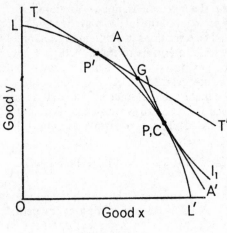

Fig. 8.1

the domestic price ratio is as given by AA'. We are assuming perfect competition in all domestic markets; therefore, where AA' just touches the production frontier, a Scitovsky community indifference curve (I_1) also just touches it. Point P,C then shows the amounts of x and y which are produced and which are also exactly equal to the amounts consumed by the whole country under autarky.

Assume now that for the first time foreign trade is permitted. If the world price ratio happens to be exactly the same as the domestic price ratio under autarky, no trade is possible. Some difference in comparative costs, and therefore the price ratios, is likely; trade should be possible. Assume the world price ratio is as given by the line TT', which is a given parameter for our small country. With free trade, the country will produce at the point (P' in fig. 8.1) where the world price line just touches the production frontier. But the consumption does not have to be at the same point; in fact, since some foreign trade takes place, some of what is produced of one commodity or another will have to be exported. The consumption point can lie anywhere on the world price line AA'.

Since the production frontier is concave from below, any straight line tangent to it passes over (or outside) all other points on the frontier. That is why in fig. 8.1 TT' passes over Point P,C (and AA', in its turn, passes over point P'). One consequence of this property of the production frontier is that no matter where on TT' the free-trade consumption point lies, we shall always be able to say that $\Sigma P_T Q_T > \Sigma P_T Q_A$, where T refers to free-trade prices and quantities and A refers to autarky prices and quantities. In other words, the value of total consumption under free trade *at free-trade prices* will always be greater than the value of total consumption under autarky. This also means that according to a current-weighted quantity index total consumption under free trade will always seem higher than under autarky. We showed in Chapter V, Section 5, that whenever the current position ranks higher than the base position according to the current-weighted quantity index the Scitovsky reversal criterion will also rank the current position as better than the base position. It follows, then, that the consumption position under free trade always passes the Scitovsky reversal criterion as compared to the autarky consumption point. If we look at TT' in fig. 8.1 we notice that no matter where a Scitovsky community indifference curve touches the straight line TT', since TT' passes over point P,C, so will the community indifference curve. This is because a Scitovsky community indifference curve is always convex from below.

But a similarly general conclusion is *not* possible about either the autarky-based quantity index number or the Kaldor–Hicks criterion. If the consumption point (in fig. 8.1) under free trade lies on TT' to the right of G, then that point will rank higher than the point P,C according to the autarky-based quantity index; i.e. in that case we shall have $\Sigma P_A Q_T > \Sigma P_A Q_A$. However, even when this is true, it does not follow that the Kaldor–Hicks criterion will be satisfied by the free-trade consumption position. For as we showed in Chapter V, Section 5, when the base-weighted quantity index ranks the current year as higher, it does not follow that the Kaldor–Hicks criterion will also necessarily do the same. If the free-trade consumption point happens to lie to the left of G on TT', then clearly we shall have $\Sigma P_A Q_T < \Sigma P_A Q_A$. When this is so the free-trade consumption position will *not* pass the Kaldor–Hicks criterion. We can sum up this paragraph thus: the free-trade consumption position as compared to the autarkical consumption position may or may not rank higher according to either the autarky-weighted quantity index or the

191

Kaldor–Hicks criterion. Our conclusions about the base-weighted and current-weighted indices of the consumption positions remain true even when more than two goods are considered.

It is the practice of a number of authors—see Johnson [12], for example—to assume that the trade-consumption point (C' in fig. 8.2) is bound to lie on a Scitovsky community indifference curve which is everywhere above the community indifference curve on which the autarky consumption point (P,C in fig. 8.2) will lie. But

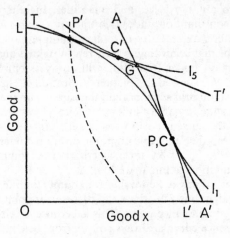

Fig. 8.2

since no well-defined social-welfare function can be assumed as given in the general, abstract case, there is no justification for assuming that the Scitovsky community indifference curves will be non-intersecting. Even if we have presumed that the social-welfare function will be Pareto-type, the Scitovsky community indifference curves might yet be intersecting. In fig. 8.2 we have drawn an intersecting community indifference curve through C'. Point C', as compared to the point P,C, passes the Scitovsky reversal criterion, as will be the case always; but it does *not* pass the Kaldor–Hicks criterion, which may or may not be the case in any given example.

We should now briefly restate some of the foregoing propositions with the help of utility possibility curves. In fig. 8.3 aa' is the utility possibility frontier of our economy under autarky; it corresponds to the production frontier LL' of fig. 8.1. When trade is allowed, though the production frontier remains the same, the consumption possibilities are expanded; they are shown by the world price line TT' in fig. 8.1. Corresponding to this outward trade consumption possibility frontier is the outward trade utility possibility frontier FF' in fig. 8.3. It may or may not touch the autarky utility frontier at one or more points, depending on the pattern of tastes of the individuals in our economy. The autarky position of individuals' utility levels is shown as C, and the free-trade position as C' in fig.

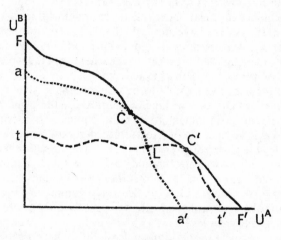

Fig. 8.3

8.3. If we compare the point utility possibility curves of free trade and autarky positions (in other words, if we compare the two positions with fixed totals of goods as we did while using the index numbers and the Scitovsky community indifference curves), then the following propositions follow from our fig. 8.3. The point utility possibility curve of autarky position can never pass over the free-trade position (because that lies on an outward *situation* utility frontier), but the point utility curve of the free-trade position may or may not pass under the autarky position. Hence the free-trade position will always pass the Scitovsky reversal criterion, but it may or may not pass the Kaldor–Hicks criterion. Further, if the Samuelson comparisons are made, then again since the *point* utility possibility frontier of the free-trade position (the curve tt' in fig. 8.3) may well intersect (as it does at L) the *point* utility frontier of the autarky

193

position (the curve *aa'* in fig. 8.3), we cannot say that the Samuelson comparisons are satisfied by the free-trade position.

There is a certain confusion in the literature about the welfare comparisons between free trade and autarky. For example, in his famous article on international trade, Samuelson [16] wrote: '... if a unanimous decision were required in order for trade to be permitted, it would always be possible for those who desired trade to buy off those opposed to trade, with the result that all could be made better off.' This amounts to the assertion that free trade satisfies the Kaldor–Hicks test as compared to autarky. But this is clearly not true if the total amounts consumed under free trade or autarky are assumed to remain fixed. As we have noticed, that indeed is the assumption whenever Scitovsky community indifference curves or the *point* utility frontiers are being used. Further, to the extent that the *a priori* comparisons on the assumption of exactly known individual utility functions were meant in principle to be only preliminary to the use of price–quantity data of the kind which are usually available, then to that extent it is logical to use the compensation-criteria-like evaluations in terms *only* of fixed totals of goods. Since there is no reason why the *point* utility possibility curves of the national products under free trade and autarky should not intersect, the foregoing statement by Samuelson (which is often approvingly quoted) is wrong. Compensation criteria relate to Scitovsky community indifference curves and the *point* utility possibility curve, but *not* to the *situation* utility possibility curves.[1]

Lastly, there is the question of feasibility. Our foregoing comparisons, whether with the help of the community indifference curves or the point utility possibility curves, have been based on the implicit assumption that lump-sum redistributions are possible. But usually they are not. As we noted in Chapter III, once we recognise the problem of feasibility, conclusions which otherwise look firm have to be modified. For example, in fig. 8.4 the free-trade consumption point lies on an outward *situation* utility possibility frontier; but any attempt to redistribute that consumption among the two individuals pushes the utility possibilities inward along the *DD'* locus; this feasibility locus intersects the situation utility possibility curve of autarky, and in fact passes under the autarky consumption point (*C*).

---

[1] In our opinion the criticism of Samuelson's claim (given as a quote in the text above) which E. Olsen made, in a Danish writing, is similar to the criticism we have advanced above. Moreover, we do not think that Samuelson in his more recent article [17] is able to answer this criticism. If the comparisons are between fixed commodity bundles, then it is not necessarily true that 'it would always be possible for those who desired trade to buy off those who opposed trade'.

Hence according to the feasibility locus, free trade may not pass either the Samuelson comparisons or the Kaldor–Hicks criterion (as it does not in fig. 8.4). However, free trade will still pass the Scitovsky reversal criterion as always (and as it does in fig. 8.4).

In the light of our foregoing results, let us evaluate the following claim made by Bhagwati [4, p. 24]: 'The policy-maker, provided he accepts the Samuelson criterion, can be confidentially told to adopt free trade in preference to no trade so long as convexity and the

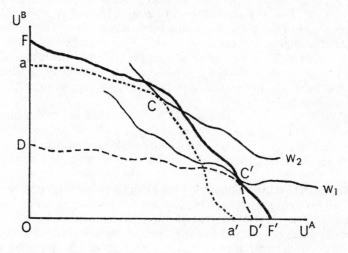

Fig. 8.4

standard "first-best" conditions are verified to hold for the economy.' There are at least three comments to be made here. First, if the comparisions between the free-trade and autarky positions are made with their *given* bundles of goods (i.e. if comparisons are made according to either the Scitovsky community indifference curves or the *point* utility possibility curves), then it does not follow that the free-trade position will pass the Samuelson comparisons. In the examples depicted in figs. 8.2 and 8.3 it does not.

Secondly, suppose we make the comparisons according to the *situation* utility possibility curves, though in our opinion such comparisons are far removed from any possible practical use and therefore even less relevant. Then, as in fig. 8.3, the *situation* utility possibility curve of free trade will always lie outside that of autarky;

on these grounds somebody might argue that free trade is potentially superior, on the Paretian value judgments, to autarky according to the Samuelson comparisons. But this is a statement about *potential* superiority; no generalisation can be obtained from it about *actual* superiority, even on the Paretian value judgments. For example, in figs. 8.3 or 8.4, though C' lies on an outward utility possibility frontier, in fact at C' individual B is worse off than he is at C. Hence without introducing a specific welfare function no comparison between C' and C in terms of *actual* superiority is possible. Depending on the social welfare function, C' may be actually superior or inferior to C. This distinction between *potential* and *actual* superiority applies even if the comparisons are made according to *point* utility possibility curves. For example, in fig. 8.3 if the point utility possibility curve of C' were to be wholly outside that of C—as is possible though not necessary—then C would be declared *potentially* better than C'; but all our foregoing qualifications about *actual* superiority would still apply.

Thirdly, if C' is *actually* inferior to C according to a given welfare function, it may also be incapable of becoming better than C through feasible redistributions. In other words, the feasible utility locus of C' may be *everywhere under* the social welfare contour that goes through C—as is the case in fig. 8.4, where DD' is the feasibility locus; C' and C are the free trade and autarky consumption points respectively.

Our foregoing comparisons have been between free trade and autarky. It is easy to see that all the conclusions that have been derived still apply if instead of free trade we compare restricted (but positive) trade with autarky, i.e. no trade at all. All we need to do is to imagine that in both figs. 8.1 and 8.2 the price line TT' is the price ratio resulting from the Government's trade-restricting action; AA', as before, is the price ratio under autarky. The free-trade world price line is now not shown in either diagram. TT' is not only *the restricted-trade* foreign price ratio but also the domestic price ratio with restricted trade. Once again the restricted-trade consumption position (which may be anywhere on TT' in figs. 8.1 or 8.2) will rank higher than the autarky consumption position (point P,C) according to both the Scitovsky reversal criterion and (restricted) trade-weighted quantity index, but not necessarily according to either the Kaldor–Hicks criterion or the autarky-weighted quantity index. Similarly, the other propositions about potential and actual superiority on the Paretian value judgments, and about the feasibility considerations, apply again.

The propositions which have been established in the last paragraph hold *so long as* the restriction on trade is of a kind which does not affect the tangency of line TT' (in fig. 8.1 or 8.2) with the production possibility frontier. Tariffs, quotas or exchange restrictions will not affect the tangency. But trade restrictions could take the form of taxes or subsidies on some exportables or importables. In this case the price line facing the consumers is different from the price line facing the domestic producers, and, therefore, *not* tangential to the production possibility frontier at any point. Even such 'general' propositions as we established above are no longer valid; now any verdict is possible on a particular case, depending on its special circumstances.

In Chapter II, Section 5, we derived the necessary conditions for a Paretian optimum in a closed economy. Once the economy is open to trade, a further element needs to be added. We shall not prove the derivation of this further element, because the need for its inclusion is quite obvious. The necessary conditions for Pareto optimality in an open economy in words are:

(1) Between any two goods the marginal rate of subjective substitution must be the same for all individuals, and this common rate should also be equal *both* to the *domestic* marginal technical rate of transforming one of those goods into the other and to the *foreign* (or through trade) marginal rate of transforming those goods.

(2) For each individual the subjective marginal rate of substitution between any factor of production and any good must be the same; and this common rate should be equal both to the *domestic* marginal technical rate of transforming that factor into that product and to the *foreign* (or through trade) rate of transforming that factor into that product.[1]

Our diagrams deal with the example of a country with just two factors, two goods, and two individuals. Going back to fig. 8.2, it is easy to see that at the free-trade consumption point C', for the two goods x and y the domestic marginal rate of technical transformation (the slope of the tangent to the production frontier at P') is equal to the foreign marginal rate of transformation (the slope of TT'), and is also equal to the slope of the marginal subjective rate of substitution (the slope of the tangent at C' to the Scitovsky community indifference curve). Hence under free trade, given all the assumptions

[1] These conditions are based on the assumption that all the traded goods are also produced at home; otherwise there is a suitably worded inequality as the necessary condition. For example, between a traded good which is not produced at home and a traded good which is produced at home the domestic marginal rate of transformation should be greater than the foreign marginal rate of transformation (through trade).

mentioned at the beginning of this section and *when the country is too small to affect the terms of trade*, all the necessary conditions for Pareto optimality are satisfied. Needless to say, when trade is restricted, the foregoing necessary conditions for Pareto optimality are violated—unless the restriction in trade takes the form of Paretian optimal tariffs which become relevant if the country is large compared to the world market. Paretian optimal tariffs are analysed in the next section.

No difference is made to any of the welfare propositions about the gains from trade proved above if we now assume that our country is large as compared to the world market for the goods it trades, so that the world prices alter as the size of its trade varies. Keeping such a large country in mind, if we refer to figs. 8.1 and 8.2 we should notice that world price line (TT') is now only the *average* price line, and *not* both the average and marginal price line as was the case before. Since world prices vary according to how much our country trades, the average and marginal prices (or the average and marginal revenues) diverge. However, trade takes place at one unique set of average prices; hence the line TT' in fig. 8.1 or 8.2 now shows the world average price ratio between the two goods x and y. The post-trade consumption point (C') has to lie along this average price ratio line. Once again the trade consumption point will always rank superior to the autarky point according to the post-trade prices, but not necessarily according to the autarky prices; similarly, the trade consumption point will always rank higher than the autarky consumption point according to the Scitovsky reversal criterion, but not necessarily according to the Kaldor–Hicks criterion. Just as when figs. 8.1 and 8.2 referred to small countries we could (on the assumption of known individual utility maps) draw in the utility space the point utility possibility curves in fig. 8.3 for the consumption points C and C' of fig. 8.2, so also now the autarky *situation* utility possibility curve aa' of fig. 8.3 can be imagined to refer to a large country with a production frontier like LL' as shown in fig. 8.2. As for the free-trade *situation* utility possibility curve of a large country, a slight difference needs to be noted. There is no reason why it should not have the general shape of the frontier FF' in fig. 8.3, and why it should not be further out than the autarky situation utility possibility frontier. However, since with a large country there is no unique world price ratio, the free-trade *situation* utility possibility curve now does not correspond to a single straight line, but to a series of varying average price lines.[1] As we have just noted, the

[1] It is possible to draw a consumption frontier under free trade for the economy for which the world prices vary with the size of its trade. See Baldwin [1]. It will

situation utility frontier will—as in the small-country case—be further out than the autarky frontier, though it may touch the latter at one or more points. Once again all the previous propositions about the *a priori* welfare comparisons on the Paretian value judgments apply. Lastly, the propositions proved about the feasibility locus in fig. 8.4 also apply to the large country. This is amply evident from fig. 8.4.

As we have already mentioned, when a country is large enough to affect world prices its equilibrium position under free trade does not satisfy the necessary conditions for Paretian optimality in an open economy. This is because the domestic marginal rates of subjective substitution and of technical transformation between any two goods are brought into equality with the foreign *average* rate of transformation rather than the foreign *marginal* rate. Paretian optimality from any single country's standpoint under such conditions can be achieved by the country only if it could adopt certain kinds of 'optimal tariffs', which are bound to be impossible to compute in practice. We turn to this topic in the next section.

8.2 PARETIAN OPTIMAL TARIFFS

As we noted in the last section, when the terms of trade of a country are variable the domestic marginal subjective and technical rates of substitution between any two goods are not equalised with the foreign *marginal* rate of transformation between those two goods but rather the *average* rate. Hence the necessary conditions for a Paretian optimum are not fulfilled. In such a situation it is possible to devise a set of *theoretical* tariffs such as would enable the economy to attain a Paretian optimum. The attainment of a Paretian optimum is not necessarily an unambiguous improvement in social welfare (i.e. is not necessarily a step to a higher social welfare contour), even on the Paretian value judgments. That proposition was proved on pp. 21–22 in Chapter II. Further, just as in a closed economy there is in principle an infinite number of Paretian optima each with a different distribution of utility levels, so also in an open economy with variable terms of trade there is an infinite number of possible Paretian optima. Hence without a specific social welfare function being given for a specific country at a specific time, the concept of an optimal tariff

---

have the general shape of the production-possibility frontier (of fig. 8.1 or 8.2), but will lie outside of it—touching it at one point. In the utility diagram like our fig. 8.3, corresponding to this free-trade consumption frontier there will be a free-trade utility possibility frontier of the same general shape as FF'.

has no more significance than that of a Paretian optimum on which the former concept is in fact based. Moreover, optimal tariffs are almost impossible to calculate in practice.

Assume that the domestic price ratio between any two goods (P_i/P_h) is equal to the domestic marginal rates of technical and subjective substitution between them. The foreign price ratio (π/π_h) differs from the foreign marginal rate of transformation between the two goods. Foreign prices cannot be changed by a country, but domestic prices can. In order to obtain a Paretian optimum, the task of the economy is to change the domestic price ratio between any two goods by as much as the divergence between the *foreign* average and marginal rates of transformation between those two goods.

Let us now see how the optimum tariff on any good i may be determined.[1] With no tariffs, the domestic price ratio between good i and any other good h is equal to the ratio between the foreign average prices; that is, we have

$$P_i/P_h = \pi_i/\pi_h \qquad (8.1)$$

Assume that z_i is the algebraic import of the ith good, so that when z_i is negative it means that the ith good is exported. Assume also that trade will always be made to balance, once provision is made for net foreign lending, which is represented by K. Though K would vary in real life according to the foreign and domestic prices, it is assumed here for simplicity that it is a constant. (Apparently little difference is made to the logic of the formula by this assumption.) We have, then, the following foreign-trade transformation function:

$$F = \Sigma \pi_i z_i + K = 0 \qquad (8.2)$$

From equation (8.2) we can derive the ratio between the marginal foreign prices of any two goods i and h, or, in other words, the marginal rate of transformation through trade between them. It can be shown that that rate is given by the following equation:

$$\frac{\partial F/\partial z_i}{\partial F/\partial z_h} = \frac{\pi_i + a_i}{\pi_h + a_h} \qquad (8.3)$$

where
$$a_i = \sum_{k=1}^{h} \frac{\partial \pi_k}{\partial z_i} \cdot z_k \quad (i \neq k) \qquad (8.4)$$

In other words, a_i shows the rate of change of the foreign prices of all the goods weighted by their quantities imported or exported—as the imports or exports of the ith good are varied. If we divide both

[1] The standard work in this field is the article by Graaff [8]. See also Scitovsky [18].

sides of equation (8.4) by π_i, then the right-hand side indicates the sum of the ordinary and all the cross-partial elasticities of foreign demand and supply for the ith good.

From equation (8.3), and also from the fact that a_i is in a sense the difference made to the balance of payments by any extra import or export, we can conclude that for a Paretian optimum to be reached for a large trading country the following equation must hold:

$$\frac{\pi_i + a_i}{\pi_h + a_h} = \frac{P_i}{P_h} \tag{8.5}$$

This implies that the foreign marginal price ratio and the domestic price ratio between any two goods have been equalised. This in fact can be brought about by changing domestic prices; but how much the price of a good i must change is decided by a_i and the foreign price π_i. Equation (8.5) suggests that the ith good must be taxed at an *ad valorem* rate of a_i/π_i, so that we have

$$\frac{P_i}{P_h} = \frac{\pi_i(1 + a_i/\pi_i)}{\pi_h(1 + a_h/\pi_h)} \tag{8.6}$$

which is equivalent to equation (8.5), and this shows that with optimal tariff on each good the necessary conditions for a Paretian optimum will be satisfied.

What is the significance of these results? Their origin is in quite an old proposition (which seems to have started with J. S. Mill) that if a country can influence its terms of trade, then it might 'benefit' from putting a tariff on its imports. But we know by now how tricky any general propositions of this kind turn out to be. All that is valid is that if the country is too large to have the foreign marginal and average prices of its exports and imports identical a Paretian optimum is not reached till the domestic price ratio for each pair of goods has been brought into equality with foreign marginal (instead of the average) revenue ratio. But it does not follow that such a movement would necessarily make everybody better off, or even that any losers could be adequately compensated (because we know from p. 101 of Chapter V, that a movement to a Paretian optimum does not necessarily fulfil the Kaldor–Hicks criterion).

Further, the Paretian optimal tariffs would in fact be impossible to calculate in practice. If we divide both sides of equation (8.4) by π_i, then the left-hand side is the expression (a_i/π_i) for the optimal tariff on the ith good, and the right-hand side then shows that the rate depends on the sum of the ordinary and all the cross elasticities of the foreign demand and supply for that good; *but* the magnitudes of these elasticities would depend on what tariff is imposed because elasticities are usually different at different prices.

Domestic prices are determined by, among other things, domestic distribution of incomes; therefore there is no unique price ratio between any two goods which is to be modified by an optimal tariff. Hence for the same *i*th good there is no unique rate of tariff; according to different income distributions, there may be a different tariff for the same good. This is not surprising when we recall that there is no such thing as a unique Paretian optimum. Finally, we have not taken into consideration the possibility of retaliation by other countries if a country adopts tariffs with a view to improving its terms of trade. We may conclude that of all the useless concepts of *a priori* welfare economics, that of a Paretian optimal tariff is perhaps the most useless; it really is a theoretical toy. It is unfortunate that the concept is so often referred to as 'optimal tariff', which perhaps raises some hope of its being a very suitable, effective tariff for some purpose. It is in fact a very limited concept. It has nothing to do with the tariff a country might adopt on infant-industry arguments (which question is to be discussed in Section 4 of this chapter); or with a 'suitable', 'optimal' short-term tariff a country may adopt to tide over temporary balance-of-payments problems. Indeed, in practice tariffs are hardly ever adopted with the aim of reaching a Paretian optimum, nor are they likely to be, because of the practical difficulties of calculating such tariffs—if for no other reason. Whether the real-world tariffs are 'optimal', i.e. 'suitable', or not can be decided only in the light of a decision-making or comment-making set of social objectives.

8.3 DOMESTIC DISTORTIONS AND GAINS FROM TRADE

The analysis of the first two sections of this chapter is based on the assumption that all domestic markets are perfect. It is now worth investigating the logic of some of the *a priori* welfare propositions about gains from trade when there are certain imperfections in the domestic markets.

Let us start with an imperfection in a factor market. Assume that due to some reason such as imperfect mobility (which may take the form of a time-lag in the response of a factor to sector differentials in its price) there are differences in the payments an exactly similar factor receives in different sectors. Hagen [10] has argued that in such a situation protection as compared to free trade will take the economy to a superior position; but a number of his critics have argued that free trade will be the superior position. However, the logic of the welfare conclusions of the participants in this controversy calls for critical scrutiny.

All the participants in this controversy have used community indifference curves to derive their propositions about welfare, but in each case the method of using them has been question-begging. Hagen is aware that there might be a problem here: 'With due recognition of the inaccuracy of assuming one set of such curves [i.e. community indifference curves] because a change in the composition of output changes the distribution of income and hence affects the shape of the curves, I use a single set for convenience in exposition. *Since it is reasonable to assume continuity in shifts in the curves, no plausible assumption about shifts in them associated with changes in the composition of output will alter the conclusions reached here*' [10, p. 505; my italics]. The claims made in the second part of the quotation are unjustified. It is not clear why shifts in the community indifference curves should be continuous, and the conclusions which Hagen (and others) reached are in fact fundamentally affected by the nature of shifts in the community indifference curves.

As we noted in Chapter II, unless a *specific* social-welfare function is assumed to be given, there is no reason why the community indifference curves should be a set of non-intersecting curves. None of the authors concerned have explicitly assumed a *specific* social-welfare function as given; and in any case, if they had, their conclusions would have been relative to that *specific* social-welfare function rather than have the kind of generality which has been quite obviously claimed by each one of them. If a *specific* social-welfare function is not taken as given, but it is only assumed that the relevant welfare function can be anything provided it is Pareto-type (which is the standard practice in theoretical welfare economics and is apparently adopted by these authors also), then any community indifference curves drawn would be the Scitovsky type.

We reproduce in fig. 8.5 the relevant parts of the diagram which Hagen uses to prove the superiority of a tariff over free trade when the industrial wage-rate in an economy is higher than the agricultural wage-rate. $AP''M$ is the economy's true technological production possibility frontier; but the economy is in fact at a point (P') within the frontier. PT represents the world price line between the agricultural and industrial products. This world price is fixed; our economy is too small to influence it. Since, under free trade, the internal and the external price ratios are the same, PT also represents the internal price ratio under free trade. The production point (P) lies where the price ratio is equal to the ratio between the marginal costs of producing the two kinds of goods; there is no reason why that point should also not be within the true technical production frontier. The country exports some of good y and imports some of good x. Its consumption point is T where it is tangential to the community indifference curve I_1.

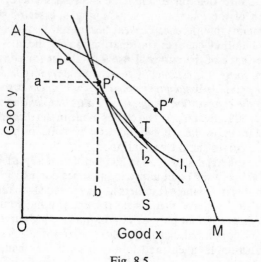

Fig. 8.5

If all trade is prevented, then though good x becomes relatively more expensive, there may yet be some demand for it. Suppose that the domestic price line is as represented by $P'S$, which is tangential to the community indifference curve I_2 at P'. Hagen draws non-intersecting community indifference curves through T and P', and has so placed these two points that the curve through P' is the higher one; from this he concludes that the position P' (resulting under protection) is superior to the position T (resulting under free trade). Bhagwati and Ramaswami [5] also draw non-intersecting community indifference curves through the free-trade and protection points in their similar diagram, and have so placed their two points that free trade is proved superior to protection. However, the real issues involved in these comparisons have not been realised. As was shown in Chapter V, so long as any two positions, A and B, being compared are such that one of them involves more of one but less of the other commodity, there is no reason in principle why according to some distribution of welfare A should not seem superior and according to some other B should not seem superior.

Returning now to fig. 8.5, the reasons for the contradictory findings of the different authors are quickly revealed. Since position P' (resulting from protection) has more of good y and less of good x than position T (resulting from free trade), there is no reason in principle why, on the Paretian value judgment, any non-contradictory welfare comparisons should be possible. Though it is by no means a necessary outcome, in our example (fig. 8.5) the position under protection (P') passes both the Kaldor–Hicks and Scitovsky reversal criteria; yet, as has just been shown, no unambiguous welfare conclusion can be drawn even on the Paretian value judgments without a *specific* social-welfare function. Only if by some chance the free-trade position were to lie within the quadrant $aP'b$ could it be said that protection was *potentially* associated with greater social welfare according to the Paretian value judgments.

Bardhan [6], who has also participated in this controversy, uses for his welfare comparisons a procedure developed by Johnson [11]. This consists of trying to break down the effect of protection (whether there are domestic distortions or not) into two categories: the effect involving a reallocation of consumption; and the effect involving a reallocation of production. However, the measurement of these two effects requires choosing one particular distribution of incomes (and hence the pattern of prices) as the most desirable; the distribution chosen by both Johnson and Bardhan is that which prevails if free trade is permitted. The effect of the reallocation of consumption then is the difference between the value of total consumption (of all commodities) under free trade and that under protection—each being valued at the set of prices which prevail under free trade. Similarly, the effect involving the reallocation of production is the difference between the value of total production (of all commodities) under free trade and that under protection.

However, it is not clear why the prices prevailing under free trade (with their implied distribution of welfare) should be the evaluating ratios for these effects. We have established in Chapter V that when two bundles of goods (one of which does *not* contain more of everything) are being compared no unambiguous welfare conclusions can in general be drawn, even on the Paretian welfare judgments, unless a *specific* social-welfare function is given. Hence though the categories introduced by Johnson are useful, they do not eliminate the need to have a *specific* welfare function if unambiguous statements about costs and benefits of protection are to be made. Johnson also mentions that if the protecting country's terms of trade are not independent of the volume of trade, then the effects of the changes in the terms of trade will have to be included along with the consumption reallocation and production reallocation effects. However, as we noted in the last section, when the terms of trade are affected by the volume of trade the optimum tariff cannot be defined without choosing a particular distribution of income as the most desirable; that is, a specific welfare function has to be given.

More needs to be said about the methods of welfare evaluation used by Bhågwati and Ramaswami [5]. Apart from working with non-intersecting community indifference curves without having assumed that a *specific* welfare function is given, they also apply an alleged corollary of the general Paretian second-best theorem [15] in order to compare different situations. According to this alleged corollary, if one of the necessary conditions for a Paretian optimum is not satisfied in one situation, and if one or more conditions are not satisfied in another situation, then there is no *a priori* way of deciding which of the two is better on any grounds. We have already, in Chapter III, criticised the use of the second-best theorem as a welfare criterion and shown that the cited corollary of that theorem is wrong. Bhagwati and Ramaswami argue thus: We know that in an economy the necessary condition for a Paretian optimum is that for any two goods and for all individuals and firms the domestic marginal rate of subjective substitution (DRS) should equal the domestic marginal rate of technical transformation (DRT) and that each should equal the foreign marginal rate of transformation (FRT) or, in other words, the world price ratio. Now if there is a wage differential at home, then with free trade, DRS = FRT ≠ DRT. Bhagwati and Ramaswami argue that since protection will make DRT ≠ FRT ≠ DRS, it is neither necessarily superior nor necessarily inferior to free trade. They wrongly go on to argue that since a tax-cum-subsidy on the use of labour combined with free trade would make DRS = FRT = DRT, it is necessarily superior to a tariff.

As we noted in Chapter III, Section 2, this procedure of using the second-best theorem as a welfare criterion is open to some serious objections. First, as was shown there, the cited corollary of the second-best theorem does not follow from the theorem. When there is a wage differential both free trade and protection involve the violation of some Paretian necessary condition; therefore, Bhagwati and Ramaswami conclude that neither is necessarily superior to the other. Yet this need not necessarily be true. If there is a wage differential between sectors the result of the distortion is described by Bhagwati and Ramaswami as DRT ≠ DRS; but this is not the basic result of the wage-differential. The basic result is that the

206

cost-minimising behaviour by the producers does not take the economy to the (true) technological production possibility frontier. In fig. 8.6, because of the wage-differential, the economy is at point L within its production-possibility frontier (and *as a further consequence* of this, the marginal rate of substitution between the two goods, even if it is equal for all consumers, cannot equal the true DRT). Suppose a subsidy on the use of labour in the high-wage sector takes the economy to its technical production-possibility curve

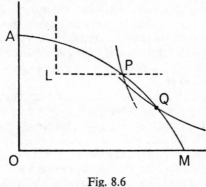

Fig. 8.6

$APQM$; but that (perhaps because of some redistributive measures) the MRS is still not equal to the DRT. The outcome in such a case might be something like the positions P or Q—at either of which a Scitovsky community indifference curve cuts the production-possibility curve. At each of the positions L, P, and Q, then, at least one necessary condition for a Paretian optimum is violated. Yet P *actually* dominates L in a technological sense, and Q *potentially* dominates L in a technological sense.

Secondly, this procedure apparently leads to the conclusion that once *all* the necessary conditions for a Paretian optimum have been fulfilled, there would necessarily be an improvement from the standpoint of social welfare. Yet it is a false conclusion, because we know from Chapter II that a Paretian optimum is not necessarily superior to any Paretian non-optimum. For example, when the price for a factor differs between sectors a Paretian optimum can be obtained by allowing free trade and by putting a rightly calculated subsidy on the use of the factor in the sector where its price is unduly high. However, it would be wrong to conclude—as Bhagwati and Ramaswami do—that the subsidy solution is necessarily superior to the other Paretian sub-optimal solutions, even on the basis of the Paretian value judgments. See Chapter II, Section 5, where it is proved that a Paretian optimum is not necessarily superior to *any* sub-optimal position; consult also fig. 2.3 and pp. 21–22.

We should now analyse the welfare conclusions which Haberler [9] arrived at in his discussion of a related problem in a famous article. It is assumed that there is complete factor immobility between the (two) sectors of an economy, but factor prices are assumed to be perfectly flexible. Haberler had claimed that under such circumstances the position under free trade is superior to that under protection. Recently Johnson [12] has made a similar claim. Once complete factor immobility is assumed, only that point on the production-possibility curve is attainable which happens to be chosen to begin with. However, if perfect flexibility of factor prices is also assumed, then that production point is compatible with any commodity price ratio.

In fig. 8.7 P is the fixed point of production. The line HH' represents the domestic price ratio with prohibitive protection. The economy then is on the community indifference curve I_1. With free trade PT is both the internal and external price ratio. Production still remains at point P, but after some trade the consumption point is T, where the economy is on the community indifference curve I_2. Haberler declared the position under free trade to be superior to the position under protection, because 'by redistributing income it would be possible to make everybody better off' [9, p. 229]. And Johnson claims '. . . the country would enjoy a consumption or exchange gain from trade even if production remained at the closed-economy equilibrium point' [12, p. 13]. However, both these claims are unjustified. Though the position after trade, as compared to prohibitive protection, will always pass the Scitovsky reversal criterion, it may or may not pass the Kaldor–Hicks criterion. In our example (in fig. 8.7, point T as compared to point P), the free-trade position does not pass the Kaldor–Hicks criterion. In other words, it may or may not be possible to redistribute, by lump-sum transfers, the income resulting under free trade to make at least one person better off and nobody worse off than they are under protection. On the other hand, it is never possible to redistribute the income resulting under protection and make at least one person better off and nobody worse off than they are under free trade; this remains true also with complete factor immobility: that is, as before, the free-trade position (point T in fig. 8.7) always passes the Scitovsky reversal criterion. In any case, as we argued in Chapter V, even if the free-trade position passed both the Kaldor–Hicks and the Scitovsky criteria, no valid comparison of the relative social-welfare merits of any two positions can be made in general, unless one position has more of at least one good and no less of any other, or unless a *specific* social welfare function is given. This latter requirement is what Balogh [3] can be interpreted to have been arguing for.

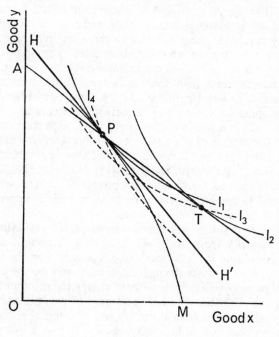

Fig. 8.7

There can be other similar distortions in the domestic economy; e.g. in the product market, prices might differ from the marginal costs. It can be shown that in all these cases as well no *general* proposition is possible about the *necessary* superiority, even on the Paretian value judgments, of the *actual* outcome of protection or free trade, or of either of these combined with action to remove the specific distortions—if such action is possible. All this does *not* amount to an argument for protection, but only emphasises the need for scrutiny of each specific case on its own merits and according to the given social considerations.

209

8.4 INFANT-INDUSTRY ARGUMENTS

The statements about the gains from trade have always been proved in a static context where no change in production techniques or tastes is allowed. But in real life these things often change through time, and sometimes how much and in what direction they would change are influenced by the extent and kind of foreign trade of a country. Through international demonstration effects in consumption, production, management methods, and research, international trade may accelerate the growth of an economy over time. On the other hand, foreign trade may sometimes thwart certain possibilities of growth; this is the basis of the infant-industry argument.

Management learns from the experience of production; in some industries and in some countries during some particular phase of their development this fact may be particularly important. To begin with, the costs in a new industry might be so high that unless it is protected (through a tariff on imports of substitutes or a subsidy on its production, etc.) for some years, it will either never get started or never get firmly established. See Viner [18]. However, this fact alone cannot be a sufficient argument for protection. There will be the further need to compare—according to some socially approved objectives and priorities as well as a rate of discount—the discounted present value of future net benefits from protection with that of future net benefits from free trade. There is an economic argument for protection only if the former value is greater than the latter.

The reduction in costs through experience may be confined to a firm itself or may be available without charge to the other firms. In the latter case they are external economies of production; whereas in the former case they are various forms of internal economies of large-scale production. It has been argued [12] that if through time only the internal (and no external) economies are generated, then there is no need for investigating the possibility of an economic (infant-industry) argument for protection, because the firms' desire to maximise profits would see to it that they expand for exploiting the future possibilities, if the discounted present value of the revenues is greater than the discounted present values of the costs.

But this argument is faulty on a number of grounds. First, firms might use a different rate of discount from what the social-welfare function lays down. Secondly, firms may lack the kind of knowledge about related investments which the authority that considers giving protection might have (see Chapter III, Section 3, for an extensive discussion of this point). Thirdly, the foregoing argument assumes well-organised, perfectly functioning capital markets.

210

But in fact this is far too unrealistic an assumption for a number of countries. The infant-industry argument for protection arises from each of these three reasons, as well as from the possible existence of external economies of production; but these reasons only establish a presumption, which then needs to be investigated in each case.

8.5 CONCLUSIONS

The main purpose of this chapter was rather abstract; it was to examine the logical foundations of some *a priori welfare* generalisations about international trade, ignoring all our fundamental objections to such *a priori welfare* comparisons. We have found that the statements about gains from trade need to be much more qualified than is the practice in the relevant literature. However, our purpose has not been to argue against international trade or even to imply that the gains in some sense from it are less frequent than economists have believed. In any case, a proper *welfare* assessment of international trade can only be done with reference to a country's specific social welfare function. This is so, if for no other reason, because the opening (or existence) of trade is likely to affect the income and wealth of some groups adversely, though it improves the economic means of some others.

REFERENCES FOR CHAPTER VIII

[1] R. E. Baldwin, 'Equilibrium in International Trade: A Diagrammatic Analysis', *Quarterly Journal of Economics*, 1948

[2] R. E. Baldwin, 'The New Welfare Economics and Gains in International Trade', *Quarterly Journal of Economics*, 1952

[3] T. Balogh, 'Welfare and Free Trade: A Reply', *Economic Journal*, 1951; also reprinted

[4] J. N. Bhagwati, 'Some Recent Trends in the Pure Theory of International Trade', in Roy Harrod (ed.), *International Trade Theory in a Developing World*, London, 1963

[5] J. N. Bhagwati and V. K. Ramaswami, 'Domestic Distortions, Tariffs and the Theory of Subsidy', *Journal of Political Economy*, 1963

[6] P. K. Bhardan, 'Factor Market Disequilibrium and the Theory of Protection', *Oxford Economic Papers*, 1964

[7] A. G. Ford, 'The Gains from Trade Yet Again', *Indian Economic Journal*, 1967

[8] J. de V. Graaff, 'On Optimum Tariff Structures', *Review of Economic Studies*, 1949–50

[9] G. Haberler, 'Some Problems in the Pure Theory of International Trade', *Economic Journal*, 1950

[10] E. Hagen, 'An Economic Justification for Protectionism', *Quarterly Journal of Economics*, 1958
[11] H. G. Johnson, 'The Cost of Protection and the Scientific Tariff', *Journal of Political Economy*, 1960
[12] H. G. Johnson, 'Optimal Trade Intervention in the Presence of Domestic Distortions', in R. E. Baldwin and others, *Trade, Growth and Balance of Payments*, Essays in Honour of G. Haberler
[13] M. C. Kemp, 'The Mill-Bastable Infant Industry Dogma', *Journal of Political Economy*, 1960
[14] M. C. Kemp, 'The Gain from International Trade', *Economic Journal*, 1962
[15] R. G. Lipsey and K. J. Lancaster, 'The General Theory of Second Best', *Review of Economic Studies*, 1956-7
[16] P. A. Samuelson, 'The Gain from International Trade', *Canadian Journal of Economics and Political Science*, 1939; reprinted in H. S. Ellis and L. A. Metzler (eds.), *Readings in the Theory of International Trade*, Philadelphia, 1949
[17] P. A. Samuelson, 'The Gain from International Trade Once Again', *Economic Journal*, 1962
[18] T. Scitovsky, 'A Reconsideration of the Theory of Tariffs', *Review of Economic Studies*, 1941; reprinted in H. S. Ellis and L. A. Metzler (eds.), *Readings in the Theory of International Trade*, Philadelphia, 1949
[19] J. Viner, 'Stability and Progress: The Poorer Countries' Problem', in D. C. Hague (ed.), *Stability and Progress in the World Economy*, London, 1958

IX

WELFARE AND ECONOMIC DEVELOPMENT

Some of what has gone before has relevance to the economics of development; this is particularly true of Chapters V, VI, and VII. To make this chapter entirely self-sufficient would require quite a lot of repetition. Hence it has been decided to refer the reader for certain details to the relevant parts of the preceding chapters, and only give an outline of some of the topics here; this applies particularly to the next two sections, which are about the concept of economic development and the relevance of the theory of resource allocation to the economics of development. On the mechanics of growth side there are unresolved controversies about the scope of planning, and who is to do the planning if there is to be any; about 'the most effective' or 'optimal' pattern of investment allocation; and about the choice of 'optimal' techniques. It is not always appreciated that no meaningful analysis of any of these subjects can proceed without relying on some explicit or implicit value judgments of one kind or another. In the fourth section we examine the normative relativity of some of the alternative measures usually mentioned for promoting economic development.

9.1 THE CONCEPT OF ECONOMIC DEVELOPMENT

Economic development obviously has something to do with the growth of national product. However, there are two sets of problems here: the first concerns the objectivity of the measurement of changes in national product, and the second is about the relation between national product and economic development.

Measurement of changes in national income or product can be looked at from at least two standpoints; they can either be thought of as measures of changes in physical production potential of an economy or as indicators of changes in the welfare level of the community. For each of these two standpoints there are again two important categories: *ex ante* evaluation and *ex post* evaluation. If the relative distribution of incomes remained the same the welfare interpretation would not be so difficult. But in practice, national product seldom changes in this way; there is always a change in the relative distribution of incomes. Again, if the outputs of some goods

213

increased without those of any other goods declining a productive potential interpretation may be possible. But even such a change in national product is rare.

Both the *ex ante* and *ex post* welfare evaluations of national-income data were examined in Chapter V. Regarding *ex ante* welfare evaluations, we concluded there that no consistent *a priori* welfare criteria are available for the purpose. Regarding *ex post* welfare evaluations, we showed that even if the national product in the second year is higher than in the first according to both the Laspeyre and Paasche quantity index numbers, then one can infer only that on the Scitovsky criterion the second year will rank higher than the first, but that on the Kaldor–Hicks criterion the second year may or may not rank higher. Only the main conclusion of that discussion is repeated here; for further details the reader is referred to Chapter V, Section 5. We have also argued against the use of *any a priori* welfare criterion; for this critique the reader is referred to Chapter VI. We can repeat here the conclusion of our arguments there that no *welfare* evaluation of national-income data is possible without a *specific* well-defined social-welfare function (or some compact list of social objectives and their relative weights). This social-welfare function may be a comment-making social-welfare function of any individual, or it might be the social-welfare function adopted by the decision-makers of the society concerned.

National-income data in most countries tend to be based on the market prices as determined by, among other things, the existing distribution of incomes; hence the need for specific welfare evaluation. Moreover, the market prices do not take into account the externalities of various kinds. As we noted in Chapter IV, some of the externalities may be very relevant to a social-welfare function. Since we have provided an extensive study of externalities already, we need not enlarge upon the subject, except to say that there can be disagreement about whether an externality exists or not. Irrespective of what the majority opinion on some such issue is and whether it has been discovered or not, for a comment or recommendation any observer is entitled to his own assessment. For example, in the economically advanced economies there is a keen debate at present about the magnitude and importance of the external diseconomies of such things as private cars, tourism, and air transport; according to some people, these things give rise to no externalities, while others think that they do.

If the *ex post* welfare evaluation is of national-income data which stretch over decades, then some further problems arise. Some old commodities are bound to have disappeared, and some entirely new ones would have appeared. The generation is likely to have changed, and it might be argued that the mental and psychological outlook of the new generation might be significantly different. Hence when price–quantity data stretching over long periods are being compared, any welfare interpretation is very much an ethical and philosophical assessment. Cf. Abramovitz [1].

Turning to the production potential interpretation, we need to note that if such an interpretation is based on the market prices, then it, too, would leave out of account external economies and diseconomies of production. For under-developed countries this may be a fairly big source of error, because in the earlier stages of economic development external economies are likely to be rather important—as we noted in Chapter IV. If we ignore this consideration, and also assume that prices reflect marginal costs then Moorsteen [7] has shown that national-product indices can be understood to measure changes in the productive potential of an economy. If it is assumed that for two years the production frontiers are convex and that the production price ratios are equal to the ratios of their marginal costs, then the base-weighted quantity index gives 'an approximation to the true index of relative potential to produce in the actual output proportions' [7, p. 455] of the second year; if a current-weighted quantity index is used, then the approximation obtained is to an index about the output proportions prevailing in the first year.

However, whenever the structure of the economy is changing rather markedly the prices of different years are likely to be so markedly different that comparisons based on different years' prices will give markedly different results. This is because often the industries which experience the largest economies of scale and the incidence of technical improvements are just the industries whose products fall most in prices. Further, for policy purposes it is the *ex ante* estimates of production potential which are often more relevant. Even if explicit welfare considerations are not brought in here, the need for explicit value judgments cannot be ruled out, because there still remains the need to decide on the sectors whose productive capacity should increase and in what proportions.

Different patterns of investment allocations are commonly discussed, assessed, and recommended for general use in the literature on economic development in the light of their assumed contributions to economic growth. This procedure assumes that whatever promotes economic growth (as commonly measured) is good, but we have just seen that it is impossible to obtain an unambiguous measure of national income even in the productive potential sense without specifying which sectors are more important than others.

Once again an explicit social objective function is needed. For example, if there is a high rate of growth (as measured by the market prices of one year or another) consisting of luxury goods it may well be less desirable, according to the appropriate welfare function, than a lower rate of growth (again as measured by the market prices) consisting largely of steel and food production. Even for the industrially advanced countries, Mishan [6] has recently argued that promoting economic growth (as measured by the market prices) may not always be equivalent to promoting welfare, according to certain value judgments.

9.2 IS *A PRIORI* WELFARE THEORY RELEVANT?

It is very common for some economists to cite the theorems of theoretical welfare economics in discussions about economic development. They tend to argue that theoretical welfare economics shows that 'the market' leads to 'the optimum'; and ask how can a poor, underdeveloped economy not require 'optimal allocation' when even the economically advanced countries depend on 'the market' to attain 'economic efficiency'. Our Chapter VI, and particularly its Section 3 on the Concepts of Efficiency, is relevant here. We showed there that the usual concept of 'economic efficiency' is by no means an objective concept, and that an emphasis on it tends to lead to the neglect of the far more important concept of technological efficiency; the latter concept implies the attainment of a country's true production frontier.

Technological efficiency does not require the value judgment of absolute consumer (and producer) sovereignty, as does the usual concept of 'economic efficiency'. The necessary conditions for it are uniform price (if there are no externalities) for a factor of production in all sectors, and genuine cost-minimising behaviour by each producer. This implies that each producer seeks out the technically most efficient production function for his process that the existing technology has to offer. Some studies were cited in Chapter VI, Section 3, which show that in fact this last assumption is very often grossly violated, and that tremendous gains in labour and capital productivity can be obtained by bringing more technical information to the producers and by encouraging them to adopt it. It was further argued in that section that perhaps even more important influences on growth are technical advance and innovations, and that the pursuit of 'economic efficiency' may in fact conflict with the aim of promoting innovations. This is because innovations probably require large firms, but large firms tend to make commodity markets imper-

216

fect. Hence our conclusion is that the concept of 'economic efficiency', and the *a priori* welfare economics as such, have no necessary relevance to the problems of economic development, whereas the concept of technological efficiency has. (For further details of this discussion, the interested reader is referred to Chapter VI, Section 3.)

The *a priori* welfare theory is based on the value judgment that each individual is to be regarded the best judge of his own welfare; hence it rules out any interference in or restriction of the individual consumption and production decisions. This value judgment, which is never very appealing in its absolute form, becomes even less so in the context of discussions about economic development. The value judgment is violated if the rate of national saving and investment is raised above what the individuals would choose on their own, if imports of unessential goods are restricted at a time of foreign-exchange crisis, or if some goods are rationed in the presence of scarcities. Yet the majority of citizens might be willing to approve of these policies *ex ante*. Sometimes the majority might be mildly opposed to some policies before they have been tried, but might be grateful some time after that they were adopted. This is what gives rise to the need for *judicious* leadership; this need exists even under a democracy. The blind repetition of the 'virtues' of the 'completely free' markets—as supposedly proved by *a priori* welfare theory—ignores these facts.

Even if we were to disregard the need for some element of leadership, our discussions of Chapter IV show that when externalities (some of which give rise to a 'public good') are present the market fails to bring about an allocation which is 'optimal' even according to the value judgment of consumer sovereignty and the other Paretian value judgments. Further, the Paretian optimal allocation brought about by the market—*when* it can bring such an allocation about—is Paretian optimal only with reference to one particular distribution of incomes. This rather obvious fact is sometimes ignored in some economists' advice to underdeveloped countries; they tend to suggest that any redistribution of incomes is itself an interference with 'the working of the market'. Of course, it is true—as we showed in Chapter III—that redistributive measures which are feasible will also violate some of the necessary conditions for Paretian optimality. It requires some further political and ethical value judgments —rather than economic expertise—to decide in such a situation that it is the redistributive aim which must be sacrificed rather than the goal of attaining a Paretian optimum.

The part of the *a priori welfare* theory which takes account of the element of time (and which was discussed in Chapter II, Section 10) has no more necessary relevance to the problems of growth than has the static form of that theory; further, this so-called dynamic form rules out uncertainty, which is a basic element in policy decisions about growth. In Chapter II we also explained how the concept of technological efficiency may be applied over time; however, since no model has so far been constructed which takes imperfect knowledge into account, their relevance is somewhat limited. Related to that model of technological efficiency over time are some theorems about Neumann balanced growth and turnpike theory; the degree of their relevance to a growth problem is to be judged according to the degree of realism of their assumptions or the reliability of their predictions. No general criticism is implied here of any *positive* dynamic theories of growth (however unrealistic their factual assumptions), but only of *a priori welfare* theory of one kind or another, static or dynamic, which might be supposed to have general policy implications for economic growth.

9.3 SOME DEVELOPMENT CONTROVERSIES

We turn now to examine the problems of investment planning and the choice of techniques, and show that the failure to recognise the necessity of starting with some value judgments or other and making them explicit has often led to controversies about the wrong points.

Writing about the time when it had been amply demonstrated that the market, working on its own, could not get the industrialised economies out of the depression, Keynes hardly needed to argue that his remedies presumed the value judgment that government interference in the national economy is not necessarily a bad thing. But his remedies do require this value judgment. A similar value judgment has to be the starting-point if government action or guidance in investment planning in the underdeveloped countries is to be accepted or advocated.

What about the degree of government interference in an underdeveloped country? In such an economy the major economic problems are not confined to avoiding fluctuations in prices and employment and a recurring deficit in the balance of payments—though these are serious enough problems—but also include the basic problem of changing a stagnant, tradition-bound economic system into an expanding one. This is a more fundamental and widespread task than is sometimes assumed. It is not simply a matter of monetary and fiscal inducements designed to raise the proportion of annual investment in the national income. Such inducements might be sufficient if there were in such a country a sufficiently large middle class, an entrepreneurial group of the required vitality in that middle class, and the necessary financial and economic institutions. This is why in an underdeveloped country a government often has to start a number of enterprises on its own. This itself would give rise to some government planning.

But what makes more detailed planning necessary is that—rather like during a war—so much needs to be done so quickly. Most economic activities are interdependent, e.g. production of steel depends on the steady availability of iron ore, coke, transport facilities for raw materials and finished goods, an expectation of steady demand, and some confidence that the necessary components which are not available at home would be importable from abroad. In a developed country a potential entrepreneur can take all these things for granted. In an underdeveloped country there are few such potential entrepreneurs, and they cannot take these things for granted. Because so much needs to be done to create new economic units in a short space of time, the repercussions are widespread and important; there could easily be substantial and unnecessary waste.

A system of exchanging information and formulating production decisions is needed which would work more promptly than the un-aided 'market mechanism'. The function of this system would be to ensure that factors are where they are needed most, so that the ratio between the marginal physical products of any two factors is the same in each use, and that there is sufficient knowledge everywhere about the best-practice techniques. In other words, the function of the system of exchanging information and co-ordinating decisions could be to ensure that the economy attains its true production frontier.

Even if our arguments (which are in fact assumptions about some empirical facts which can in principle be tested) establish a technical case for some form of planning and co-ordination, a value judgment is required about whether such a means of attaining the economy's production frontier is acceptable or not; and a further value judgment is required for choosing between planning by a private body or a government—and again about choosing the form of government itself.

The next decision to make is, of course, about the amount of investment to be undertaken. This is so obviously a matter which depends on value judgments that few economists fail to realise that it is not a matter of economics so much as politics. Though the rate of growth (somehow measured) partly depends on the rate of invest-ment, investment itself implies foregone consumption. It is a matter of weighing the claims of the present against the future. Some economists think that the best policy is for individuals to be able to decide this on their own, whereas others consider that in the interests of the future generations it is the government which should decide on the claims between the present and the future. It is also pointed out by some that there is an important direct *non-market* relationship among individuals here. We have already discussed this topic in some detail in Chapter VII, Section 3; the interested reader is referred to that discussion.

We turn now to the problem of the sectoral allocation of investment and the choice of techniques. These two problems are different in principle, yet merge into each other in practice. The difference in principle is this: apart from comparing costs of producing something at home with the costs of importing it (which is an economic consideration—though the costs may have some non-economic aspects requiring value judgments), the problem of sectoral allocation is largely a problem of politics; it depends more on having a set of social objectives and their relative weights than on anything else. Sectoral allocation is a matter of guns or butter: it concerns questions such as how much to spend on heavy industry, consumer industry, and agriculture, etc. Here economics *can* help in reaching decisions only after some sort of social aims and their relative weights are given. The conflict between the future and present consumption also comes in here—for example, in the choice between heavy industry and consumer industry.

Choice of techniques, on the other hand, can in principle be a matter of only technical or just economic considerations. Given the decision on what has to be produced (or on some social objectives), they need to be so produced that the combinations of factors used would minimise costs at the properly adjusted prices of the factors. Carefully adjusted prices of factors are such as properly reflect their relative scarcities, in the sense that at that set of prices all factors or at least labour is fully employed. But, of course, labour may be so abundant relative to capital that its price would have to be lower than even a subsistence wage. Under such circumstances family enterprises may shelter disguised unemployed, even though their marginal product may be less than the village wage-rate for labour, and some urban employers might pay a higher wage-rate than that at which they can get all the labour they need because they want to ensure a certain minimum of physical efficiency from their workers.

Because of the need, then, to 'adjust' factor prices, the problem of the choice of techniques does not remain a purely economic one in the context of a labour-surplus economy. Further, often the technical range of combining factors in the production of certain industrial products is more or less fixed—especially for the underdeveloped countries, which have to import the machinery to make such goods, and consequently have little say in the initial designing and development stages of the equipment. Because of these limited opportunities of substitution, decision to produce a certain product also fixes the choice of techniques of production—and the two problems of sectoral allocation and the choice of techniques tend to merge into each other. Yet the two problems are different in principle and must be kept distinct. We shall examine now some of the criteria which have been proposed for the choice of techniques.

The Rate of Turnover Criterion

In the controversy about criteria for the choice of techniques the very first proposed criterion (the rate of turnover) slurred over the distinction between the two problems of the choice of techniques and sectoral allocation. It was proposed by Polak [12] that a war-devastated economy trying to make a quick recovery should undertake only such investments as maximise the output–capital ratio. The most serious criticism of this criterion has been that such an economy may well be in urgent need (value judgment of course!) of building up public utilities (railways, etc.) which are very capital intensive, and this criterion would be against them. Now it is—as we have seen—no business of an economic criterion to lay down what sectors should be chosen. But once the sectors have been chosen, it does make fairly good economic sense in an economy with acute shortage of capital, but not of labour, to choose such combinations of factors as maximise output–capital ratio. However, on technical grounds, too, this criterion had the fault that it would discriminate too heavily against the kind of techniques which give rather a little return for the first two or three years but then a great deal more than any rival techniques. It is essential to have a criterion which incorporates some rate of discount for net annual return in each year of the lives of the projects being compared. See Chapter VII, Section 3.

Discussions in this field have tended to suffer in clarity due to a lack of explicitness about the assumed aims of social policy. It should have been obvious that alternative investment criteria cannot be compared unless the assumed aims and constraints of social policy are explicitly mentioned. This confusion is to some extent a hang-over of the confusion between 'economic efficiency' and 'technological efficiency' which we came across in Section 2. It is likely that the rules for 'optimal' allocation of resources of the *a priori* kind of welfare economics have inspired the confidence that in development economics, too, there ought to be generally valid rules of optimal allocation of investment. But this search is equally futile. There can only be rules of efficient allocation of investment in the light of some given aims of social policy; these rules would be relative to those aims—not generally valid. Indeed, in the context of growth economics, more value judgments are required (e.g. regarding the choice of the time profile of consumption) than in static economics.

The Rate of Surplus Criteria

It is instructive to examine a common characteristic of the contributions in this field of Galenson and Leibenstein [5], Dobb [3], and Sen [13]. In their view, 'maximisation of output' and 'maximisation of the rate of growth of output over say the next 10 years' are taken to be conflicting aims. At first sight this conflict appears odd, because normally with net output at its maximum in any year absolute net investment can be as great as possible under the circumstances. In other words, with a full-employment-like situation in the economy the amount of investment that can be undertaken (at constant prices) is a function of the real natural product. Other things being equal, maximisation of the rate of investment should then help in maximising the rate of growth of national product. But a special set of assumptions was introduced. It was assumed that workers consume all their wages and that all savings came out of profits. With this special assumption, it is no longer true that the set of techniques which maximises output leads to maximum rate of growth, but that set of techniques which maximises the share of profit in the national product. It may be that with the given endowments of capital and labour, etc., more output would result from some relatively labour-intensive techniques. But since this would mean a relatively large share of wages in the product, the investible surplus will be smaller than with an alternative technique which provides a smaller total output but a greater relative share of profits. This is because it has been assumed that all wages are consumed and all profits saved.

The implied factual assumption is that the rate of savings and, therefore, investment in an underdeveloped economy is a function of only the distribution of national income between wages and profits; that fiscal policy cannot do the job at a lower social cost. The social cost would take into account such things as effects on the distribution of incomes and the administrative machinery, etc. It has been made out, by Sen [13], for example, that to deny that the rate of savings depends only on the distribution of national income between wages and profits is to assume that there is no conflict between present and future consumption. But this is incorrect; for, even if

222

from some special kind of allocation there were no profits at all, but only wages, there would still be the need to decide on how much taxation (or deficit financing) to undertake to provide for investment. (It is to be remembered that deficit financing is basically another form of taxation—though often not so desirable a form.)

We come now to the most important aspect of this kind of criterion. This aspect is normative and political, but has gone unnoticed so far. The criterion also implies a special value judgment: namely that the relative distribution of income among families is not a relevant consideration, or at any rate not an important consideration, for the social welfare function; because, otherwise, as we choose the kind of techniques which maximise the relative share of profits, we are also making the distribution of real income less equal than before. (Though, of course, we do satisfy the Paretian criterion of some persons better off without anybody being worse off.) This is obviously a value judgment—there is nothing in positive economics itself to justify it.

Another criticism of this rate-of-surplus criterion is that, since everything is measured in money terms (and presumably at market prices), investible 'surplus' becomes a uni-dimensional concept; any equal rise in the value of the surplus is equally welcome. Yet a rise in the surplus of certain goods (e.g. basic consumption goods and capital goods) may be considered by a social-welfare function much more important than that of, say, certain luxury or semi-luxury goods, even though the money value of the surplus as determined by the market prices is the same. This is because market prices only reflect relative scarcities as determined, among other things, by the present distribution of incomes. Social values of goods may be different from their market values. Further, sometimes it is easier to take decisions in terms of the different kinds of surpluses needed rather than in uni-dimensional value terms. This would be the case in times of acute scarcities when possibilities of extensive and quick exchange of goods through foreign trade are limited.

In short, though, from the social-welfare standpoint 'investible surplus' may be an important consideration, there may also be other important considerations, such as the distribution of incomes and the choice of which kinds of surplus; these other considerations must also be mentioned in a logically consistent analysis of the role of surpluses.

The Maximising of Employment Criterion

At the other extreme we have writers like Fei and Ranis [4], who advocate the criterion of maximising employment in the industrial sector, subject to some output constraint. Now in an industrially advanced country, given a certain state of knowledge of techniques, maximising employment is normally a condition of being able to maximise total output. (This is an empirical judgment, not necessarily always true.) But in the context of a labour-surplus economy it is possible to argue that this correspondence breaks down because of the imbalance in the factors' proportions. There is so much labour as compared to the other factors of production that, given the present state of techniques, an attempt to give employment to everybody would result in total output less than it would be otherwise. This is because capital will have to be spread thinly and inferior techniques will have to be adopted. In such an economy, then, a choice has to be made between maximising employment and maximising output.

If full employment were desired in such an economy it would obviously be not for the economic reason of increasing output, but for the social reason of wanting a more equal distribution of incomes. If it could be assumed that a desired distribution of incomes is possible to achieve through administrative measures, then the rational policy would still be to maximise output (assuming that investible surplus is a function of administration as well and not just the techniques). However, in an underdeveloped country with limited administrative resources and exceedingly large numbers of the unemployed of various categories it is difficult to organise unemployment relief of any kind. Therefore, it is possible that in such an economy, particularly during periods of pronounced stress among the poorer classes, society might choose techniques (in some sectors) which are a compromise between maximum output and maximum employment, but which help to bring about the desired redistribution of real incomes.

We might sum up this section thus. Our argument has been that in the development field, as much as in any other, no *practical* economic problem can be meaningfully discussed without *explicitly* starting with some social objectives and some idea of their relative weights. Arguments and criteria which are paraded as technical, economic, or non-controversial tests of suitability or efficiency, etc., inevitably beg a number of value judgments which need to be made explicit. In the problem of choice of techniques, one fundamental element is that some costs and returns will be stretched over several future time periods, so that the use of some socially approved rate of discount is essential. Further, other than just commercial costs and returns need to be taken into account. In short, investment sectors and the techniques have to be chosen on the basis of suitably designed cost–benefit analysis, as was argued at length in Chapter VII.

The irony is that we are sometimes presented with accounts of cost–benefit analysis which seem to suggest that such an analysis must necessarily proceed on the basis of the market value of things; but there is no such necessity in logic. What elements are to be considered as costs and what are to be considered as benefits and how they are to be evaluated are questions which can be answered only by a specific social welfare function of a given country in a given situation. See Chapter VI.

CONCLUSIONS

We have given reasons to show that the concept of economic development is properly regarded as a normative concept—especially when it is viewed as an objective of *ex ante* policy. We have also argued that the concept of 'economic efficiency'—as defined in theoretical welfare economics—has no necessary relevance to the policies for promoting economic development, whereas the concept of technological efficiency has. Finally, we have shown that some of the controversies in the development literature have been about the wrong points, because the underlying value judgments were not made explicit.

REFERENCES FOR CHAPTER IX

[1] M. Abramovitz, 'The Welfare Interpretation of Secular Trends in National Income and Product', in M. Abramovitz, *The Allocation of Resources*, Berkeley, 1959

[2] A. Bergson, *The National Income of Soviet Russia Since 1928*, Cambridge, Mass., 1961

[3] Maurice Dobb, 'A Note on the So-called Degree of Capital-Intensity in Underdeveloped Countries', *Economic Applique*, 1954; reprinted in his *On Economic Theory and Socialism*, London, 1955

[4] J. C. H. Fei and G. Ranis, 'Innovation Capital Accumulation, and Economic Development', *American Economic Review*, 1963

[5] W. Galenson and H. Leibenstein, 'Investment Criteria, Productivity and Economic Development', *Quarterly Journal of Economics*, 1955

[6] E. J. Mishan, *The Costs of Economic Growth*, London, 1967

[7] R. H. Moorsteen, 'On Measuring Productive Potential and Relative Efficiency', *Quarterly Journal of Economics*, 1961

[8] C. A. Moser, *The Measurement of Levels of Living, with Special Reference to Jamaica*, London, 1957

[9] H. Myint, 'Economic Theory and Underdeveloped Countries', in K. Martin and J. Knapp (eds.), *The Teaching of Development Economics*, London, 1967

[10] S. K. Nath, 'The Theory of Balanced Growth', *Oxford Economic Papers*, 1962

[11] S. K. Nath, 'Welfare Economics, Economic Growth and the Choice of Techniques', *Journal of Development Studies*, 1968

[12] J. J. Polak, 'Balance of Payments Problems of Countries Reconstructing with the Help of Foreign Loans', *Quarterly Journal of Economics*, 1955

[13] A. K. Sen, *The Choice of Techniques*, Oxford, 1960

X
CONCLUSIONS

A question of policy in any subject can only be discussed in the light of what is to be the *aim* of action; some statement about what is suitable or desirable is needed. We may choose to examine economic policies according to their effects on the welfare of the individuals composing a certain social group. This is not the only possible stand that an economist could take; for example, somebody might want to analyse the economic policies of a country according to their effects on 'military strength' somehow defined. But let us adopt the value judgment that economic policies in any country should be judged according to their effects on general welfare, because any other aim for social policy is bound to be ethically less attractive. To this extent it seems justified to use the label 'welfare economics' for the part of economics where the *application* of positive economic theories to actual problems is considered.

The determinants of welfare, or the social objectives, can only be decided with reference to a particular social context, and on the basis of some explicit political, social, and ethical considerations. We have distinguished between the comment-making and decision-making roles of a social-welfare function; and argued that for the former role everybody is entitled to his value judgments, whether they are 'widely acceptable' or not, whereas for the latter the established decision-making mechanism is the arbiter. We have further argued that for either of these roles a social-welfare function need not always be a precisely defined mathematical function; often only an explicit statement of the more important aims of social policy, with some idea of their relative weights, is all that is required. In particular, the concept of something called an 'economic-welfare function', expressed in terms of the individual utility indicators, is not likely to be of any practical use; these individual utility indicators (unless they are ethical assessments by the comment-maker or the decision-maker) can in fact never be known. We also argued that it is much more meaningful and practical to adopt the convention that distributive judgments are to be expressed in terms of money incomes (with some eye on prices). See Chapter VI, Section 2, for further discussion of these points.

Since the aims of social policy are necessarily political and ethical and may vary from one society to another, there can be no *general*

227

principles regarding desirable allocations of economic resources—except perhaps at the technological level on certain assumptions; see Chapter II, Section 2 and Chapter VI, Section 3. *A priori* welfare economics is based on an attempt to get round this difficulty by deriving general, non-controversial, and (almost) objective principles of 'optimum' allocation from some seemingly 'widely acceptable' value judgments. We have argued (in Chapter VI, Section 1) that this attempt is based on doubtful logic. The derived principles of allocation are necessarily political and ethical. Moreover, it has never been shown by anybody that the relevant value judgments really are more widely acceptable in some society than any other conceivable set of value judgments; nor has it ever been convincingly argued in the light of all their implications that they are morally impelling. (If we adopt a series of economic policies which make the richer group richer but leave the poorer group at the same absolute level then according to a Pareto-type social welfare function—i.e. a function which conforms with all the Paretian value judgments—we would be necessarily raising the level of social welfare.) Our conclusion, then, is that any *a priori welfare* model—static or dynamic—is invalid. It is to be emphasised that our arguments have not been against dynamic positive theories but only against *a priori* welfare economics, dynamic or static. Incidentally, we also showed (in Chapter III, Section 3) that the standard static model of welfare—even if all its other presumptions were granted—is inapplicable once the inevitable imperfections of knowledge which are likely to exist in any real situation are recognised.

At a number of points in this book we have sought to evaluate the efficacy of the market to achieve certain objectives. Indeed, traditional welfare economics is a system designed to show that *on certain assumptions, and on certain value judgments*, the market mechanism at equilibrium is some sort of an 'optimum'. If the assumed initial conditions of the theory could be empirically verified and if the underlying Paretian value judgments (specified in Chapter II, Section 1) of the theory could be justified with reference to a particular society, then the workings of the market mechanism might be said to be particularly useful to the society concerned.

Of course, even for such a society the market mechanism working entirely on its own would not necessarily take it to *the* social optimum—i.e. the unique arrangement of factors and goods which is considered the most desirable in the light of the basic value judgments accepted by the society. For, even when those value judgments are Paretian, it does not necessarily imply that the state of the relative distribution of incomes and wealth (or of utility, economic welfare, or welfare) among the individuals does not matter at all; such a supposition is not true of even the Pareto-type social welfare functions. (See Chapter II, Section 5.) When all the Paretian value judgments are acceptable and feasability problems do not exist, the socially most desirable state of affairs has to be a Paretian optimum. *However,* this does not mean that just any equilibrium set of prices, salaries, and wages that is brought about by the market is the social optimum. There might still be a need for taxes and subsidies to alter the distribution of incomes. It may be that such transfers of purchasing power would spoil some of the necessary marginal conditions for Pareto optimality. A popular way of expressing this possibility is to say that the Government's attempt to change the distribution of incomes might adversely affect some groups' economic incentives to work, save, and invest. However, as we showed in Chapter II, even if that possibility exists, the socially most desired position for the economy, even when the Paretian value judgments are accepted, might yet require fiscal and other measures to change the distribution of incomes from the pattern that the market-mechanism on its own would bring about. Thus the social optimum may well not coincide with a Paretian optimum. What this establishes, then, is that even if there were to be perfect competition in all markets, no uncertainty, and no unemployment, and even if all the Paretian value judgments were acceptable (and none other)—even then there is no case for completely undiluted *laissez-faire* of a kind which would rule out even distributive measures.

But of course, for a realistic evaluation we must remove the assumptions of perfect knowledge and perfectly competitive markets. If some firms are rather large compared to the size of the industry, then—whatever the other merits of the situation—the price of the commodity may no longer be equal to the marginal cost, and the market mechanism will therefore not result in an allocation of resources which is optimal in the Paretian sense. Now, only if the State interferes with the market and somehow compels each producer to charge a price equal to marginal cost, could a Paretian optimum emerge.

Similarly, when the assumption of perfect knowledge is dropped there is no longer a guarantee that a unique price would always emerge for a homogeneous product. Moreover, with uncertainty, sometimes even some important interdependence of the profitability of some economic ventures may remain unknown to individual producers so that they fail to expand when in fact they need to if the society is to reach its technological frontier. The third consequence of recognising uncertainty is that information (about new techniques, etc.) now

229

becomes a commodity; since the marginal cost of the dissemination of information is almost zero, technological efficiency requires that information about all inventions and innovations should be freely available to all producers. But this is not compatible with patent rights, nor perhaps with any private business at all, because with a private business there will always be a motive to keep discoveries secret, whether there is a patent right or not. Each one of the three difficulties raised by uncertainty can be removed *in theory* by state intervention. The state could require to see all major investment proposals and also explore investment possibilities itself—and then make all the relevant information available to all potential entrepreneurs or its own managers. Similarly, the state could undertake all scientific research and then make its results freely available to all; or it could buy new discoveries and inventions from whoever made them and then make them freely available. (For a further discussion of the consequences of recognising uncertainty, see Chapter III, Section 3.)

If externalities (which were analysed in Chapter IV) are present, then for the more important of them at least, state needs to impose some carefully defined taxes and subsidies, even if all social decisions are to be based on the Paretian value judgments. A special form of consumers' externalities on consumers leads to the existence of 'public goods'; if such a good is made available for anyone it becomes available for all. (This kind of externality also arises from the possible existence of envy or compassion.) Other examples of public goods are defence, police protection, conservation of natural scenery, afforestation, flood control, removal of litter, and so on. No private business can provide these things, because it will not be able to charge a price to all those who consume them. Hence if they are to be provided they must be provided by the State. When externalities exist, Pareto optimality itself requires active fiscal or other intervention by the State. However, even if the social action is *not* to be *only* on the Paretian value judgments (given in Chapter II, Section 1), the decision-makers or comment-makers may want to take action due to the existence of some externalities. See Chapter IV, Section 7; Chapter VI, Section 2a; and Galbraith [4].

The frame of reference has been largely static so far. Let us now consider economic growth. All the three points mentioned in connection with uncertainty above are again relevant, because uncertainty is particularly important in the context of change and growth. *In theory*, then, there are arguments in favour of state intervention in order to promote economic growth, even on the Paretian value judgments, when uncertainty is recognised. Moreover, as we noted in Chapter VII, Section 3, it may well be that in a number of countries

230

businessmen use a much higher rate of time discount than is desirable according to the adopted social objectives. To the extent that this is true there is again an argument *in theory* in favour of state intervention in the investment decisions in order to promote growth. However, when we are considering economic growth the question of economic incentive becomes very important. Nothing much can be said on this question in theory; it is a problem which needs to be studied with reference to particular countries in the light of their special circumstances. Yet perhaps one can generalise and say that most economic growth springs from the exercise of the economic motive by individuals. Even if this is true, it is not necessarily an argument against state intervention in the market, because even with such intervention various kinds of economic incentives can be given to managers, researchers, and workers. Yet it may be that, as some people argue, the restrictions imposed on the economic motive under some forms of state intervention—such as the inability to accumulate personal property beyond certain limits or buy for one's children 'superior' education—do significantly weaken the possibilities of economic growth. Actual examples can perhaps be found both to support and to contradict this contention. Another unproven, but possibly sometimes true, contention is that under a rather large degree of state intervention there is very little 'freedom' left for the man on the spot to exercise imagination and strike out new paths because there is too much centralisation.

As we noted in Chapter II, the traditional theory of resource allocation is based on the assumption that full employment of all resources is always maintained because all markets are cleared at equilibrium; only *voluntary* unemployment of resources is possible in this system. *This is the assumption of the classical school that Keynes had such a difficult time dislodging.* (See Keynes [7, specially ch. 2].) However, today hardly anybody believes that the market mechanism, working entirely on its own, can be relied upon never to let rather large-scale *involuntary* unemployment arise and be perpetuated.

In our discussion above we have italicised the fact that the various arguments hold *in theory*; *practice* is, of course, a different matter. (See the discussion of practicability of economic policies in Chapter VI, Section 2c.) If in the light of certain value judgments, certain theories, and some knowledge of the relevant empirical conditions a social policy seems the best it does not necessarily follow that the policy will also work out to be the best in actual practice. There is always the need also to examine the practicality of a policy. To some extent this practicality aspect forms a part of the examination of the relevant empirical conditions; but the practicality cannot be fully examined except with special reference to a particular country at a particular time. Hence, it is possible that some of the arguments in favour of state intervention that we established above—on certain value judgments and assumptions—would need to be qualified when administrative possibilities are taken into account. There can be little doubt that some countries are more competent than others in handling certain complications of administration.

This last point links up with an issue which was hotly debated in the thirties: could a socialist economy actually function in practice? Mises[1] had argued that since factors of production would not be privately owned under socialism, no prices could emerge, and hence no rational calculation would be possible. However, it was agreed by most of the participants by the end of the controversy that even if there is no private property, marginal-value productivities of factors could be calculated on the basis of the existing technology and the given final bill of goods. It would have to be an iterative process to make sure that in the final solution there is full employment of the factors. The marginal-value product of a factor (the same wherever it is used) was then also its price; another, and modern, name for this is the shadow or accounting price of the factor. The prices of final goods would also be determined in the same iterative process—in order to equate amounts supplied with amounts demanded. Unless there is structural disequilibrium in the economy, there would be a unique set of accounting prices at which all factors are fully employed.[2] 'Decentralised decision-making' would then imply giving managers of plants freedom to take output decisions in order to maximise profits at the accounting prices of inputs and outputs which would have been handed down to them from a higher authority.

In our discussions in this concluding chapter, we have so far neglected the political and cultural means to welfare. These are matters of opinion even more. Some people would argue that different degrees of state intervention in the market economy need to be compared on the basis not so much of what they do to the economic means to welfare as what they do to the political and cultural

---

[1] For an excellent review of this controversy—which also includes an examination of certain aspects of the *a priori* welfare theory of allocation—see Dobb [3]. Also relevant are Lange [8], and Bergson [1].

[2] Needless to say, the techniques of activity analysis have an application here. However, it would seem that in countries where most of the means of production are state owned prices are determined by a process of trial and error in the field and over time rather than in a theoretical iterative model. Cf. Chapter II, Section 7. For an account of the actual practices in some countries, see Hague [6].

means to welfare. But perhaps a rational approach is to compare the effects of the different types of policies on all the different kinds of means to welfare. Any assessment of their effects on the non-economic means may be very much a value judgment. On the one hand, there are people who argue that democracy is safe only with *laissez-faire* or slightly modified *laissez-faire*; on the other hand, there are those who maintain that democracy begins to be real only under an advanced form of socialism. Cf. Schumpeter [10].

A question we have not discussed so far in this chapter is that of the distribution of the economic means to welfare. There can be little doubt that the market mechanism working on its own cannot be relied upon to bring about a distribution of incomes that necessarily would be considered desirable by all social welfare functions. This is almost a truism. (If nothing else, the market mechanism would leave out in the cold all those who have nothing or very little to sell—the handicapped, the disabled, the aged, and so on.) Hence, some inter-ference in the market mechanism in the interests of smaller inequali-ties is often necessary. Socialists have often maintained that their system would guarantee greater equalities of incomes; but it is far from a proven proposition that a greater degree of state ownership of economic resources has been associated with greater equality of incomes.

One of the Paretian value judgments is that complete consumer (and producer) sovereignty is desirable. This implies that each individual is supposed to be the best judge of his own welfare, and is sometimes referred to as the individualist value judgment. This is a value judgment which sounds attractive in the abstract, but when the realities of everyday life are recalled it is not difficult to see that some individuals do need some guidance and even a certain amount of compulsion in their own interests. It is this argument which justifies compulsory education, compulsory health insurance, old-age pension schemes, and so on. Further, it is also possible to argue that since an individual does not live in a vacuum, often his judgment may be clouded by commercial publicity media which do not always work in his best interests. Finally, it has recently been argued that since the initiative to supply certain kinds of goods is taken by the producers in a capitalist country, it is rather question-begging to claim that under capitalism consumer is king. See Galbraith [5]. As for the socialists, they believe in a certain amount of guidance and control of consumers' decisions. Whether the amount of guidance and control is judicious or abhorrent in theory—or in practice in a particular country—each person needs to decide on his own.

We should say a few words about the scope of welfare economics.

If we grant that economic policies are to be judged by the comment-makers and decision-makers according to their consequences for social welfare, any application of economic theory is a problem in welfare economics. The range of what is at present designated welfare economics has come to be largely restricted to the problem of making a choice from among the various combinations of outputs that an economy can produce with a given amount of resources under the assumption of full employment. But this problem is of exactly the same type as some other problems of applied economics—for example, the choice among the various levels of employment and the various possible ways of maintaining a certain level of employment, the choice of the national rates of investment and growth, the problem of deciding on the right amount of nationalisation or social security, regional distribution of industry, and so on. Each one of these problems, including the problem which has been the concern of the traditional welfare economies, requires more than just either economic theories or economic considerations (or considerations about something called 'economic welfare') for a rational decision; they all require positive economic theories, empirical data, and some explicitly stated social objectives with some idea of their relative importance. There is no logical reason for placing the considerations of any one practical problem into a separate category to be called welfare economics.

In short, according to our arguments, applied economics, welfare economics, economic policy, and applied welfare economics—all these names describe the same field of study. Ignorance of this fact has been responsible for a chief mischief (this is a value judgment). Economic problems which come under the umbrella of the allocation of economic resources are discussed with the appearance of scientific objectivity. But there is a tendency to shy away from some other economic problems which are no less *economic* and no less relevant to welfare; this is an attitude which can only be described as pseudo-scientific. For example, there is no reason why in applied economics, welfare economics or economic policy (according to our arguments all these are equivalent name-tags) such a question as the following should not be discussed. Is the wage this man (or this group of men) gets a fair wage—in the light of some explicitly stated ethical considerations, the relevant positive economic theories, and empirical data? This is of course in direct contrast to those who have made the untenable (for reasons given in Chapter VI) distinction between welfare economics and applied economics in general. Consider the following: '. . . someone may think that whether or not a man gets a fair wage is a matter of economic welfare. But we exclude this, since

234

CONCLUSIONS

we concern ourselves only with how much he gets and what he does, and not with the question whether one is fair in relation to the other' [9, p. 82].

The reader would perhaps be able to recall for himself many instances of this kind of pseudo-science. A recent example which turns up in a number of learned economics seminars is that of considering the policy measures designed to facilitate world trade as 'proper', 'scientific', 'welfare-economics-type' questions and therefore worth a discussion by academic economists; but *not* the policy measures designed to facilitate aid from the developed countries to the developing countries: it is claimed that the former discussion relies on *no* value judgments while the latter does! In fact a discussion of either problem must start from some explicitly stated or implicitly assumed value judgments. Why increase world trade if it does not increase any individual's or group's *welfare*? Further, an increase in world trade may well reduce the economic means to welfare of those groups which have been hitherto protected from foreign trade: an attempt to justify an increase of world trade (in spite of this fact) by invoking the compensation criteria—or by any other method of welfare evaluation—*must* again presuppose some value judgments. Of course it can be argued that the value judgments required to justify international aid do not coincide with the value judgments required to justify world trade, but it is silly to argue that one is a 'scientific' question and the other is not.

Human welfare is important (this is a value judgment). There is no such thing as 'economic welfare'. Whenever an economic theory is applied to a practical problem, we are in the realm of welfare economics. Though the traditional, *a priori* welfare economics has proved barren, *ad hoc* welfare economics is fertile. We have defined *ad hoc* welfare economics as a study of problems of applied economics in the light of positive economic theories and some *explicit* value judgments which an economist introduces on his own or which—*if he is doing an assigned job*—are given to him by 'parliament'; in *either* case the value judgments *are* value judgments.

REFERENCES FOR CHAPTER X

[1] A. Bergson, 'Socialist Economies', in H. S. Ellis (ed.), *A Survey of Contemporary Economics*, Philadelphia, 1948; also reprinted in his *Essays . . .*, Cambridge, Mass., 1966
[2] Maurice Dobb, *Political Economy and Capitalism*, London, 1937
[3] Maurice Dobb, 'A Review of the Discussion concerning Economic Calculation in a Socialist Economy (1953)', in his *On Economic Theory and Socialism*, London, 1955

235

[4] J. K. Galbraith, *The Affluent Society*, London, 1958.

[5] J. K. Galbraith, *The New Industrial State*, London, 1967

[6] D. C. Hague (ed.), *Price Formation in Various Economies*, Proceedings of a Conference held by the International Economic Association, London, 1967

[7] J. M. Keynes, *The General Theory of Employment, Money and Interest*, London, 1936

[8] Oscar Lange, 'On the Economic Theory of Socialism', in B. Lippincott (ed.), *On the Economic Theory of Socialism*, Minneapolis, Minn., 1938

[9] I. M. D. Little, *A Critique of Welfare Economics*, 2nd edn., Oxford, 1957.

[10] J. A. Schumpeter, *Capitalism, Socialism and Democracy*, London, 1943

INDEX

Abramovitz, M., 187, 215, 225
Accounting Prices, 34–5
Activity analysis and *a priori* welfare theory, 33–5
and accounting prices, 34–5
and the assumption of convexity, 33–5
and 'decentralised decision-making', 34–5
and an objective function, 34–5
Ad hoc welfare economics, 2, 149
and a basic value judgment, 126
includes all applied economics, 130–1, 233–6
Applied economics, 2
A priori welfare criteria, 8, 94–123
compensation criteria, 95–101
and assessment of the right amount of compensation, 96n.
Kaldor–Hicks criterion, 95–9
applications in the theory of international trade, 189–99, 205, 208–9
and the Laspeyre quantity index, 118–20
as used to compare Paretian optima, etc., 101
and the interpretation of the utility curves, 97–8
and the quantity index numbers, 117–22
Samuelson's criticisms, 101–5
Scitovsky reversal criterion, 99–101
applications in the theory of international trade, 189–99, 205, 208–9
and the Paasche quantity index, 119–21

as used to compare Paretian optima, etc., 101
the two-way compensation criterion, 100–1
definition, 94
distinguished from a social welfare function, 94n., 139
in the form of an alleged corollary of the second-best theorem, 50–4, 123, 206–8
Little's criterion, 105–16
and the assumption of transitive social welfare functions, 113
its basic statement, 106
the judgment about distribution, 108
its three possible interpretations, 108–16
and Pareto-type social welfare functions, 112
its value judgments, 106
Pigou's proposition about distributive transfers, 94
and inter-personal comparisons of utility, 94–5
'Samuelson criterion', an unfortunate description, 104
its misuse, 195–6
A priori welfare economics, 2, 5
and activity analysis, 33–5
and the calculus, 32–3
and ordinal utility, 4, 22, 144
Arrow, K. J., 34n., 42, 62, 110n., 123, 131–3, 135–6, 145, 161

Bailey, M. J., 123, 187
Baldwin, R. E., 123, 198n., 211–12
Balogh, T., 125, 161, 209, 211
Barone, E., 7

237

Bator, F. M., 42, 62, 92
Baumol, W. J., 85, 92, 140n., 161
Beckman, M., 170n., 187
Bergson, A., 4, 7, 22, 42, 142, 161, 225, 232n., 235
Bergson curves, easily misused, 139
Best-practice techniques, 156n.
Bhagwati, J. N., 195, 206–8, 211
Bhardan, P. K., 205, 211
Boulding, K. E., 92
Braybrooke, D., 145, 161
Buchanan, J. M., 64, 65n., 68n., 70, 71, 92

Capital punishment, 128
Chenery, H. B., 62, 187
Coase, R. H., 71n., 92
Coleman, J. S., 133n., 161
Comment-maker, 4, 41, 153, 230
    comments as distinguished from decisions, 128–31, 137–8
    (see also Recommendations)
Community indifference curves
    (see Scitovsky community indifference curves)
Comparative costs, and international trade, 190–2
Compassion, when untraded is an externality, 74
    and the alleged distinction between economic and general welfare, 140–2
    modified necessary conditions for Paretian optimality, 76
    (see also Envy)
Consumers' Surplus, 165–7, 177–8
Compensation criteria
    (see A priori welfare criteria)
Consumer sovereignty, 9, 174, 216, 233
Corner solution for a Paretian (overall) optimum, 33
Corlett, W. J., 46, 62
Cost accountants, 173
Cost minimisation, 12
    non-cost-minimising behaviour, 16

Cost-benefit analysis of investments, 173–86, 224
Criterion
    (see A priori welfare criteria and Investment criteria)

David, P. A., 62
Davis, O. A., 54n., 62, 71, 85, 92
Debreu, G., 34n., 42, 60, 62
Decision-maker, 4, 41, 153, 230
    decisions as distinguished from comments and recommendations, 128–31, 137–8
Decision-making mechanism, social, 144–6
    (see also Decision-maker and Comment-maker)
'Decentralised decision-making', 34–5
Differentiation of product, 48
Disagreements, why they are so frequent among economists, 149–52
Distributive judgments, 142–9
    distribution of welfare v. that of the means to welfare, 142–4
Dobb, M., 43, 123, 161, 222, 225, 232n., 235
Dolbear, Jr., F. T., 65n., 69n., 92
Dorfman, R., 38n., 43
Double-index-number-criterion, the, 121–2
Domar, E. D., 176
Dupuit, 165
Duesenberry, J. S., 74, 75, 92, 140n.

Eckstein, O., 175, 187
Economic development, concept of, 213–16
    analysis of some controversies, 218–26
    ex ante and ex post evaluation of national income data in terms of production potential, 215–16
    ex ante and ex post evaluations of national income data in terms of welfare, 213–15

238

Hickman, B. G., 162
Hicks, J. R., 43, 95, 102, 123, 142n., 145, 162, 166n., 187
Hildrith, C., 133n., 162
Hirshleifer, J., 187
Homogeneous factors, 11
Hotelling, H., 165, 187
Hume, David, 127
Hutchison, T. W., 151n., 162

'Ideal output', see Pigovian ideal output
Imperfect knowledge, 16, 55–61, 218
  and co-ordination of large investments, 60
  due to possible changes in tastes, technology and weather, etc., 60
  implications for competitive equilibrium and Paretian optimality, 55–61
  and the inequality of marginal cost with price, 56
  information now becomes a good, 57
  may prevent reaching the economy's production frontier, 57–60
  and mutual repercussions on profits, 58–60
  and the problematic concept of a pecuniary external economy, 59, 63n.
Imperfections in factor markets, 16, 48
  and gains from trade, 202–9
Incomes, distribution of
  (see Money incomes, distribution of)
Individual (ordinal) utility functions, 4
  assumed as known, 4, 22, 144
Indivisibility, 11, 32, 163
  and pricing policy for public enterprise, 168–9, 170
  and the social optimum, 32

Industrial engineers, 173
Interdependence
  (see Non-market interdependence)
Interest rates, differences in, 176
Internal rate of return criterion
  (see Investment criteria)
Investment criteria
  benefits/costs ratio criterion, 183–4
  internal rate of return and net discounted present-value criteria compared, 178–83
  maximisation of employment criterion, 222–5
  net discounted present-value criterion, 178–83
  pay-back-period criterion, 177
  profitability criterion, 178
  rate of surplus criteria, 222–3
  rate of turnover criterion, 221–2
  (see also Time; Saving, the social rate of; Uncertainty; Public goods; Externalities; Merit goods; and Efficiency, concepts of)

Johnson, H. G., 192, 205, 208, 212

Kahn, R. F., 31n., 43
Kaldor, N., 95, 96, 102, 123
Kaldor–Hicks criterion
  (see A priori welfare criteria)
Kemp, M. C., 212
Kenen, P. B., 43, 162
Kennedy, C. F., 109, 114, 123
Keynes, J. M., 213, 218, 236
Kirschen, E. S., 162
Knapp, J., 225
Knight, F. H., 63, 92
Koopmans, T. C., 34n., 38n., 43, 61n., 62, 187
Krutilla, J. V., 187

Labour-surplus economy, 224
  disguised unemployment, 220
Laissez-faire, 229, 233

INDEX

(*see also* Double-index-number criterion, the)
applications in the theory of international trade, 189–99
Paretian exchange optima, 16–18
and value judgments, 16–17
necessary conditions for, 17–18
Paretian overall optima, 18–28
and corner solution, 33
and the Kaldor–Hicks criterion, 101
necessary conditions for, 23–4
in an open economy, 197–8
second-order necessary conditions, 31–2
not necessarily 'superior' to any non-optimum, 21–2
and ordinal utility, 3–4
Paretian trend in welfare economics, 5
and *the* Paretian value judgment, 10
and Paretian value judgments, 18–20
and perfect competition, 28–31
and the Scitovsky reversal criterion, 101
and social welfare function, 22–4
total conditions for, 33
Paretian value judgments
(*see* Value judgments)
Pareto, 3
(*see also* Paretian)
Pareto-superiority, 97, 102
(*see also* Potential (Pareto) superiority)
Patent rights, 230
Pay-back-period criterion
(*see* Investment criteria)
Pearce, I. F., 162
Perfect competition and Paretian optima, 28–31
'Perfect knowledge about the present', 11
Pigou, A. C., 7, 35, 37, 43, 63, 78, 92, 94, 95, 124, 140, 144, 162, 165, 175

Pigovian, trend in welfare economics, 5
ideal output, 35
rule for, 36
similar to a Paretian optimum, 35–7
proposition about distributive transfers, 94–5
remedies for externalities, 64, 69–72, 78–9, 84, 85n.
and second-best problems, 87–8
Pitchford, J. D., 188
Point utility possibility curve, 20–1
and compensation criteria, 97
Polak, J. J., 221, 226
Popper, K. R., 128, 150, 162
Positive economics, 2, 149–51
Potential (Pareto) superiority, 96, 102
a sufficient condition for it, 103
Practicability of economic policies, 150–1
Prescriptions, 1
Prest, A. R., 188
Price, equality with marginal cost
achievement of it wherever possible, once considered desirable, 49
a critique of it as a pricing rule, 164–73
not essential for technological efficiency, 171–3
only relevant to Pareto-type social welfare functions, 170–1
and Paretian optimality, 29–31
and the second-best theorem, 169–70
and taxes, 45
under perfect competition, 29–31
not necessarily if the assumption of perfect knowledge dropped, 56
Producer sovereignty, 9, 216, 233
Producers' surplus, 166
Production possibility frontier, 15–16, 157–8, 191, 219
Profit maximisation, 12

243

and separable utility and transformation functions, 54–5
and specificity of factors, 54
and technological efficiency, 50–4
Sen, A. K., 110n., 113n., 124, 175n., 188, 222, 226
Sengupta, Jati K., 161
Similar tastes, 94–5, 133–5, 143–4
Situation utility possibility frontier, 20–4
also called the utility, economic welfare, or welfare frontier, 21
and compensation criteria, 97
and lump-sum redistributions, 46–7
and monopoly, 154
relevant only when the social welfare function is Pareto-type, 24
Slasor, G., 110n., 124
Social indifference curves, arbitrary, 139
easily misused, 139
less useful than Scitovsky community indifference curves, 139
Social objectives, 144–52
and relative social welfare weights, 145–9
Social optimum, the, 22–4, 153
changes in, 146
distinguished from a Paretian optimum, 24, 147, 153, 228–9
and externalities, 89
the feasible, 47–8
and indivisibilities, 32
the necessary conditions for when the social welfare function is Pareto-type, 22–3
the necessary conditions for with any type social welfare function, 23–4
Social welfare function, 2–5, 10n., 145
and activity analysis, 34–5
and Arrow's theorem, 131–8
the analysis of its relevance and significance, 135–8
the majority paradox, 135–6

not true if ethical assessment of inter-personal utility allowed, 133–4
which is possible because welfare is distinguishable, 135
and the assumption of transitivity, 113
distinguished from a priori sufficient welfare criteria, 94n., 139
and Duesenberry-like externalities, 115–16
and ethical considerations, 4
forms of social welfare functions, 138–52
and indivisibilities, 32
maximising the expectation of, 148–9
a non-Paretian social welfare function, example of, 115–16
and Paretian optima, 22–4
Pareto-type, monotonic increasing function of individual utility, and consistent with the other Paretian value judgments, 10, 22–4, 32, 48
and the Little criterion, 112
necessary basis for the marginal-cost pricing rule, 170–1
and the second-best theorem, 55
and widely accepted value judgments, 128–9
realistic social welfare functions, 146–9
and social objectives, 144–52
social welfare contours, 22–4
sources of, 125–38
and technological efficiency, 42
three possible interpretations of, 137–8
Social wants, another term for public goods, 164
Social welfare contours
(see Social welfare function)
Socialised economy, a, 34–5
Socialism, 232–3

not the only possible set of
value judgments for defining
the social optimum, 23–4,
147, 153, 228–9
and Paretian overall optima,
18–20
and Pareto-type social welfare
functions, 10
and the second-best theorem,
55
and technological efficiency, 12–
14
'widely acceptable', 2
Viner, J., 210, 212

Welfare
defined as an ethical term, 1
economic means to, 77, 142–4
distribution of, 142–4

not equal to market choices, 139–
40
measurement of, 1
no such thing as economic welfare, 139–42
non-economic causes of, 8
non-market interdependencies in
individual welfares, 74–7, 140–2
political means to, 77, 142–3
Welfare frontier
(see Situation utility possibility
frontier)
Wellisz, S., 85n., 93
Whinston, A. B., 54n., 62, 71, 85,
92
Williams, B. R., 177n., 188
Winston, C. B., 187
Wiseman, J., 165n., 188
Wolfe, J. N., 62